**Microsoft Money**

# Guide to Personal Finance

## SECOND EDITION

PUBLISHED BY
Microsoft Press
A Division of Microsoft Corporation
One Microsoft Way
Redmond, Washington 98052-6399

Library of Congress Cataloging-in-Publication Data pending.

Printed and bound in the United States of America.

1 2 3 4 5 6 7 8 9   QEQE   1 0 9 8 7 6

Distributed to the book trade in Canada by Macmillan of Canada, a division of Canada Publishing Corporation.

Library of Congress Cataloging-in-Publication Data pending.

Microsoft Press books are available through booksellers and distributors worldwide. For further information about international editions, contact your local Microsoft Corporation office. Or contact Microsoft Press International directly at fax (206) 936-7329.

**Acquisitions Editor:** Lucinda Rowley
**Project Editor:** Maureen Williams Zimmerman

# Acknowledgments

A heartfelt thank-you to Lucinda Rowley, Microsoft Press Acquisitions Editor; Stephen Guty, Microsoft Press Acquisitions Director; John Pierce, Project Editor; and Maureen Zimmerman, Project Editor; all of whom nurtured and nursed this project as an idea became an outline, an outline became a manuscript, a manuscript became pages, and, finally, as the pages became a book.

Thank-you to Clay Martin, Microsoft Money project team member, who enthusiastically wrote the chapters covering the online services in the first edition of this book. (Clay also wrote Money's online help.)

Thank-you to Saul Candib, who revised this book for the most recent version of the Microsoft Money software.

A special thank-you to Jim Brown, Publisher at Microsoft Press, who simultaneously organized the major parts of this book, selected topic areas, and helped me with my golf swing one hot July afternoon.

# Contents at a Glance

Introduction                                                    xix

## Part 1    Money Basics

| | | |
|---|---|---|
| Chapter 1 | Setting Up and Starting Out | 3 |
| Chapter 2 | Keeping Your Checkbook | 13 |
| Chapter 3 | Printing Checks | 25 |
| Chapter 4 | Printing Reports | 33 |
| Chapter 5 | Balancing Your Bank Accounts | 45 |
| Chapter 6 | About the Plastic | 53 |
| Chapter 7 | Mortgages and Loans | 63 |
| Chapter 8 | Homes, Boats, and Cars | 89 |
| Chapter 9 | Getting Wired | 95 |
| Chapter 10 | Paying Bills Online | 111 |
| Chapter 11 | Banking Online | 123 |

## Part 2    Personal Finance and Money

| | | |
|---|---|---|
| Chapter 12 | Personal Financial Planning | 135 |
| Chapter 13 | Retirement Planning | 153 |
| Chapter 14 | Planning for College | 169 |
| Chapter 15 | Getting Started with Your Investments | 187 |

Chapter 16    Mutual Funds    201

Chapter 17    Stocks and Bonds    211

Chapter 18    Real Estate    223

Chapter 19    Special Investments
and Common Problems    241

Chapter 20    Online Quotes    251

Chapter 21    Researching Investments Online    257

Chapter 22    Income Taxes and Money    263

## Part 3    Managing a Small Business with Money

Chapter 23    Running Your Business from a Checkbook    277

Chapter 24    Billing and Collecting from Customers    287

Chapter 25    Payroll    299

Chapter 26    Measuring Profits, Cash Flow,
and Net Worth    313

Glossary    321

Index    325

# Contents

**Introduction**                                                    **xix**
What This Book Assumes
   about Your Computer Skills                        xix
What This Book Assumes
   about Your Financial Savvy                        xx
How This Book Is Organized                                          xx
Conventions Used Here                                               xxi
A Final Comment                                                     xxii

**Part 1   Money Basics**

**Chapter 1   Setting Up and Starting Out**                         **3**
Installing Money                                                    3
Strategies for Starting Out                                         6
Setting Up Your Accounts                                            7
   Setting Up Accounts the
      First Time You Start Money      8
   Setting Up Accounts Sometime Later               11
A Few Words about the
   Account Manager Window                            11
In Conclusion                                                       12

**Chapter 2**  **Keeping Your Checkbook**  **13**

Recording Checks and Deposits  14
    Displaying the Account Register  14
    Entering Your First Check  15
    Recording Your Second and Subsequent Checks  16
    Recording Deposits  17
The Best Category Trick  18
Account Transfers  19
If You Ever Make Mistakes…  20
Backing Up Your Financial Records  21
About the Account Register's
    Other Bells and Whistles  22
    A Nice View  22
    A Few Details  23
In Conclusion  23

**Chapter 3**  **Printing Checks**  **25**

Should You Even Print Checks?  25
Choosing the Right Check Form  26
Ordering Your Checks  28
Describing the Checks You Want to Print  28
Printing Checks  29
Check Printing Tips and Tricks  31
In Conclusion  32

**Chapter 4**  **Printing Reports**  **33**

Viewing Reports On-Screen  33
Reviewing the Microsoft Money Reports  35
Printing Reports  36
Your Personal Archives  37
    Banking Records  38
    Tax Records  38
    How Long Should You Retain Records?  38

A Few Words on Exporting Reports                                39
Creating Customized Reports                                      40
    Changing the Date                        40
    Summarizing Accounts                     42
Other Changes You Can Make to Reports                           43
In Conclusion                                                   43

**Chapter 5**    **Balancing Your**
            **Bank Accounts**                                **45**
How to Balance a Bank Account                                   45
What to Do When
    an Account Won't Reconcile                48
Errors That Balancing Won't Catch                               50
    Uncleared Transactions You Forget to Record   50
    Fictitious Transactions                  51
Preventing Forgery                                              51
In Conclusion                                                   52

**Chapter 6**    **About the Plastic**             **53**
Tracking a Credit Card with Money                               53
Tracking Credit the Lazy Way                                    54
Tracking Credit the Accountant's Way                            55
    Setting Up a Credit Card Account         55
    Recording Credit Card Charges            58
    Recording Credit Card Credits            59
    Recording a Credit Card Payment          59
Getting Out from under
    Your Credit Card Debts                   61
In Conclusion                                                   62

**Chapter 7**    **Mortgages and Loans**           **63**
How to Track a Loan                                             63
    Setting Up a Liability or a Loan Account 63
    Recording Loan Payments                  72
    Fixing Loan Account Balance Errors       74

How to Shop for a Loan   76
   Calculating a Loan Payment   77
   Making Extra Principal Payments   78
   Comparing Two Loans with the Loan Calculator   80
   Creating an Amortization Schedule   80
Using the Mortgage Planner   81
   Comparing Two Mortgages   82
   Refinancing a Mortgage   87
In Conclusion   88

**Chapter 8   Homes, Boats, and Cars   89**
Setting Up an Asset Account   89
Tracking an Asset with Money   92
Tips for Tracking Assets   93
   Your Home   93
   Cars, Boats, and Other Personal Property   94
   Asset Lists for Property and Casualty Insurance   94
In Conclusion   94

**Chapter 9   Getting Wired   95**
Overview of Money's Online Services   95
Modems   96
   Modem Speed   97
   Installing a Modem   98
   Making Your Modem and System Work Together   99
Online Services   100
   Is It Safe to Use Online Banking Services?   101
   Setting Up Online Services   102
In Conclusion   109

**Chapter 10**    **Paying Bills Online**    **111**

How It Works    111

Entering an Electronic Payment    112

Sending Electronic Payments    115

What If I Need to Cancel
a Payment after It's Sent?    117

What If the Payee Doesn't Receive the Check?    118

Creating Automatic Payments    119

Canceling an Individual Automatic Payment    121

Permanently Canceling an Automatic Payment    121

Checking on the Status of a Payment    122

In Conclusion    122

**Chapter 11**    **Banking Online**    **123**

How It Works    123

Should You Keep Entering
Transactions Manually?    124

Downloading Your Bank Account Records    125

Making the Connection and Downloading    126

Adding the Transactions to the Account Register    128

Transferring Money between Accounts    131

In Conclusion    132

**Part 2**    **Personal Finance and Money**

**Chapter 12**    **Personal Financial Planning**    **135**

Arranging Your Day-to-Day
Financial Affairs    135

Five Budgeting Tips    136

Seven Ways to Stretch
Your Budget Dollars Farther    138

Budgeting with Money    142

Plotting a Course Toward
    Your Long-Term Financial Goals    144
Creating a Financial Safety Net    145
    Make a Will    145
    Create a Rainy-Day Fund    146
    Get Earnings Insurance    146
    Protect Your Assets    151
In Conclusion    152

**Chapter 13**    **Retirement Planning**    **153**
The Good News and the
    Bad News about Social Security    153
A Few Words about Employer Pension Plans    154
Setting a Retirement Income Goal    156
Calculating Retirement Savings    157
A Few Words on Rates of Return    162
Ideas on Coming Up with
    the Money You Need to Save    164
    Get the Government's Help    164
    Get Your Employer's Help    165
    Make Healthy Choices    165
    Make Your Big Decisions Carefully    166
In Conclusion    167

**Chapter 14**    **Planning for College**    **169**
Is College a Good Investment?    169
What Will College Cost?    170
Do You Need to Save?    170
But What about All That Financial Aid?    171
    Determining Eligibility    171
    Reviewing Financial Aid Programs    171

Saving Money for College ............................................ 173

Where Should You Save? ............................................ 179

   In Whose Name Should
     You Put the College Savings? ............................ 179

   Where Should College
     Savings Money Be Invested? ............................ 180

What to Do If You Can't
   Possibly Afford College ........................................ 184

In Conclusion ............................................................ 186

**Chapter 15 Getting Started with Your Investments 187**

Why You May Not Want to Do This ............................ 187

Setting Up an Investment Account ............................ 189

Describing Your Current Portfolio ............................ 192

Updating the Prices in Your Portfolio ........................ 196

Viewing Your Portfolio ............................................ 198

In Conclusion ............................................................ 199

**Chapter 16 Mutual Funds 201**

Recording Mutual Fund Purchases ............................ 201

Recording Mutual Fund Sales .................................... 203

Recording Mutual Fund Dividends ............................ 205

Reinvesting Mutual Fund Distributions ...................... 206

Recording Other Income
   and Other Expense Amounts ................................ 208

In Conclusion ............................................................ 209

**Chapter 17 Stocks and Bonds 211**

Recording Stock and Bond Purchases ........................ 211

Recording Stock and Bond Sales .............................. 213

Recording Dividends ................................................ 214

Reinvesting Dividends .............................................. 215

Recording Stock Splits 217
Recording Bond Interest 218
Recording Brokerage Account
  Fees and Miscellaneous Income 219
Working with Money's
  Associated Cash Accounts 220
In Conclusion 221

**Chapter 18  Real Estate                223**
Passive Real Estate Investments 223
Recording Passive Real Estate
  Investment Purchases 224
Recording Real Estate Investment Sales 226
Recording Real Estate
  Investment Distributions 227
Return of Capital Transactions 228
Active Real Estate Investments 229
  Setting Up Your Property Accounts 230
  Setting Up Your Property Classifications 231
  Tracking the Adjusted Cost of a Property 233
  Recording Depreciation on
    a Property's Asset Account 234
  Tracking a Property's Mortgage 236
  Keeping Records of a
    Property's Income and Expenses 236
  Reporting on Your Active
    Real Estate Investments 239
In Conclusion 240

**Chapter 19**  **Special Investments
and Common Problems**                                    **241**

Stock Dividends                                          241
Liquidating Dividends                                    241
Handling Short Sales                                     242
Buying on Margin                                         243
Derivatives                                              243
    Selling Puts and Calls           244
    Buying Puts and Calls            244
    Exercising Puts and Calls        244
Employee Stock Options                                   245
Accrued Interest on Bonds                                245
    Accrued Interest on Bonds You Purchase   245
    Accrued Interest on Bonds You Own        246
Bond Premiums                                            246
Handling Bond Discounts                                  248
Certificates of Deposit                                  250
Zero-Coupon Bonds                                        250
Precious Metals and Commodities                          250
In Conclusion                                            250

**Chapter 20**  **Online Quotes**                       **251**

How It Works                                             251
Setting Up Your Account
  to Use the Service                           252
Entering Market Symbols
  for Stocks and Mutual Funds                  252
Electronically Downloading Market Prices                 253
In Conclusion                                            256

**Chapter 21**  **Researching Investments Online**          **257**

On the Internet                                              257

   A Review of Available Newsgroups              257

   A Review of Available Mailing Lists           259

   Reviewing World Wide Web Sites                259

On the Outernet                                              262

In Conclusion                                                262

**Chapter 22**  **Income Taxes and Money**                  **263**

Building the Perfect Categories List                         263

Summarizing Your Income
   and Deduction Data at Tax Time                266

Should You Export Data
   to a Tax-Preparation Package?                 268

The Five Best Tax-Saving Gambits                             269

   Take Every Deduction You're Entitled To       269

   Bunch Your Deductions                         270

   Exploit Retirement Savings Options            272

   Don't Use Nondeductible Consumer Credit       272

   Use Specific Identification for Your Investments  273

In Conclusion                                                274

**Part 3**  **Managing a Small Business with Money**

**Chapter 23**  **Running Your Business from a Checkbook**  **277**

Understanding the Big Picture                                277

   Printing Business Forms                       278

   Tallying Business Income and Expenses         279

   Keeping Records of Assets,
      Liabilities, and Owners Equity  279

   Simplifying Financial and Accounting Calculations  280

Keeping Your Books with Money                                    280
   Preparing for Business Accounting                       280
   Recording Business Income                              283
   Recording Business Expenses                            284
If Money Doesn't Work for Your Business                          285
In Conclusion                                                    286

**Chapter 24**   **Billing and Collecting from Customers**   **287**
A Look at the Big Picture                                        287
Preparing for Accounts
   Receivable Accounting                                  288
Tracking Accounts Receivable                                     289
   Using Cash-Basis Accounting                            290
   Using Accrual-Basis Accounting                         292
Monitoring Accounts Receivable                                   295
In Conclusion                                                    298

**Chapter 25**   **Payroll**   **299**
Becoming an Employer                                             299
   Federal Payroll Tax and Reporting Requirements         300
   State and Local Payroll Tax
      and Reporting Requirements                        301
   Other Employee Reporting Requirements                  301
Setting Up the Payroll Accounts You Need                         302
Setting Up the Payroll Categories You Need                       303
Preparing Payroll Checks                                         305
Making Tax Deposits                                              308
Filing Quarterly and Annual Tax Returns                          308
Preparing W-2 and W-3 Forms                                      309
In Conclusion                                                    312

**Chapter 26  Measuring Profits, Cash Flow, and Net Worth**                                **313**

Measuring Profits                                                313
Measuring Cash Flow                                              316
Measuring Your Net Worth                                         318
In Conclusion                                                    320


Glossary                                                         321
Index                                                            325

# Introduction

**J**ust for the record, I don't believe that money buys happiness. I've seen too many people with vast amounts of money and little else. But that philosophical admission aside, I have to tell you something: You can improve your life dramatically by being smart about your financial affairs. For example, you can build your assets and net worth so that a personal or professional setback such as an illness or being unemployed won't cause a financial disaster. You can plot a course toward long-term financial objectives—a course that almost always assures that you'll succeed financially. And you can live better in a material sense by stretching your income.

As a practical matter, however, it's tough to be "smart" about money. To be smart about money in your day-to-day activities, you need to keep detailed financial records. To be smart about money in your long-range planning, you need to make rather complicated financial calculations and projections. Fortunately, Microsoft Money is a wonderful tool for doing these tasks. This book is about how to organize and manage your financial affairs better, to see where you are financially, and to start planning so you can go, financially speaking, where you want to go.

## What This Book Assumes about Your Computer Skills

You don't need to know much about using a computer to make good use of this book, but you should know a few things: how to turn on your computer, start a program (such as Microsoft Money), choose menu commands, and work with dialog boxes. If you don't already possess this knowledge, you can acquire it by viewing the Microsoft Windows 95 online tutorial or by reading one of the short tutorials on Windows 95.

## What This Book Assumes about Your Financial Savvy

You don't need to know anything about personal finance, budgeting, investments, or anything like that to make good use of this book. It doesn't hurt if you know something about those topics, of course, but you don't need to have any prerequisite knowledge. I assume you purchased this book to get that information.

## How This Book Is Organized

This book is organized into three parts:

➤ Part 1, "Money Basics," describes how to use the Money program for personal financial record-keeping: things like setting up an account, reconciling an account, printing checks, and so on. This part also explains how you use Money's new electronic banking and bill-paying features.

➤ Part 2, "Personal Finance and Money," explains how to do personal financial planning and investment record-keeping with Money. For example, how to use Money to track investments in stocks and bonds or real estate and how to use Money to plan for retirement income or college savings.

➤ Part 3, "Managing a Small Business with Money," provides information about how small business owners and managers can use the Money program for business financial management.

I've also included a glossary that explains many of the financial terms you'll encounter in this book.

One other point: Don't feel obliged to start with Chapter 1 in Part 1 and then plod through the remaining chapters and parts in order. I wrote this book with the assumption that you'll read a chapter or two up front to learn how to start using Money and then jump around to the chapters that describe in more detail the information that you want to know.

# Conventions Used Here

To make this book easier for you to use, I've employed several conventions. Whenever I use a glossary term for the first time in a chapter, the term appears in **boldface**. If you don't know the meaning of the term, you can get a quick definition by looking in the glossary.

I've also made comments in the margins of most pages. These margin notes contain a variety of interesting or useful information that adds to the main themes in the chapters. To help you identify the kind of information that a margin note includes, I've attached an icon to each one so you can tell at a glance what kind of topic it covers:

| Icon | Description |
| --- | --- |
| | Offers a technique, tip, or trick for using the Microsoft Money program. |
| | Provides personal financial advice or a useful financial fact. |
| | Points you to another chapter that contains related information. |
| | Alerts you to a problem that is particularly serious. |

## A Final Comment

Let me make a final comment: I applaud your decision to actively manage your personal finances. I really do. Many, many people choose not to manage—or even think about—their personal finances. As a result, they bumble from one financial problem to another and then count themselves lucky if they just avoid some financial disaster.

You're different, however. You've decided to take responsibility for yourself, to get ahead by your own hard work and careful planning. I assure you that your decision to take this step will dramatically improve your finances over time. Congratulations!

# Part 1

# Money Basics

# Setting Up and Starting Out

**G**etting started with Microsoft Money isn't difficult. It's really very easy. But that much said, let me suggest that you'll benefit by having a little friendly help. That way, you'll get up and running more quickly, and you won't make simple mistakes that cause you to waste time later or miss out on some neat benefit.

## Installing Money

To use Money, of course, you first need to install it. If you're not sure whether or not Money is installed, just click the Start button and then choose Programs.

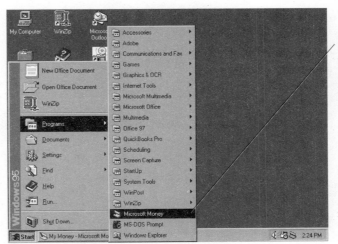

If you see the Microsoft Money command on your Programs menu, Money is already installed on your computer.

If Money isn't already installed, you can install it in the same way that you install any other Windows-based application. If you know how to do this, go ahead. Then continue reading at the next section, the one titled "Strategies for Starting Out."

If you don't know how to install a Windows-based application, just follow these steps:

**Installing Windows Programs.** *You use the Control Panel's Add/Remove Programs tool to install Money and other programs, too.*

1 Click the Start button.

2 Choose the Settings menu.

3 Choose the Control Panel command. Windows 95 displays the Control Panel window.

The Add/Remove Programs tool

4 Double-click the Add/Remove Programs icon. Windows 95 displays the Add/Remove Programs dialog box.

5 Click the Install/Uninstall tab in the Add/Remove Programs Properties dialog box if it isn't already showing.

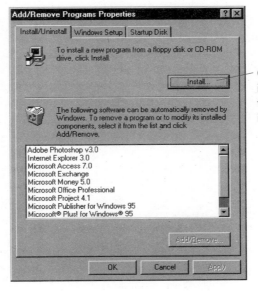

Clicking Install tells Windows 95 to install whatever program is on the floppy disk or CD-ROM you've just inserted.

**What Else Can I Use the Add/Remove Programs Tool For?** *You can also use the Add/Remove Programs tool to uninstall programs. To uninstall a program, display the Add/Remove Programs Properties dialog box, select the program or programs you want to uninstall, and then click the Add/Remove button.*

**6** Insert the first Money disk in your floppy disk drive or insert the Money CD-ROM in your CD-ROM drive.

**7** Click the Install button.

Once you click Install, Windows 95 goes to work. (Follow the instructions on the screen and press Enter when you are requested to.) Windows copies the files it needs and puts them on your hard disk. If you install Money from floppy disks, you'll be prompted to replace floppy disks one or two times during the installation. If you are installing Money from a CD-ROM, it will contain all of the files you need.

*Microsoft Money uses wizards to step you through and simplify most tasks. Wizards display a series of dialog boxes. To use a wizard, you answer the questions asked by its dialog boxes.*

*If you have questions about how some Microsoft Money command works, refer to Money's excellent online help system.*

When Windows 95 finishes installing Money, it places a listing for Money on the Programs menu.

When you start Money the first time, Money wants you to begin setting up an account or two, but you should probably stop and think for a minute before you do that. It really makes sense for you to decide up front how you want to begin using Money and what you want to get out of it. So read the next section before you set up an account.

## Strategies for Starting Out

There isn't only one correct way to use a program like Money. That's the first thing you should know. Some people use the program only to track their tax-deductible **expenses** or to make it easier to reconcile their checkbooks (if they even do reconcile their checkbooks). Some people use Money to monitor the ways they spend their money and to keep records of their bank accounts and **investments.** (I fall into this group.) And then there are the financial fanatics who use Money to keep a tight rein on their finances and to constantly monitor the pulse of their cash flow and net worth. (My father-in-law falls into this group.)

Predictably, the less you want to accomplish with Money, the less work you have to do. If the only work you want to do is track tax deductions and reconcile checking accounts, you can be up and running in a few minutes. No joking. All you need to do is set up a bank account or two (I describe how to do that in the next section) and then learn how to do the stuff described in Chapter 2.

However, if you want to use Money to monitor the ways you spend your money and to keep good records of your cash and investment accounts, you need to do a little more work. You need to set up accounts for your **assets** and refine the **income** and expense categories that Money initially provides. And that means you should read or skim most of the chapters in Part 1.

**Should I Track All My Accounts?** *You don't need to track every account with Money. You should track accounts that have a lot of activity or a significant balance. For example, I have a savings account that is attached to my regular checking account, but my checking-savings account pays a woefully inadequate interest rate and I don't store much money in it. (The account balance is around $.80, I think.) I keep my extra cash in a money market account. So, for me, it would be a waste of time to set up a Money account for my $.80 checking-savings account. If you have similar accounts that are inactive, it really doesn't make any sense to formally track them.*

If you want to use Money as a personal business manager—as a tool to run your financial life—then you need to learn more about the way the Money program works. I suggest that you carefully read all of the chapters in Part 1 and then skim the rest of the book, swooping down to take a closer look anytime you see information that relates to your specific situation.

If you don't know what you want to do with Money—if you just know you want to manage your finances better than you've been managing them in the past—let me suggest that you take the middle ground. Use Money to monitor the ways you earn and spend your money and to keep track of your bank accounts and any investments you have. Using Money in this way isn't difficult. It isn't time-consuming. And it doesn't require you to be or become a financial wizard—or a computer genius.

## Setting Up Your Accounts

For every bank account you want to track, you set up a Money account. A Money account lists the transactions, or changes, that are made to an account—for example, when you make a deposit, when you make a withdrawal, when the bank hits you with a service charge, and so forth. So, if you have a checking account you want to track with Money, set up a Money account for it. If you have a money market account and a savings account you want to track, set up a Money account for each of them as well.

You have a choice as to when you set up the accounts you want to use. You can set them up the first time you start Money, or you can set up your accounts sometime later. But you need to set up an account before you can start any record-keeping.

## Setting Up Accounts the First Time You Start Money

The first time Money starts it opens the Sample data file that comes with the program, and displays the Welcome To The Money 97 Tour dialog box. If you want to take the tour, click Next and follow the directions. If you want to open your own file and get started setting up your accounts, click Cancel. In the next dialog box, select the Create A New Money File option and click OK. Money opens a new file that it calls My Money. The Contents Window appears, displaying a message that reads "Click here to create new accounts." If you do as Money suggests, Money displays the Account Manager window, which is blank. Click the New Account button and Money starts the New Account Wizard and displays the first New Account dialog box.

**Starting Microsoft Money.** *If you've just installed Money, the installation program starts Money for you. If you need to start Money yourself, click the Start button, choose Programs, and then choose Microsoft Money.*

Wizards, as you might already know, are pretty slick. All you have to do to set up an account with the New Account Wizard is answer the questions posed in a series of dialog boxes. To answer these questions, you fill in text boxes—input blanks, really—and you click buttons.

**Accounts You Can Track Besides Bank Accounts.** *You can also set up accounts for tracking assets (things you own), liabilities (money you owe), and your investments. How you set up and use these other accounts is described in future chapters. This chapter just describes how you set up your checking, savings, and other bank accounts.*

 *The first account you set up should probably be a checking or savings account at a bank or other financial institution. If for some reason you want to set up some other kind of account first (say an asset or liability account), see the section of this book dealing with that kind of account. But I don't recommmend it.*

To use the New Account Wizard, follow these steps:

**1** Read the introduction and click Next. Enter the name of the bank or financial institution where you keep your account in the combo box in the dialog box. Then click Next again.

**2** In the next New Account dialog box, the Wizard asks what kind of account you want to set up. Click Checking if you're setting up a checking account, click Savings if you're setting up a savings account, or click Bank if you're setting up some other kind of bank account that isn't a checking or savings account.

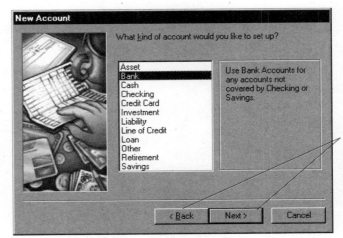

To move between the Wizard's dialog boxes, you click the Back and Next command buttons.

**A Friendly Reminder.** *Don't worry about remembering that you need to include all of the uncleared transactions (the transactions that weren't included on the last bank statement). I'll remind you to do that in the next chapter.*

**3** Click Next. The Wizard asks what name you want to give your new bank account.

You don't have to give it a fancy name. But if you (or your spouse) have more than one bank account, give the new bank account a name that easily and uniquely identifies it. That way, everybody who uses your Money program will know exactly what this account is. For example, you might name the account after the bank it's kept in ("Big National") or after the person who uses it ("Steve's checking").

**4** Click Next. If you know your account number, enter it in the next dialog box. If not, leave the text box blank. You can enter the number later.

**5** Click Next. The Wizard asks for the account's opening balance.

You can enter the account's current balance if you've got that figure handy. But you know what? It turns out that it's a better idea to enter the account's ending balance listed on your last bank statement and then enter all of the uncleared transactions that weren't included on the last statement.

By entering the balance as of your last statement, you start your record-keeping with your records balanced with the bank's records. And that makes reconciling your account a lot easier.

**6** Click Next. Money asks if you have other accounts at the bank that you want to set up at the same time. If you do, Money takes you back to step 2 for the next account.

**7** Click Next. Money asks if you would like to find out about the Online Services offered through the bank. If you click yes, you can get set up for online banking, but for now, click No, Not Now. (Online Banking Setup is discussed in Chapter 9.)

**8** Click Finish. A new icon for the account appears in the Account Manager window.

## Setting Up Accounts Sometime Later

The New Account Wizard appears automatically the first time you start Money, but you also use it to set up new accounts you want to track at a later date.

To use the New Account Wizard to set up another new bank account, follow these steps: click the Account Manager command button. When Money displays the Account Manager window, click the New Account button near the bottom of the screen. Money starts the New Account Wizard, which you use in the way I described in the preceding section.

## A Few Words about the Account Manager Window

You don't need to know anything more than I've already told you to use the Account Manager window. In fact, unless you add new accounts on a regular basis, you'll rarely look at this window. So if you're the sort of person who can't be bothered with the little details, or you don't like cluttering your head with information you won't use very often, stop reading. But if you don't mind cluttering your head with all the little details, review the figure that follows. It describes the Account Manager's buttons and its View triangle menu.

## Using the Account Manager's Buttons and View Menu

The View triangle menu lets you choose how Money lists accounts and how much detail Money shows for each account.

Click the New Account button to start the New Account Wizard.

By clicking the Account Manager window's Account Details button, you can store additional information about an account you've selected.

To remove an account you don't need, click the account's icon in the Account Manager window, and then click the Delete button.

To display the selected account's transactions in a register, click the Go To Account button.

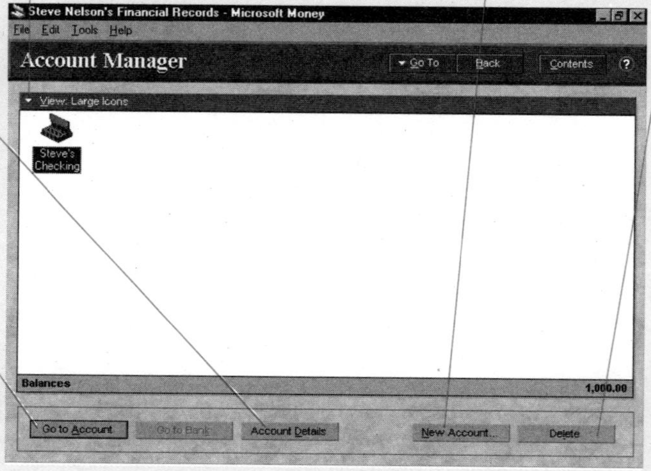

**Steve Nelson's Financial Records - Microsoft Money**

File  Edit  Tools  Help

**Account Manager**

Go To    Back    Contents    ?

View: Large Icons

Steve's Checking

Balances                                        1,000.00

Go to Account    Go to Bank    Account Details    New Account...    Delete

## In Conclusion

Once you've installed Money and set up an account or two, you've done the hard part. Now you're ready to begin using Money to keep your financial records. If you're ready to take a break, go ahead and take one. This is a good stopping point.

If you want to keep working, however, flip ahead to the next chapter. It describes how you use Money to track your income and spending.

# Keeping Your Checkbook

**A**t its core, Money is a computerized checkbook, so instead of keeping track of your checks and deposits in a paper register, you use an on-screen register. You get several very important benefits from computerizing your checkbook records:

➤ Your computer calculates your account balances so that as long as you enter the correct numbers, your account balance is correct.

➤ You can tag, or describe, checks as falling into specific **income** and **expense** categories. That way, you can see how much you spent for, say, utilities. All you have to do to find out how much you spent in a certain category is click the mouse a couple of times.

➤ You can reconcile, or balance, your account in roughly two minutes.

➤ You can print checks or transmit payments electronically, which makes paying bills much easier and much quicker.

In this chapter, I'll describe how to track your account balances and categorize your income and spending. (In the three chapters that follow this one, I'll describe how you print checks, print reports, and reconcile bank accounts.)

**A Few Addenda.** *In addition to its computerized checkbook features, Money also provides tools for tracking other assets and liabilities, including credit card transactions and investments. And it provides a powerful set of financial planning wizards as well. Later chapters describe these features.*

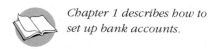

*Chapter 1 describes how to set up bank accounts.*

# Recording Checks and Deposits

To use Money, you set up an account for each bank account you want to track. Then you record the checks you write and the deposits you make for each account. You already know most of what you need to know to record these transactions. Money doesn't change the way you record checks and deposits; it simply provides an on-screen form for you to use in place of the paper register that the bank gives you when you open a new account.

## Displaying the Account Register

To display an account register, start Money, and then click the Account Register button in the upper-left corner of the Money Contents window. Money displays the Account Register window.

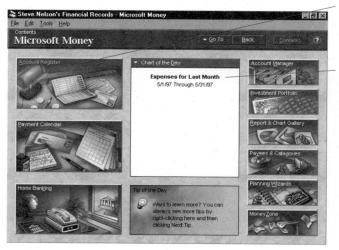

Click here to display an account register.

Until you start entering some real data, the Chart of the Day won't show anything.

*You'll find it easiest to set aside a regular time for entering transactions— perhaps when you pay bills or on Saturday morning.*

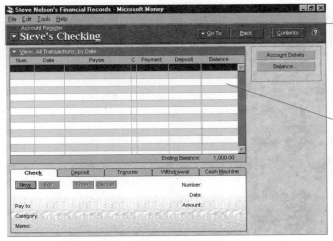

This is the triangle menu you use to select the account you want to see.

This register lists all the checks and deposits for an account and the account balance after each check or deposit.

**It's Easy to Adjust Check Numbers and Dates.** *You can press the + key to add 1 to the check number or to move the date one day forward. You can press the - key to subtract 1 from the check number or to move the date one day backward.*

Each register lists the transactions for a single account. But you can use the triangle menu near the upper-left corner of the Account Register window to display a list of accounts and select the one you want to see.

## Entering Your First Check

When you enter a check, you use the data input area at the bottom of the Account Register window. In a nutshell, what you do is click the Check tab and then describe the check by filling in the blanks. To move between the blanks, press the Tab key or click the mouse on the blank you want to fill in. When you finish, click Enter. Money records the check and recalculates the balance. The steps are described in detail on the next page.

## Recording a Check

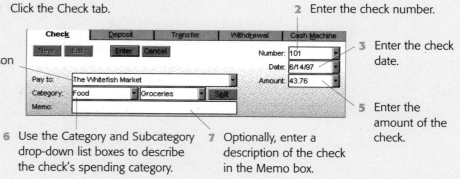

1 Click the Check tab.

2 Enter the check number.

3 Enter the check date.

4 Enter the name of the person or business you're paying.

5 Enter the amount of the check.

6 Use the Category and Subcategory drop-down list boxes to describe the check's spending category.

7 Optionally, enter a description of the check in the Memo box.

**What If I Can't Find a Category That Describes My Check?** *If you can't find a category that correctly describes the check, enter a new category in the Category box. Money then displays a dialog box that asks you to name and describe the category.*

**Subcategories Are Categories within Categories.** *The second category box is for recording a subcategory, which is a category within a category. A few of the categories on Money's starting category list use subcategories. For example, the Insurance category contains the following subcategories: Automobile, Health, Homeowner's/Renter's, and Life.*

# Recording Your Second and Subsequent Checks

Recording your second and subsequent checks works the same way as recording your first check. However, after you record a check to a particular person or business, Money performs a nifty trick to help you the next time you write a check to that same person or business. By activating the Pay To drop-down list box and selecting the payee from the list, you can have Money fill in the rest of the check blanks with the same information you used the last time you entered a check to this payee.

For example, suppose you're writing a check to Puget Power, the local electric company, and the last time you did this the check amount was $45 and the category was Bills. When you activate the Pay To drop-down list and select Puget Power, Money fills in the check amount as $45 and the check category as Bills. If you included something in the Memo field (perhaps your account number), that bit of information gets copied, too.

**What If I Make a Purchase Using Another Currency?**

*Money supplies a Currency Converter calculator that you can use to convert foreign currency amounts to dollars or pounds (or whatever other currency you bank in). To use the Currency Converter calculator, press F8 when an Amount field is selected.*

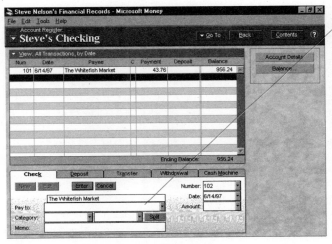

When you are entering a payee, you can type the first few characters of the name of a person or business, and when Money recognizes the name, it fills in the rest.

This "filling in the blanks" trick, which goes by the name AutoComplete, can seem sort of goofy at first. But it's a very handy tool. The reason it's so handy is that when you write a check to someone you've paid before, much of the information will be the same. Sometimes, in fact, almost all of it will be the same. And that saves you the trouble of having to fill in everything all over again.

## Recording Deposits

Once you get the hang of entering checks in the Account Register window, deposits are a snap. You describe the date of the deposit, who paid you, the amount of the deposit, and, finally, the category that the deposit falls into. All the same data-entry tricks that work for checks also work for deposits. You can move between fields by using the tab key or clicking the mouse. You can press the + and - keys to adjust the deposit number and date, for example. The steps you follow are shown in detail on the next page.

**Handling Withdrawals and Cash Machine Transactions.**

*The Account Register window also provides Withdrawal and Cash Machine tabs. You can use these to record cash machine withdrawals as well as other withdrawals you make. Predictably, recording a withdrawal or cash machine transaction works the same way as recording a check.*

**Recording a Deposit**

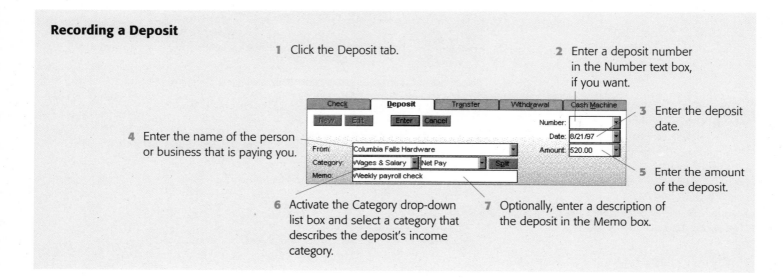

1 Click the Deposit tab.

2 Enter a deposit number in the Number text box, if you want.

3 Enter the deposit date.

4 Enter the name of the person or business that is paying you.

5 Enter the amount of the deposit.

6 Activate the Category drop-down list box and select a category that describes the deposit's income category.

7 Optionally, enter a description of the deposit in the Memo box.

**Splitting Your Gross Pay.**
*If you enter Gross Pay in the Subcategory box, Money displays the New Paycheck Wizard, which shows you how to split your gross paycheck into categories like net pay, taxes, and retirement fund contributions.*

# The Best Category Trick

You know what? I can guess what you're thinking right now. You're thinking that this computerized check register business seems pretty darn good. But you've also identified a problem. "What," you're wondering to yourself, "do I do about checks and deposits that fall into more than one category?"

Fortunately, Money does let you record a check that pays for items that fall into more than one expense category. Say, for example, that you've just written a check to The Whitefish Market, the local grocery store, but that your $91.76 didn't buy just one thing. You bought some groceries. You had a drug prescription filled. And you bought some motor oil for your car. Can you record this sort of check? You bet you can.

To record this sort of check, you click the Split command button rather than enter a category. When you click Split, Money displays the Split Transaction dialog box.

## Splitting a Transaction

2 Optionally, enter a memo description of the first spending category.

3 Enter the first spending category's amount on the first line, too.

1 Enter the first category here, on the first line.

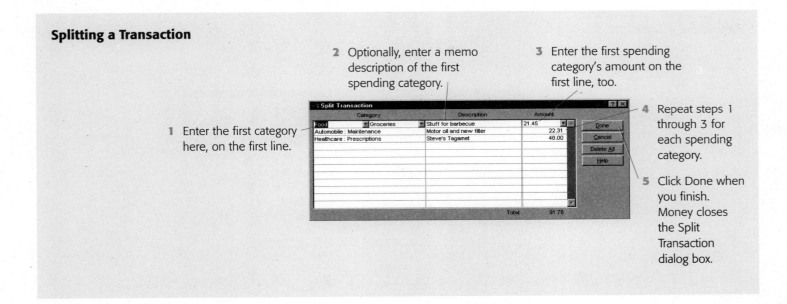

4 Repeat steps 1 through 3 for each spending category.

5 Click Done when you finish. Money closes the Split Transaction dialog box.

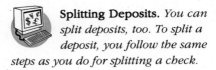

**Splitting Deposits.** *You can split deposits, too. To split a deposit, you follow the same steps as you do for splitting a check.*

# Account Transfers

There's a good chance that you have both a checking account and a savings account. If this is the case, you should know how to record one other type of bank account transaction, an account transfer. This works pretty much like you'd expect: You need to identify the accounts you're moving money between, the date of the transfer, and the amount of the transfer. Follow the procedures illustrated on the next page.

## Recording a Transfer

**1** Click the Transfer tab.

**2** Activate the drop-down list box next to Number and choose Electronic Transfer (Xfer).

**4** Enter the name of the account you're moving money from.

**3** Enter the transfer date.

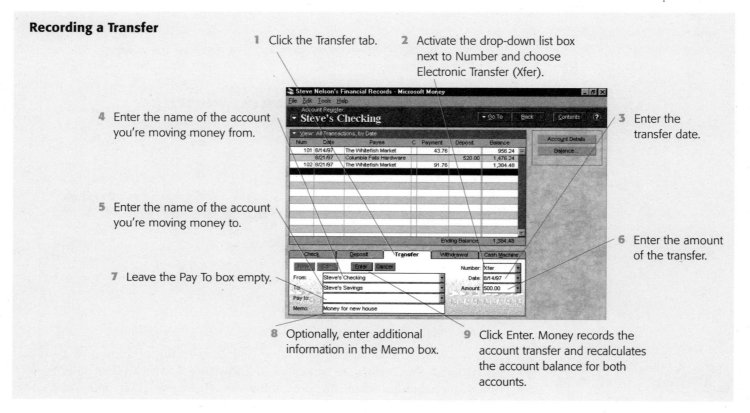

**5** Enter the name of the account you're moving money to.

**6** Enter the amount of the transfer.

**7** Leave the Pay To box empty.

**8** Optionally, enter additional information in the Memo box.

**9** Click Enter. Money records the account transfer and recalculates the account balance for both accounts.

# If You Ever Make Mistakes...

It is easy to fix mistakes you happen to make while entering checks, deposits, and account transfers. To change a piece of data in a transaction, make sure the Account Register window shows the right account and then click the transaction. This tells Money to display the transaction on the Check, Deposit, or Transfer tab. Next, click the Edit button on the Check, Deposit, or Transfer tab and then make your changes by entering the correct information in the box where the incorrect information is. If the amount shows as $42.13 instead of as $41.23, for example, click the amount field and then type 41.23.

Deleting a transaction is even simpler. Just select the transaction by clicking it, and then press the Delete key on the keyboard. Money will ask if you really want to delete the transaction. If you do, click Yes. Otherwise, click No.

## Backing Up Your Financial Records

As soon as you start using Money, you'll want to begin backing up the financial information you collect. (Backing up just means to make a separate copy of your financial records in case something destroys or corrupts the original copies.)

To back up your financial records, make sure you have a floppy disk available that you can keep your backup file on. (You can reuse the same one, if that's convenient.) It's not usually wise to keep the backup file on your hard disk, since the backup file is meant to protect you if the hard disk should fail for some reason.

Choose Backup from the File menu. Money displays a dialog box that lets you specify the name of the backup file and where the backup file should be created. Money suggests you use your original file name and the word "backup" to name the backup file.

For example, if your original file is named "Steve's Records," the suggested name for the backup is "Steve's Records Backup." Money also suggests you backup to the same folder on your hard drive where your original file is kept so that you can backup automatically whenever you exit Money. You'll have to decide between security and convenience. You can choose another name and location for the backup file, however, by replacing the contents of the Back Up text box.

If you need to use your backup copy, choose Open from the File menu. When Money displays the Open dialog box, use it to identify the backup file and describe its location.

**Don't Be Without a Backup.** *It's a good idea to back up your Money financial records each time you finish using Money.*

# About the Account Register's Other Bells and Whistles

If you've been reading this chapter from the start, you know how to use Money's account register. Nevertheless, you probably won't be surprised to learn that there is a lot more to the account register than I've described thus far. Money's account register is packed with all sorts of extra bells and whistles for doing sophisticated record-keeping.

Most people, however, don't need to know about these other bells and whistles. So if you know how to do what you want to do, stop reading.

If you haven't stopped reading, I'm going to assume that you want to learn more about the account register. And that's what I'll do in laundry-list fashion in the remaining pages of this chapter.

## A Nice View

*You'll usually want to view transactions in order of their dates because that's the way they clear the bank.*

*Chapter 5 describes how to reconcile bank accounts.*

The View triangle menu lets you choose which transactions are listed in the account register and how you view them. You can choose, for example, to list transactions by date, number, or entry order. You can list all the transactions in an account or only those that weren't cleared when you reconciled the account. You can view more information about a transaction, instead of just the date, payee, and amount. And you can remove the Transaction Forms. (The Transaction Forms are the data-entry forms that initially appear at the bottom of the Account Register window.)

The View triangle menu options aren't complicated or difficult to use. So if you're interested, you may as well just experiment with them. (The default account register view, by the way, is to list all transactions by date and show only the top line of each transaction.)

*Chapter 9 describes how to set up Money and your personal computer for online banking.*

**What about Those Other Buttons?** *There are a handful of other buttons scattered across the Account Register window. At the top are the Go To, Back, and Contents buttons, for example. If you want to learn how these buttons work, just experiment with them. You'll see how they work after about sixty seconds of noodling around.*

*Don't forget to record the checks and deposits that have cleared the bank since the ending bank statement date. Your account balance is wrong until you enter these transactions.*

## A Few Details

Click the Account Details button to display boxes you can use to collect and store general account information. You can store the bank's name, an account number, or what the minimum balance is. There's also a button to click if you want to set up an online banking account.

When you click Account Details, Money also displays a chart that shows your account balance over the year. I'm not going to show this stuff in a figure. I'll let Money surprise you.

## In Conclusion

With the information in this chapter, you can begin your financial record-keeping with Money. You'll have no problem, for example, recording the checks you write on a bank account and the deposits you make to a bank account.

I do have two other points to make, however, before the chapter ends. First of all, if you followed my suggestion (and Money's suggestion!) to enter your starting account balance as the ending balance shown on your last bank statement, you need to record any checks or deposits that had not cleared the bank by the date of the ending statement. You can do this by using your own records, if they're complete and accurate, or you can wait until next month's statement arrives and use it to record these missing transactions.

You should also know where you can continue learning about Money: Chapter 3 describes how to print checks with Money, Chapter 4 explains how to print reports, and Chapter 5 shows how to reconcile bank accounts.

# Printing Checks

**Y**ou don't need to print your checks with Microsoft Money, but many Money users do. The idea is that you save time—and produce neater check forms—by doing so. When you choose to print checks with Money, Money takes the information that you enter when you record your checks and uses that information to print your checks.

*Chapter 2 describes how to record checks.*

## Should You Even Print Checks?

Good question. There are advantages and disadvantages to printing checks with Microsoft Money. The big disadvantage of check printing is the cost. Check forms are quite expensive. Before you dismiss this point as the penny-pinching complaint of an accountant, let me review a few numbers. If you buy 200 checks from your bank, you pay somewhere between $8 and $10, depending on the type of check you order and how much your bank charges. Computer check forms run between $40 and $60 for 250 checks, plus a few dollars for shipping. So instead of paying $.04 to $.05 for each check, you pay $.16 to $.24. The difference can be measured in pennies, but if you write a couple hundred checks a year, you'll spend $35 to $50 more for computer checks.

*Chapter 10 describes another way to pay your bills—electronically.*

Check forms aren't bad, however. In fact, they provide three advantages over handwritten and typewritten checks. One advantage is obvious: If you print large numbers of checks—say, several hundred a month—the time savings can be huge. If you can batch all your check writing and print all your checks only once or twice a month, you can save several hours each month.

*Chapter 25 describes how to calculate payroll amounts and prepare payroll checks with Money. The information described there applies both to small businesses and to people who have household employees such as nannies.*

*The business check forms some banks sell can be as expensive or almost as expensive as the ones used for printing checks.*

Another advantage of computer-printed checks is that the final product—neat, computer-printed checks—is more professional-looking than handwritten ones. Especially if your handwriting is, uh, less than perfect. For some individuals and especially for businesses, appearance is very important. Spending extra money to look more professional might be a wise investment if you're trying to build credibility among your business contacts.

The third advantage of computer-printed checks is that some check forms provide stubs, or vouchers, on which you can describe what the check is for. For example, if you use Money to produce a check to pay several invoices, you can use the voucher to note the invoice numbers. If you use Money to prepare payroll checks, you can describe employees' gross pay and deductions.

How do the advantages and disadvantages of computer-printed checks stack up? It depends on your specific needs. My guess is that most home users, and even some small businesses, won't find it worthwhile to use computer-printed checks. The time savings don't justify the cost. On the other hand, any business with more than a few dozen checks to write each month will probably benefit from the time saved and the usefulness of the vouchers.

## Choosing the Right Check Form

Impact printers let you print wallet-size checks, standard checks, and voucher checks. Wallet-size check forms make the most sense for home users and home-based businesses. Here's why: Wallet-size checks, at only 2.83 inches by 6 inches, are smaller than standard checks. It's easy to slip one into a shirt pocket or your wallet for a trip to the grocery store or local Chinese restaurant. And they have a 2.5-inch stub. The stub makes it easier to load wallet-size check forms into a printer. In addition, wallet-size check forms are less expensive than other choices.

*An "impact printer" is any type of printer for which the character is printed on the paper by some sort of impression, similar to the way a typewriter key hits the ribbon and paper to print a letter. This category includes dot-matrix printers and daisywheel printers, for example.*

Standard and voucher checks are good choices for businesses because these checks are larger. In both forms, the check is 3.5 inches by 8.5 inches. The only difference between them is that a voucher check has an attached 3.5-inch-by-8.5-inch voucher, or check stub. Microsoft Money prints split-transaction information on the voucher, so any information that you enter in the Split Transaction dialog box to describe the check appears on the voucher as well.

A wallet-size check

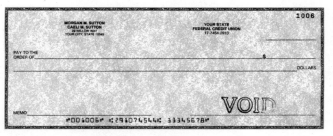

A standard-size check

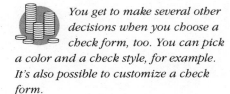

*You get to make several other decisions when you choose a check form, too. You can pick a color and a check style, for example. It's also possible to customize a check form.*

With an inkjet or laser printer, you have the same basic choices that you have if you own an impact printer: laser wallet, laser standard, and laser voucher. (The only difference is that the check forms look a little different because they're fed through the printer as individual sheets rather than as a continuous strip of check forms.) When you choose a particular check form to use with a laser printer, you should consider the same factors I discussed for an impact printer check form.

# Ordering Your Checks

*You can also find information on ordering checks in the booklet that comes with Money.*

Once you pick the kind of check form you want, you can order checks from Deluxe Business Systems by filling out the paperwork that comes inside the Money box. You can either mail the paperwork to Deluxe or fax it to them at (800) 531-1931.

If you got Money in some other way, you can also order check forms by calling Deluxe at (800) 432-1285. If you telephone Deluxe Business Systems, you need your bank account number, bank name and address, and starting check form number. (You can get the bank account number and the bank name and address from one of your existing check forms.)

# Describing the Checks You Want to Print

*Recording a check is described in detail in Chapter 2.*

When you want to print a computer check (I'm calling it a computer check to distinguish it from a check you write by hand), you first record the check in the register, as shown in the following figure.

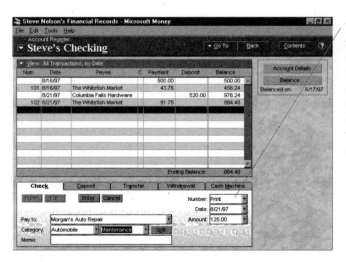

You describe a check that you want to print using the Account Register window. Be sure to specify the Number as "Print" by selecting Print This Transaction from the drop-down list.

# Printing Checks

To print computer checks, you display the Account Register window. Then you follow these steps:

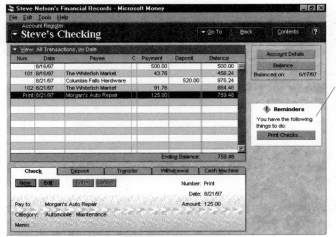

This message and button show when you have checks to print.

**How Often Should I Print Checks?** *You'll probably want to print checks every time you regularly pay your bills. For example, if you pay your bills every Saturday morning, you might want to print your checks then, too.*

1 Click the Print Checks button on the right side of the screen. (This button appears only after you've described a check you want to print.) Money displays a dialog box that asks which type of check form you've selected and loaded in your printer.

2 Select a check form and click Next. Money displays a dialog box that asks whether you want to print all your checks or only selected checks and what number it should use for the first printed check.

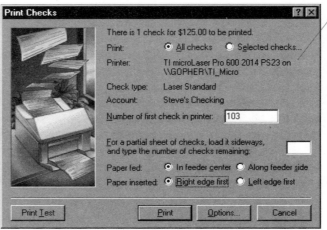

Money uses this dialog box to ask which checks you want to print and how it should number those checks.

3 If you want to print only some of the checks, click the Selected Checks button. When you do, Money displays the Select Checks dialog box. Click the computer checks you want to print, and then click OK to close the Select Checks dialog box.

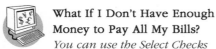

**What If I Don't Have Enough Money to Pay All My Bills?**

*You can use the Select Checks dialog box to pay those checks that you do have money to pay. Note that the bottom of the Select Checks dialog box shows the total dollar amount of the checks you've selected to print.*

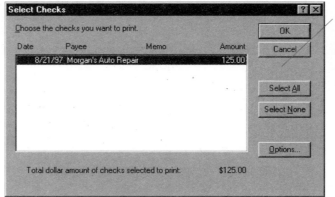

Money uses this dialog box if you decide to print some, and not all, of your checks.

**4** Look at the preprinted number of the first check form you loaded in your printer, enter this number in the Print Checks dialog box, and then click Print. Money prints your computer check or checks. Then it displays the next dialog box, which asks whether the computer check or checks printed correctly.

**5** If the computer checks did print correctly, click Finish. If they didn't, click Reprint.

If you click Finish, Money updates the account register so that the checks now show the check numbers. If you click Reprint, Money restarts the check printing process with step 3.

## Check Printing Tips and Tricks

If you have extra check forms that didn't get used, just stick them in your wallet and use them the next time you go to the grocery store. Or the office supply store. Or wherever. Of course, you'll have to remember to write down a description of the check so you can enter it in the account register. The main thing to realize is that you aren't required to print computer checks with a computer. You can fill them out by hand with a pen.

If you have check forms that print incorrectly or get messed up in some way, be sure to mark the check form as void. To do this, write the word "VOID" in large letters across the face of the check. Use a pen. Basically, you just want to make sure that neither you nor anyone else uses the check form again. You don't, for example, want to accidentally send the check. And you don't want some dishonest soul to try to cash the check. (You should store voided checks with your canceled checks.)

If you want to record a voided check, select the check in the account register and choose Mark As Void from the Edit menu. Recording voided checks is a darn good idea. Money ignores voided checks when it calculates your account balance. And it doesn't include the check amount in any reports. By voiding a check, you keep a record of it in your account register.

**A Bit of Check Form Trivia.** *Check forms don't actually need to be neat-looking, well-organized paper forms. In theory, you could use just about any type of material to provide the payee and bank with the information needed to cash and process the check. Rumor has it, in fact, that a Montana cattle rancher has even used a cowhide as a check form.*

*It's a good idea to carefully sign your checks using a signature that isn't easily duplicated. Signatures that consist of just a wavy line and some squiggles are more easily forged.*

# In Conclusion

Check printing with Money is easy. It's fast. But it isn't for everyone. The cost and extra formality of computer check forms mean that some people—and I'm in this group—don't need to print computer checks.

I do have a suggestion, however. If you're intrigued by the idea, if you're someone who likes to be neat, or if you print a lot of checks each month, check printing is something you should try. If you're in this group, go ahead and place a small order for some checks. Then try printing computer checks for a month or two. You may really find it useful. A lot of people do.

*Keep your computer check forms locked up in a desk or cabinet. Professional forgers often steal blank check forms as a first step in the theft.*

# Printing Reports

U sing Money only for financial record-keeping delivers some benefits. Money, for example, calculates account balances automatically and accurately. It prints checks for you. And after you begin using Money, you'll discover that reconciling a bank account takes only a couple of minutes. Literally.

But the biggest benefit of using Money isn't that it allows you to do all of these things. The biggest benefit is that Money lets you sort and summarize the financial information you collect in a bunch of different ways. Using Money's reports, for example, you can see how much you're really spending on housing, groceries, work expenses, and so forth. You can easily track and tally tax deductions. And you can compare your actual income and expenses with whatever amounts you budgeted.

## Viewing Reports On-Screen

To produce an on-screen report, click the Report And Chart Gallery button on the Money Contents window. Or, if you're working in a different window, click the Go To triangle menu and choose the Report And Chart Gallery command. Money displays the Report And Chart Gallery window, as shown on the next page.

*Chapter 5 describes how to reconcile bank accounts with Money.*

**Setting Up Your Printer.** *You can change the way Windows 95 prints. To do this, choose the Print Setup from the File menu, and then from the submenu choose Report And Chart Setup. When Money displays the Report and Chart Setup dialog box, use the Orientation options to specify whether Money should print pages in a portrait orientation or a landscape orientation. Use the Options button to change the way the printer works. You'll see a Properties dialog box, which provides a bunch of buttons and boxes you can use. Depending on the type of printer you're using, you can usually change things like the paper size your printer expects, the printer's print quality, and so forth.*

## Producing an On-Screen Report

Click these buttons to see reports and charts that summarize a particular aspect of your finances—such as your spending habits.

Money displays a sample of the selected report here.

Select a specific report or chart by clicking one of the items listed in this box.

Click the Go To Report/Chart button to have Money produce the selected report or chart.

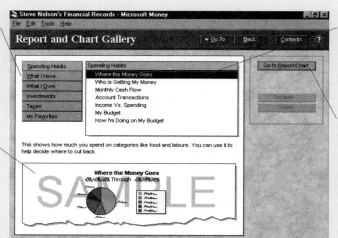

Once you select a report or chart and click the Go To Report/Chart button, Money produces the selected report or chart and displays it in its own window, as shown on the next page.

## Working with On-Screen Reports

The window shows most of the report or chart, but usually the report doesn't fit entirely within the window, and you have to scroll up, down, left, or right to read all of it.

Click these buttons to display the same basic information in a chart (if a report is showing) or in a report (if a chart is showing).

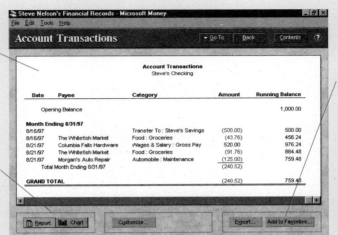

Click this button to add this report or chart to a list of personal favorites. This Favorites list can be displayed by clicking the My Favorites button in the Report And Chart Gallery window.

# Reviewing the Microsoft Money Reports

Money provides five basic report categories: Spending Habits, What I Have, What I Owe, Investments, and Taxes. Each category of report conveys different information and serves a different purpose. As a result, you might not be sure—particularly when you're first working with Money—which report category you want in a given situation.

To address this initial confusion, the table on the next page summarizes the five categories of reports. The table describes the information that reports within a category provide and gives brief descriptions of how reports within a category can be used.

| Category | Description | Purpose |
|---|---|---|
| Spending Habits | Summarizes transactions by payee or category and compares actual income and spending with budgeted income and spending | Allows you to see how you earn and spend your money, where you earn and spend your money, and how your actual earnings and expenditures compare to your plans |
| What I Have | Summarizes account balances at a point in time or over a period of time | Allows you to estimate your net worth and to see the estimated value of your assets and liabilities |
| What I Owe | Summarizes liability account balances and post-dated payment transactions | Allows you to gauge the magnitude of your debts and to plan repayment strategies |
| Investments | Summarizes investment account and transaction information | Allows you to assess the profitability of your investments and to perform year-end investment tax planning |
| Taxes | Summarizes tax-related transactions | Shows you what taxable income and tax deductions you'll report on your year-end tax return and allows you to perform year-end tax planning |

**My Favorites List.** *A little later in this chapter, in the section titled "Your Personal Archive," I describe a short list of the reports that I think you should add to your Favorites list, print regularly, and permanently file away someplace.*

# Printing Reports

When you produce a report or chart that you want to print, choose Print from the File menu. Money displays the Print Report dialog box. Usually, when Money displays this dialog box, you simply click OK to have Money produce the report (with Windows 95's help).

But if you want to, you can use the buttons and boxes in the dialog box to print multiple copies of the report or to print the report at a higher print quality, or resolution, as my "Account Transactions, Steve's Checking" report shows.

## Printing a Report

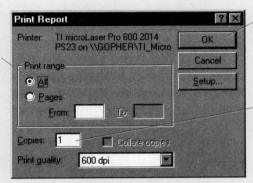

Click OK when you're ready to print.

You can specify that only some of the pages in a report print by using the Print Range options.

Use the Copies text box to print multiple copies of the report.

The Account Transactions reports lists all the checks, deposits, and transfers for an account.

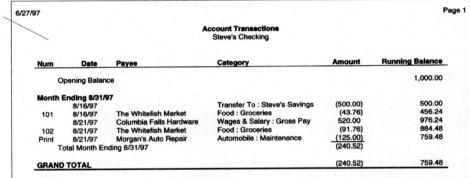

| | | | | | |
|---|---|---|---|---|---|
| 6/27/97 | | | | | Page 1 |

**Account Transactions**
Steve's Checking

| Num | Date | Payee | Category | Amount | Running Balance |
|---|---|---|---|---|---|
| | | Opening Balance | | | 1,000.00 |
| **Month Ending 8/31/97** | | | | | |
| | 8/16/97 | | Transfer To : Steve's Savings | (500.00) | 500.00 |
| 101 | 8/16/97 | The Whitefish Market | Food : Groceries | (43.76) | 456.24 |
| | 8/21/97 | Columbia Falls Hardware | Wages & Salary : Gross Pay | 520.00 | 976.24 |
| 102 | 8/21/97 | The Whitefish Market | Food : Groceries | (91.76) | 884.48 |
| Print | 8/21/97 | Morgan's Auto Repair | Automobile : Maintenance | (125.00) | 759.48 |
| | | Total Month Ending 8/31/97 | | (240.52) | |
| **GRAND TOTAL** | | | | (240.52) | 759.48 |

# Your Personal Archives

Money is capable of producing a bunch of different reports and charts—more than two dozen in all. As a result, deciding which reports to print and which to save permanently can be a bit overwhelming. Fortunately, you can apply some good rules of thumb in this area.

## Banking Records

You should print out an Account Transactions report at the end of every month and file it with your bank statement and canceled checks. An Account Transactions report shows all the transactions in your register and, as such, provides a complete record of all the transactions you entered. In a pinch, if you forget to back up your Money data, you could use your Account Transactions report to rebuild your financial records. (You would do this by reentering all the transactions shown on the report.)

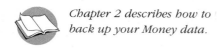

*Chapter 2 describes how to back up your Money data.*

## Tax Records

Money's reports provide an excellent way to track tax deductions. (To get to these reports, click the Taxes button in the Report And Chart Gallery window.)

While you may have reason to use all four of the Money tax reports, only the Tax-Related Transactions report is essential for your personal archives. You should print one copy of a Tax-Related Transaction report at the end of each year and store it with a copy of your tax return. In this way, you'll be able to answer any questions about, for example, the individual transactions that make up your charitable contribution deduction.

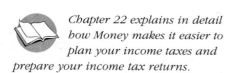

*Chapter 22 explains in detail how Money makes it easier to plan your income taxes and prepare your income tax returns.*

## How Long Should You Retain Records?

People throw around many different rules for retaining canceled checks, bank statements, copies of old tax returns, and other financial records. I suggest that you keep everything for seven years after you file a tax return. If you filed 1991's tax return in April of 1992, you should keep all your 1991 tax return stuff until April of 1999.

The reason you should hang on to the stuff for so long is that the Internal Revenue Service can examine returns as old as seven years. The IRS can't go back any further than that, except in a handful of very special cases. So as long as you keep everything together for at least seven years, you'll almost certainly be okay. (The "handful of very special cases" have to do with businesses with net operating loss carry-forwards and taxpayers with foreign tax credits. If you don't know what these are, they probably don't apply to you anyway. But consult a tax advisor if you're not sure.)

**Which Records Should I Retain for Seven Years?** *When I say to hold on to your records for seven years, I'm referring to financial records. Some documents should be saved for much longer than seven years. Hang on to insurance records permanently, for example, because it's possible in some circumstances to file a claim against a policy from years and years ago. Many legal documents should also be retained permanently. (Consult with an attorney for information on this.)*

# A Few Words on Exporting Reports

*Exporting* means to move a report to another application. If you take a report and move it to Microsoft Excel, for example, you're exporting a report. You export reports so you can manipulate the data in some way or use the data in another document. For example, you might export a report so you can analyze it in a spreadsheet application. Or you might want to include a report in a word-processing document you're working on, in which case you would export it to the word-processing application.

When you export a report, Money creates something called a *tab-delimited text file*. Tab-delimited text files are easy for spreadsheet applications to import and open, and they can also be imported and opened by most word-processing applications.

**Exporting a Report**

1 Display the report in a window.

2 Click the Export button. Money displays the Export Report dialog box.

3 Use the Save In box to specify where Money should locate the exported report.

4 Use the File Name box to name the new file.

5 Click OK.

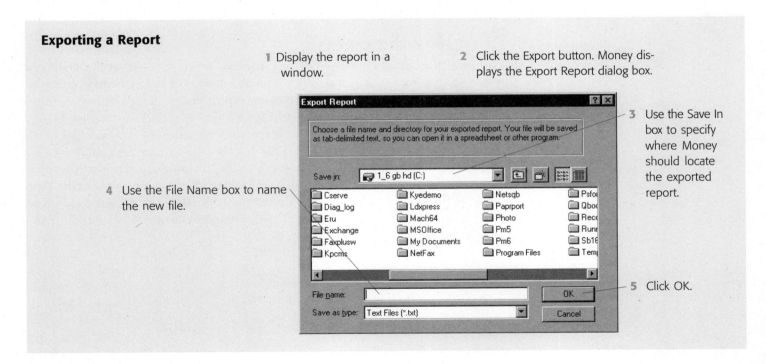

**How Do I Use an Exported File?** *To use a file you've created by exporting a Money report, you open the file within the other program. For example, if you want to import a file into Microsoft Excel, you would start Excel and choose Open from the File menu.*

To import the tab-delimited text file into another application, just open it from the other application. (You may need to indicate that the exported file uses the *.txt* extension.) If the application requires additional information from you about how to open the file, it will ask for that information when it tries to open the file.

# Creating Customized Reports

Since Money offers more than two dozen reports, you can usually find one that answers the questions you have. Nonetheless, Money gives you a rich set of customization options that you can use to change the appearance of reports. I could spend chapters and chapters describing Money's report options, but rather than provide encyclopedic descriptions of every customization option, I just want to describe the most important and useful ones.

## Changing the Date

The most important change—one you'll make frequently—is to the Date options. Money makes assumptions about the range of dates that each report should cover. For an Account Transactions report, for example, Money assumes you want to list every transaction. And for a Monthly Cash Flow report, Money assumes you want the report to summarize the previous month's financial transactions.

By using the Dates options, however, you can produce reports that cover any date range you want. The Dates drop-down list box provides many date range options: All Dates, All to Date, Current Month, Current Year, Month to Date, Year to Date, and so forth. You can also enter your own dates in the From and To boxes.

To have a report summarize a different range of dates, follow these steps:

1 Produce the report on-screen so that Money displays the report in a window.

2 Click the Customize button. Money displays the Customize Report dialog box.

**The Customize Report Dialog Box.** *Which options appear in the Customize Report dialog box depend on the report. Different reports have different customization options.*

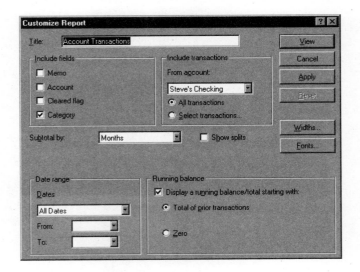

3 Activate the Dates drop-down list box and select one of the date ranges.

4 Click View to close the Customize Report dialog box and update the report.

# Summarizing Accounts

Typically, Money summarizes transactions from all the accounts you've set up when it generates a report. But this isn't always appropriate. For example, if you're married and you and your spouse have separate checking accounts, you may want a report that summarizes only your account's activity, not the activity in both your account and your spouse's.

To select accounts to summarize in a report, follow these steps:

1 Produce the report on-screen so that Money displays the report in a window.

2 Click the Customize command button. Money displays the Customize Report dialog box.

3 In the Include Transactions area, activate the From Account drop-down list box and select the Multiple Accounts option. Money displays the Select Accounts dialog box. Initially, all of the listed accounts are selected.

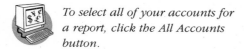

*To select all of your accounts for a report, click the All Accounts button.*

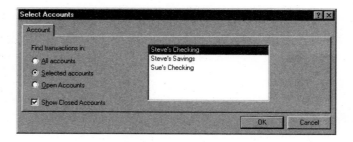

4 Remove the accounts you don't want to include on the report by clicking on them.

5 Click OK to close the Select Accounts dialog box.

6 Click View to close the Customize Report dialog box and update the report. Note that a little graphic and note appears next to the Customize button to alert you that this report has been customized.

*Remember, you can't hurt your data by summarizing it in reports or by depicting it in charts, so you should feel free to experiment on your own.*

# Other Changes You Can Make to Reports

Besides changing dates and the accounts that are summarized, there are other ways to customize reports. As a general rule, you can customize a report so it includes only the information you want and organizes that information in specific ways. The common customizations are pretty straightforward and easy to understand.

Here is a list of some of the other changes you can make to your reports using the Customize Report dialog box:

*Some customization options are not available for some kinds of reports.*

➤   Click the Widths button to display another dialog box that lets you change the widths of the columns in a report.

➤   Click the Fonts button to display a dialog box that lets you change font styles and point sizes.

➤   Use the Rows drop-down list box to choose how you want Money to summarize report information using the report's rows.

➤   Use the Columns drop-down list box to choose how many columns of financial information you want Money to display and what you want those columns to show.

➤   Click the Reset button to undo the effect of all your customization changes.

# In Conclusion

Microsoft Money provides many features that are much flashier than financial reporting, including bank account reconciliation, planning wizards, sophisticated investment analysis tools, and so on. In the coming chapters, I'll talk about those features. But Money's most useful feature is its ability to summarize financial affairs in reports and charts.

A Monthly Cash Flow report is a great resource for figuring out how you spend money and for budgeting next year's finances. A Tax-Related Transactions report makes preparing your taxes, if not painless, at least expeditious. And charts like Where The Money Goes can deliver financial insights that you'd never glean from a report.

# 5 Balancing Your Bank Accounts

**It Can Happen Here!** *In a crazy twist of fate, I have to tell you that long after I started writing about the importance of balancing bank accounts and how you might even catch an embezzler or forger this way, it actually happened to me. I came back from a short vacation and, by reconciling my bank account, found that an employee I'd recently hired had forged several checks. I talk more about that experience and what it taught me at the end of this chapter.*

L et's face it. One of the most tedious tasks in keeping a checking account is balancing, or reconciling, the account. Yet it's extremely important to do so. By comparing your records with the bank's, you can catch errors you've made in recording transactions and usually catch errors made by the bank as well. Only by regularly balancing an account can you protect yourself against problems such as forgery and embezzlement.

Fortunately, balancing an account with Money is a snap. By keeping your checkbook records with Money, you already have all the information you need. So balancing your account requires, quite literally, a few mouse-clicks. No joking.

## How to Balance a Bank Account

To balance a bank account (also known as reconciling a bank account), you need to have been using Money to keep track of the account for a month or so. After you've used Money for more than a month, you can balance the account by taking the following steps:

1 Display the account register for the bank account you want to reconcile. If you just started the Money program and the Contents window shows, you can do this by clicking the Account Register button. Money displays the Account Register window.

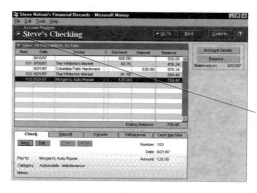

Use this triangle menu to display another account if the account currently shown isn't the one you want to reconcile.

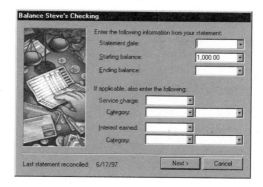

*Money uses the name of the account you're balancing in the dialog box name. In the figure shown here, for example, the dialog box title is "Balance Steve's Checking" because the name of the account is "Steve's Checking."*

2 Click the Balance button in the upper-right corner, below the Account Details button. Money displays the Introductory Balance Checking dialog box. Click Next.

3 In the next dialog box, enter the bank statement ending date in the Statement Date text box.

4 Enter the bank statement opening, or starting, balance in the Starting Balance text box.

**5** Enter the bank statement closing, or ending, balance in the Ending Balance text box.

**6** If your bank statement shows a monthly service charge, use the Service Charge text box and the drop-down list boxes to describe this expense.

The service charge amount, of course, goes in the Service Charge text box. The service charge category goes in the first drop-down list box. (In Money's initial list of categories, there is a Bank Charge category for recording just these sorts of charges.) If you're using subcategories, the subcategory goes in the second drop-down list box.

**7** If your bank statement shows any interest income, use the Interest Earned text box and the drop-down list boxes to describe this income.

The interest income amount goes in the Interest Earned text box. The interest income category goes in the first drop-down list box. As with a service charge, if you're using subcategories, the subcategory goes in the second drop-down list box.

**8** Click Next when you've correctly entered all the little bits of information that the Balance Checking dialog box asks for.

Money updates the account register so it shows only the unreconciled transactions in the account.

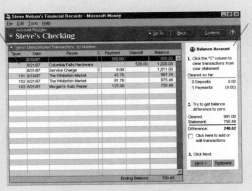

To the right of the register, Money displays instructions that explain how to go about balancing an account.

**What "Reconciling" Is.** *When you reconcile a bank account with Money, what you're really doing is recalculating your account balance on the basis of the transactions that have cleared the bank. If the "cleared transactions balance," or "cleared balance," equals the bank statement balance, your account reconciles.*

**9** Mark the checks and deposits that have cleared the bank. To do that, click in the C (for cleared) column for all transactions that show on your bank statement. When you do, Money places a *C* in this column to signal that this transaction has cleared the bank.

**10** When the difference between the cleared balance and the bank statement balance equals zero, click Next.

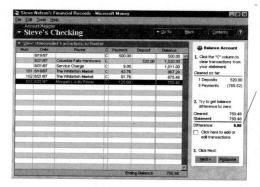

The cleared balance and bank statement balance, and the difference between these two amounts, all appear in the lower-right corner of the screen. They're labeled "Cleared," "Statement," and "Difference."

After you click Next, Money displays another dialog box congratulating you for for balancing your account.

**11** Click the Finish button. Money redisplays the account register in its usual format. You're done.

*If you look closely at the account register after you've reconciled an account, you'll notice that it changes the Cs you placed in the Cleared column to Rs. Those Rs mean that you've already used these checks and deposits in a reconciliation. Be careful, therefore, that you don't change them.*

# What to Do When an Account Won't Reconcile

If, after you complete the step-by-step process described in the preceding paragraphs, the cleared balance still doesn't equal the statement balance, the problem probably lies in one of the following places:

> You made a mistake marking transactions as cleared

> The register is missing one or more transactions

> You or the bank recorded a transaction incorrectly

If you find yourself in this situation, your best bet is first to be sure that your account register isn't missing a transaction. You can do this by checking that every transaction that appears on the bank statement also appears in the account register. I find, for example, that it's really easy to miss an automated teller machine (ATM) transaction or two (or three). You can add a missing check or deposit transaction directly in the Account Register window that shows when you're reconciling an account.

When you're sure that you've entered any missing transactions, verify that each transaction you recorded as "cleared" has really cleared. If you incorrectly marked an uncleared transaction as cleared, unmark it. If you accidentally left a cleared transaction marked as uncleared, by all means clear it.

Finally, compare the transaction amounts shown in your register with the transaction amounts shown on your bank statement. If you discover that you've entered one of your checks or deposits incorrectly, you can fix it by editing it in the list of unreconciled transactions. For example, you can change check or deposit information by clicking on the incorrect information and then editing or typing over the existing text or number.

One other tidbit I'll mention is this. Remember that in setting up your accounts, you need to begin with an accurate account balance, preferably a just-reconciled account balance. If you don't begin with an accurate balance, you might not be able to reconcile the account balance because your starting balance is wrong. In this case, there's not much you can do unless you want to go back to your old banking records and try to find the error or errors that made your starting account balance wrong. If you do find yourself in this situation, by the way, I suggest that you attempt to balance your bank account every month—and then give up once you can't go any further. (By clicking the Postpone button, Money saves your work and returns you to a regular view of the account register.)

**Two Notorious Bank Account Errors.** *Two types of bank account errors are notoriously difficult to catch, so let me tell you what they are and how you catch them. Transposed numbers are the first such error. For example, say you enter a check as $21.34 when it really should have been entered as $23.14. Do you see the problem? You've entered the correct digits, but in the wrong order. This error is tough to catch because as you look through your checks and deposits, you see the transaction, see that it has all the right digits, but fail to notice the transposed 1 and 3. Another common error is to enter a check as a deposit or a deposit as a check. People make this error when they enter a transaction in the register but stick the amount in the wrong column. You can usually catch this error by marking your checks and other withdrawals as "cleared" in a batch, and then marking your deposits as "cleared" in a batch.*

This sounds lazy and perhaps crazy, but here's my logic. If you can't balance the account but the difference is the same every month—$41.35 in January, $41.35 in February, and $41.35 in March, for example—you'll know that the account won't balance because of errors you made at least as early as January. And in this case, I think it makes more sense to adjust the account balance so your account does balance rather than waste any time looking for the error or errors that explain the mysterious $41.35. Money is, after all, supposed to make managing your finances less work, not more work.

To adjust the account balance, click Finish, even though Money still shows a difference between your records and the bank's. When Money displays the Balance Account dialog box, click the Automatically Adjust The Account Balance option button, use the Category boxes to categorize the adjustment, and click Next.

**How Do I Categorize Balance Adjustments?** *It's sometimes tough to categorize balance adjustment transactions. You may want to create a new category, for example, or you may want to use whatever category describes the largest share of your expenses. (You can justify this second approach by saying that if you've forgotten to record some transaction or made an error in recording some transaction, the transaction mostly likely affects your largest expense category.)*

**What Should I Do If I Can't Reconcile?** *Select the Automatically Adjust The Account Balance option button to tell Microsoft Money to add a cleared transaction that makes the cleared balance equal to the statement balance.*

# Errors That Balancing Won't Catch

The main reason that you should balance bank accounts is to find errors you or the bank made in recording checks, deposits, and other transactions. But a reconciliation won't catch bookkeeping errors.

## Uncleared Transactions You Forget to Record

One such error is a transaction that you've forgotten to record in your account register and that hasn't yet cleared the bank. Obviously, because neither your account register nor the bank statement includes the transaction, it can't be the reason for a difference between your records and the bank's. If the missing transaction is a check (and it most likely is a check, since you usually have more checks than deposits), you think you have more money in your checking account than you actually do. Unfortunately, the only thing you can do to avoid this error is to be diligent about recording your transactions.

## Fictitious Transactions

Another type of error a reconciliation won't catch is a fictitious transaction you inadvertently recorded. Because the transaction is fictitious, it never shows up on a bank statement and is always listed as outstanding. Although the possibility of recording a fictitious transaction seems extreme, it can occur. You might, for example, record a weekly check to your daughter's piano teacher without actually printing the check.

Fictitious transactions have the opposite effect on your account balance than do uncleared transactions that you have forgotten to record: A fictitious check erroneously decreases the account balance, and a fictitious deposit erroneously increases the account balance. To prevent these errors, you simply need to be careful not to record transactions until they occur.

## Preventing Forgery

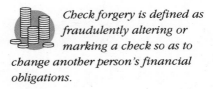

*Check forgery is defined as fraudulently altering or marking a check so as to change another person's financial obligations.*

At the start of this chapter, I mentioned that you can take steps when you reconcile your account to protect against forgery. Although taking these steps isn't part of balancing an account, it's easiest to perform them while you're doing just that. So let's talk about how you can prevent forgery while you balance an account.

First of all, you should carefully review the face and the back of each canceled check to be sure that you actually signed it and that someone didn't fraudulently alter it. If you find evidence of forgery, report it to the bank immediately. (And then call the police, of course.) Usually, if you alert the bank immediately, you won't have to absorb the loss. However, if you procrastinate for a few days or weeks (or months!), you might forfeit all or most of your rights to recover the stolen funds from the bank.

The other step you can take is to keep good records. That sounds obvious, but if you keep messy financial records, a theft like forgery will very likely get hidden in the mess.

Because it's instructive and mildly interesting, I'll tell you about my personal experience as a forgery victim. What the forger who stole from me did was steal a blank sheet of manual checks from the back of my checkbook. Then, every week, he wrote himself a second, bogus payroll check and signed my name to it. (I was paying him weekly.) His forged signature was actually pretty good. It looked very similar to mine. In fact, when I first saw it, I thought that maybe the funny-looking checks were ones that I'd dashed off quickly on a poor writing surface. But then I noticed that I'd never recorded the checks in my register—and that was kind of weird, because I try to keep really clean, accurate financial records. And then I started looking more closely at the checks and realized they all paid the same person—this one employee—and that I had already paid the employee for the weeks the forged checks purportedly paid for. At this point, I put two and two together: The guy had stolen around $700 from me by forging three checks over a five-week period.

When the police called on my now ex-employee (I'd terminated his employment by this time), he confessed. Ultimately, he was sentenced to four months for the felony.

In hindsight, I'm still not sure that there was much I could have done to prevent the theft. I had checked the person's references, and his former employer gave him the thumbs-up sign. And part of the person's job was to do a little bookkeeping for me, so he had access to the blank check forms he needed for his theft. So my only real recourse was to be vigilant about watching for it.

## In Conclusion

The most impressive timesaving task that Money provides is reconciling, or balancing, bank accounts. Reconciling an account by hand can easily take an hour instead of the minute or two it takes with Money. Accordingly, you'll want to reconcile your bank account using Money.

# About the Plastic

**A**lmost every time I hear of someone in financial trouble, the person's credit cards seem to be one of the main culprits. Credit card companies, I'm sure, would disagree with me on this point, but credit cards are by their very nature problematic. You're carrying around a little piece of plastic that can be used at whim to respond to the explicit and the implicit messages that exist in every piece of slick advertising. And once you've got that brand-new credit card and a high starting credit limit, there aren't really any obstacles to keep you from purchasing leather shoes you can't afford or expensive stereo gear you don't need. Then, after you fall behind and begin carrying a balance (or start taking cash advances) on the credit card, breaking out of the credit card trap becomes more and more difficult. And once you're paying interest on the interest, of course, you're in pretty serious trouble.

## Tracking a Credit Card with Money

Believe it or not, Money can help you deal with your credit cards by letting you track the money you're spending with a credit card and the balance you've accumulated. Keeping these records produces a couple of interesting benefits.

The first and most obvious benefit is that you know where you're spending money and how much you owe on your credit card. (If you've been using Money to track a bank account, of course, you already know this.)

There's also a second and more subtle benefit to using Money to track your credit card spending: If you're someone who finds it easy to spend freely with credit cards, the simple act of recording each and every credit card purchase will very likely help you become more disciplined. If, after you go shopping, you sit down at your computer and record the effects of saying "Charge it," you become much more sensitive to how you use your credit card. I'm not sure why this works, but it does.

## Tracking Credit the Lazy Way

You can track credit card spending with Money in two ways: the quick-and-dirty way, which I've labeled the "lazy way," and a more precise way, which I've labeled the "accountant's way." If you don't carry a balance on your credit card and you're already disciplined about how you use it, the lazy way is for you.

If you do carry a balance on your credit card or you're not disciplined about how you spend with credit cards, you're better off using the accountant's way. If that's the case, skip ahead to the next section in this chapter.

To use the lazy way, record the check to the credit card company in the same way that you record any other check. When you get to the category boxes, split the transaction so that each of the categories for the items you purchased over the month with your credit card appears as a separate line in the Split Transaction dialog box. The figure shows how I filled out the Split Transaction dialog box to summarize the amounts I charged over the month on my credit card.

*Some research suggests that people spend, on average, 23 percent more when they shop with a credit card than they do when they shop with cash.*

This line of information summarizes the charges for gasoline.

This line of information summarizes the charges for dining out.

# Tracking Credit the Accountant's Way

The lazy way of tracking credit card charges is easy to implement, but it has its weaknesses. You don't keep track of where you spend your money—only of how much you've spent in various categories. Also, you don't really know how big a balance you're carrying on your account. With the lazy way, the monthly statement's balance can be an unpleasant surprise, and you can bump up against the credit card limit in months when you charge many large purchases.

Fortunately, Money lets you employ a much more precise way of tracking credit card charges. With the accountant's way, you set up an account for your credit card and use its account register to record your charges and payments.

## Setting Up a Credit Card Account

To set up a new credit card account, follow these steps:

1 With the Money Contents window displayed, click the Account Manager button. Money displays the Account Manager window.

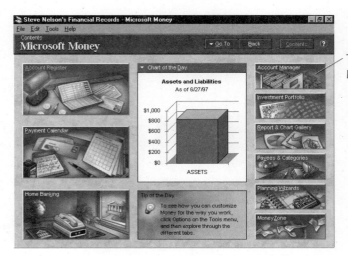

This is the Account Manager button.

You can change the way accounts are displayed on the Account Manager window by using the View menu.

**Removing an Account.** *To remove an account you don't need—say you make a mistake adding a credit card and want to start over—click the account in the Account Manager window, and then click the Delete button.*

**2** Click the New Account button near the bottom of the screen. Money starts the New Account Wizard. In the first New Account dialog box, enter the name of the bank or financial institution that issued your card.

**3** Click next. When the Wizard asks what kind of account you want to set up, click Credit Card and then click Next.

**4** The Wizard asks what name you want to use for your bank account. Enter a name and click Next.

**5** The Wizard asks for an account number. If you know the number, enter it and click Next.

**6** The Wizard asks for the credit card's current balance. Enter the ending credit card balance from your last statement and click Next.

**7** The Wizard asks whether you want Money to remind you of this credit card bill and, if so, when. If you do want to be reminded to make the credit card payment, check the Yes Remind Me When The Bill Is Due box. Then enter the payment amount you'll probably have to make in the Estimated Monthly Amount text box. Specify the date by which you'll next have to make a payment on the credit card balance in the Bill Is Due Next On text box. Then indicate from which bank account you'll write a check for your credit card purchases by using the Pay Bill From Account drop-down list box.

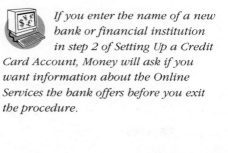 *If you enter the name of a new bank or financial institution in step 2 of Setting Up a Credit Card Account, Money will ask if you want information about the Online Services the bank offers before you exit the procedure.*

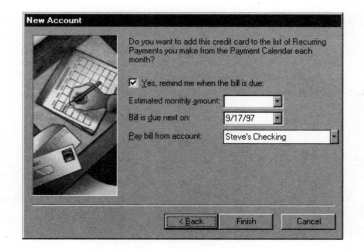

 *You can display the Account Manager window by clicking the Contents window's Account Manager button or by activating the Go To triangle menu and choosing its Account Manager command.*

8 Click Next. If you need to set up additional credit card accounts, click the I Have Other Accounts At This Bank button, and click Next. Money will lead you back through steps 4 through 7. If you don't need additional credit card accounts tell Money so and click Finish.

Would you like to store additional information about the credit card account you just created? No problem. Click the Account Manager window's Account Details button and Money displays a dialog box you can use to store some more information about the account. You can store the name of your credit card company, your account number, the opening balance, the credit limit, and so forth.

When you finish working with the Account Manager, you can return to the Money Contents window by clicking the Contents button.

# Recording Credit Card Charges

To record a credit card purchase (or any other credit card transaction, for that matter), you display the account register of the credit card account. You can do this in several different ways, but the easiest is to display the Account Manager window, click the credit card account, and then click the Go To Account button. When you do this, Money displays an account register for the credit card.

A credit card account register works the same way as a bank account register. To enter a credit card charge, you use the area at the bottom left of the Account Register window.

## Entering a Credit Card Charge

1 Click the Charge tab.

2 Enter the reference number for the charge.

4 Enter the name of the business you paid with your credit card.

3 Enter the charge date.

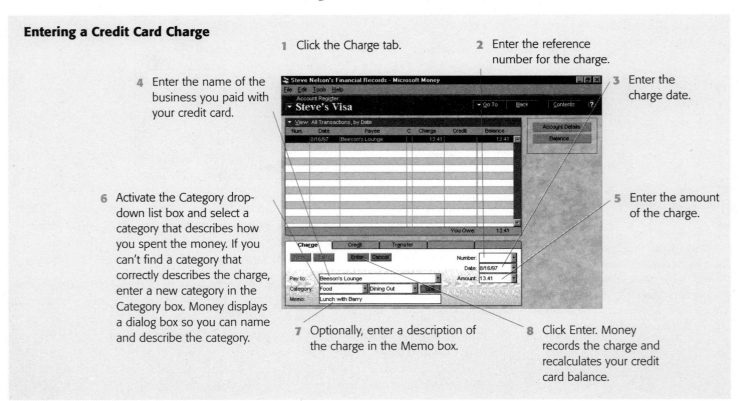

6 Activate the Category drop-down list box and select a category that describes how you spent the money. If you can't find a category that correctly describes the charge, enter a new category in the Category box. Money displays a dialog box so you can name and describe the category.

5 Enter the amount of the charge.

7 Optionally, enter a description of the charge in the Memo box.

8 Click Enter. Money records the charge and recalculates your credit card balance.

Recording your second and subsequent charges works the same way as recording your first charge. After you record a charge to a particular business, you can activate the Pay To drop-down list box and select the payee from the list. SuperSmartFill, that feature with the strange name, fills in the rest of the charge blanks with the same inputs you used the last time you entered a charge for the payee. If you need to make changes to this information, simply replace or edit the contents of the text boxes.

## Recording Credit Card Credits

To record a credit card credit, such as you might get when you return an item you bought with a credit card, you display the account register for the credit card, click the Credit tab, and fill in the blanks. You do this the same way you fill in the blanks of the Charge tab, so I won't repeat my earlier description of the process.

## Recording a Credit Card Payment

To record a credit card payment, you record the check that you use to pay the credit card bill in the appropriate bank account register. For example, if I am going to pay my VISA bill by writing a check on a bank account that I named "Steve's Checking," I just write and record the check in the usual way. Then, rather than categorize the check, I transfer the money to the credit card account. The figure on the next page shows how to do this.

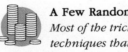

**A Few Random Thoughts.** *Most of the tricks, tips, and techniques that I've discussed in the context of bank accounts and bank account registers also work for credit card accounts and credit card registers. You can use the same date-editing tricks for the transactions in a credit card account as you can for the transactions in a bank account. You reconcile a credit card account in the same way that you reconcile a bank account. You can print reports of the activity in a credit card account just as you print reports of the activity in a bank account.*

## Recording a Credit Card Payment

**1** Click the Transfer tab.

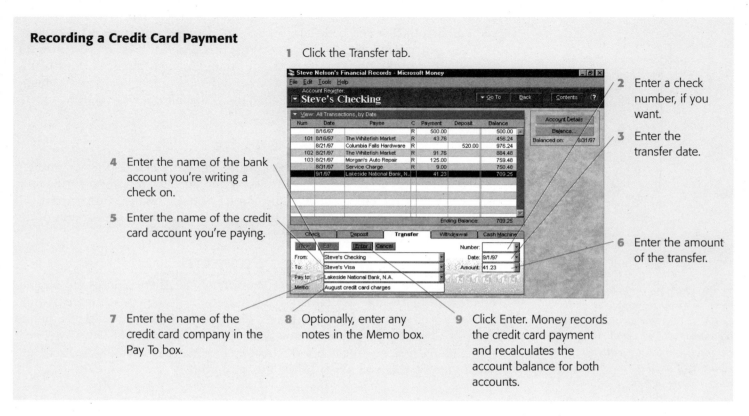

**2** Enter a check number, if you want.

**3** Enter the transfer date.

**4** Enter the name of the bank account you're writing a check on.

**5** Enter the name of the credit card account you're paying.

**6** Enter the amount of the transfer.

**7** Enter the name of the credit card company in the Pay To box.

**8** Optionally, enter any notes in the Memo box.

**9** Click Enter. Money records the credit card payment and recalculates the account balance for both accounts.

Once you record the credit card payment by describing an account transfer, Money enters a payment transaction into both the bank account register and the credit card account register. The transaction reduces your bank account and your credit card balance to show the effects of the payment.

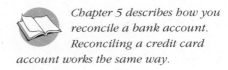

*Chapter 5 describes how you reconcile a bank account. Reconciling a credit card account works the same way.*

**The High Cost of Credit.** *You can see the total cost of your credit card by looking at the Total Interest amount. It shows your interest costs over the time it takes to repay the loan.*

# Getting Out from under Your Credit Card Debts

Once you start using Money to monitor your credit card spending and your credit card balances, you'll find it much easier to be disciplined about the money you spend with credit cards. If you've been carrying a balance, you may even want to begin paying it down.

If you're curious about how long it would take to pay down a credit card's existing balance, follow these steps:

1 Click the Planning Wizards button, which appears on the Money Contents window. Money displays the Planning Wizards window.

2 Click the Loan Calculator button. Money displays the Loan Calculator dialog box.

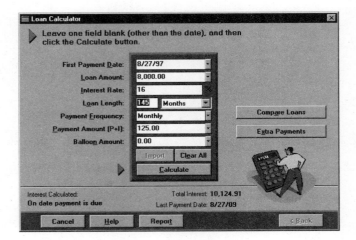

3 Enter the current credit card balance in the Loan Amount text box.

4 Enter the credit card interest rate in the Interest Rate text box.

5 Specify the payment frequency as Monthly. You do this by activating the Payment Frequency drop-down list box and selecting Monthly.

6 Enter the monthly payment you'll begin making on the credit card in the Payment Amount text box.

7 Click the Calculate command button.

If your payment amount is large enough to pay off more than just the interest charges, Money calculates how many months of payments you have to make to pay off the balance. If your payment amount isn't large enough to pay off more than just the interest charges, Money tells you, "You have entered loan values that don't work together."

# In Conclusion

One of the prerequisites of getting your financial house in order is keeping a tight grip on credit card spending. That sounds harsh and maybe a bit compulsive, but it's true. By the time you figure in the extra amount that people spend when they make purchases using a credit card (on average, 23 percent more) and the interest charges that often approach 20 percent annually, it's easy to pay close to 50 percent more for everything you charge on a credit card: food, clothing, automobile expenses, and so on. You won't be surprised to hear that you ain't gonna get ahead by paying an extra 50 percent for everything you charge.

All of the above is bad news if you've gotten in over your head with credit cards, but I have some good news for you. Money can be a marvelous tool for getting back on track to financial success. If you take advantage of Money's record-keeping tools, you should find it easier to bring discipline to your spending. And by using the Planning Wizards—specifically, the powerful Loan Calculator—you can start to map a way out of any credit card mess you find yourself in.

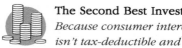

**The Second Best Investment.** *Because consumer interest isn't tax-deductible and because credit card interest rates are usually very high, paying off a credit card balance is usually the second best investment you can make. (The best investments are tax-deductible investments like 401(k)s and Individual Retirement Accounts, or IRAs.) If you want to pay off your credit cards, start with the credit card that charges the highest interest rate.*

# Mortgages and Loans

**M**icrosoft Money comes with powerful tools for analyzing loans and for monitoring the money you borrow. Using these tools as part of your regular financial record-keeping can deliver enormous benefits. By monitoring the money you borrow and what that money costs you (in interest), you can do a much better job of planning and managing your day-to-day financial affairs. You'll also be able to calculate your net worth more accurately. By using Money to carefully analyze the loans you consider, you can easily save thousands of dollars in interest and finance charges.

## How to Track a Loan

Tracking a loan with Money is very easy, especially if you're already familiar and comfortable with tracking a bank account and you know how to transfer money between accounts. To begin tracking a loan, all you need to do is find the paperwork that describes the loan and its current balance (probably the last monthly statement) and then use the New Account Wizard to set up an account for the loan.

### Setting Up a Liability or a Loan Account

Money provides two different account types for tracking loans: a **liability** account and a loan account. Which one you set up depends on whether the loan you'll track will be amortized. If a loan will be amortized, you set up a loan account. If a loan won't be amortized, you set up a liability account.

**Why an Amortizing Loan?** *You need to set up a special type of account for an amortizing loan because Money needs to break down your payments into their interest and principal portions.*

If you're not familiar with the word "amortized," let me explain it. **Amortization** means that your loan payments include not only the interest but also the principal. Over time, as the principal payments reduce the loan's balance, more and more of each payment goes toward reducing the loan's balance. Conventional home mortgages are amortizing loans. So are most car loans. But many loans aren't amortizing. Some home equity loan payments, for example, include only interest.

## Setting Up a Liability Account

Setting up a liability account works very much like setting up other accounts. To use the Account Manager to set up a new liability account, follow these steps:

 *If you enter the name of a new bank or financial institution in step 3 of setting up a Liability Account, Money will ask if you want information about the Online sources the bank offers before you exit the procedure.*

1 With the Money Contents window displayed, click the Account Manager button. Money displays the Account Manager window.

2 Click the New Account button. This tells Money to start the New Account Wizard.

3 Enter the name of the bank or financial institution to whom you'll make your payments. Click Next.

4 The Wizard asks what kind of account you want to set up. Select Liability and then click Next.

5 The Wizard asks what name you want to use for your liability account. Enter a name and click Next.

6 When the Wizard asks for the account's opening balance, enter the ending liability balance from your last statement. In other words, enter the amount you still owe.

7 Click Next. If you need to set up additional accounts, click I Have Other Accounts At This Bank to repeat steps 2 through 6. Otherwise, indicate that you don't. Click Finish.

## Setting Up a Loan Account

Setting up a loan account differs only slightly from setting up a liability account. The differences stem from the fact that Money collects the loan information it needs to break down your loan payments into interest charges and principal reductions.

To use the Account Manager to set up a new loan account, follow these steps:

*If you have questions about how the Account Manager window works, refer to Chapter 1. It describes the Account Manager in more detail.*

1 With the Money Contents window displayed, click the Account Manager button. Money displays the Account Manager window.

2 Click the New Account button. This tells Money to start the New Account Wizard.

3 Enter the name of the bank or financial institution to whom you'll make your payments. Click Next.

4 The Wizard asks what kind of account you want to set up. Click Loan and click Next.

5 Money starts the New Loan Account wizard and displays a dialog box that tells you what's about to happen. Click Next.

6 Money displays another page of information in the New Loan Account Wizard dialog box. Click Next again.

7 Money asks whether you're borrowing money or lending money. Click the Borrowing Money button and click Next.

8 Money asks for the name of the loan and the name of the lender to whom you'll make your payments. Fill in this information and click Next.

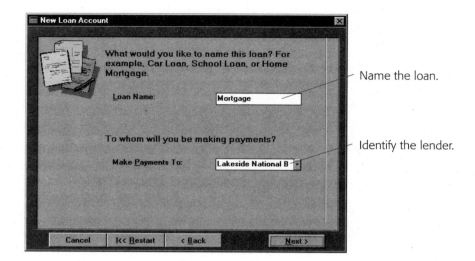

Name the loan.

Identify the lender.

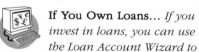

**If You Own Loans...** *If you invest in loans, you can use the Loan Account Wizard to set up special accounts for tracking the loans you own. You do this by following the same process described here—except that basically, you end up with an investment account that pays you regular loan payments.*

9  Money asks whether you've already made any payments on the loan. Answer this question by clicking the Yes Payments Have Been Made or No Payments Have Not Been Made option button. Click Next.

10  If you click the Yes Payments Have Been Made option, Money asks how far back it should go to calculate loan payments and loan amortization: to the beginning of the loan or only to the beginning of the year. It doesn't really matter which option you select. Once you answer this extra question, click Next.

11  Money asks when you will make or when you made the first loan payment. Enter this date in the text box provided and click Next.

12  Money tells you that it's collected all the general information it needs for tracking the loan and that it now needs specific information about the loan itself. Click Next.

13  Money asks how often you'll make your payments. Using the drop-down list box provided, indicate the payment frequency: Monthly, Biweekly, Semi-monthly, and so on. (The Paid How Often drop-down list provides a bunch of different options.) Click Next when you're done.

**How Different Loans Calculate Interest.** *Interest on home mortgages is usually calculated based on the date the payment is due—so you don't save interest by paying the loan payment a few days early, for example. Interest on most consumer credit loans, car loans included, is calculated based on the date the loan payment is received. The Two Times Per Year interest calculation, as suggested, applies to Canadian mortgages. If you have a question about how interest on your loan is calculated, call your lender or read the loan contract.*

**14** Money asks how interest is calculated on the loan: Based On Date Payment Is Due, Based On Date Lender Receives Payment, or Two Times Per Year (Canadian Mortgage). Click the option button that corresponds to the interest calculation method. Click Next again to keep moving.

**15** The Wizard asks for the loan's balance. Enter it in the Loan Amount text box and click Next.

**16** When the Wizard asks for the loan's interest rate, enter it in the Interest Rate text box. Be sure to enter the loan interest rate, however, and not the Annual Percentage Rate, or APR. The APR, which I talk about later in this chapter, is different from the interest rate. Click Next.

**17** The Wizard asks for the scheduled length of the loan. Use the Loan Length text box and drop-down list box to provide this information. For example, if you'll make monthly payments over the next five years, enter 60 in the first box and specify Payments using the second box. When you're done, click Next.

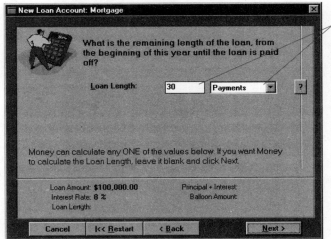

You need to tell Money how long you'll be making loan payments.

**18** The Wizard next asks for the regular principal and interest loan payment you'll make on the loan. If you know this bit of information, you can enter it in the Principal + Interest text box. However, as the figure shown here indicates, you aren't required to enter this piece of information if you've already entered each of the other bits of loan information. Money can calculate your payment based on the loan amount, interest rate, and scheduled length. Click Next to keep going.

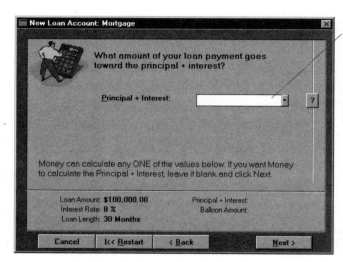

You can enter the principal and interest amount or have Money calculate this piece of information for you.

**Calculating the Five Loan Variables.** *Loan calculations use five variables, or inputs: the loan amount, the loan interest rate, the scheduled length of the loan (or its term), the loan payment, and the balloon payment. If you enter any four of these inputs, Money calculates the fifth. Typically, people calculate the payment amount because they know the loan balance, interest rate, and term—and because there usually isn't a balloon payment. But you could calculate any of the five variables by leaving it blank and providing the remaining four values.*

**19** When the Wizard asks whether or not there's a **balloon payment** associated with this loan, enter the amount in the Balloon Payment text box. If your loan doesn't include a balloon payment, leave this input set to zero. Click Next.

**20** Money displays a message box that provides whatever loan variable you didn't enter. For example, if you didn't enter the loan payment amount, this message box shows your loan payment. Click OK. Money displays a page of information about the loan. If a part of the loan information is incorrect, click Back to return to the page where you entered the incorrect data, correct it, and then click Next to return to this dialog box.

**Interest Rates and the Cost of Loans.** *Tiny differences in interest rates can make a big difference in the overall cost of a loan. Suppose, for example, that two homeowners both get a $100,000 mortgage and both make the same monthly payment. Suppose further that the first person borrows money at 7.75 percent interest while the second borrows at 7.875 percent interest. The first person will pay about $10,000 less in interest than the second person—all because of the 1/8-percent difference in the interest rate.*

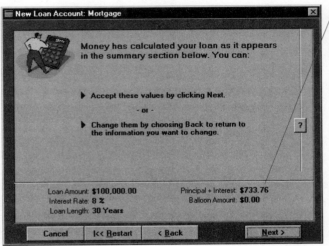

Once you describe the loan, Money calculates the loan payment.

**21** Click Next. Money tells you that it's collected all the loan information and that it wants to know which categories you'll use to track your loan payments. Click Next again.

**22** When the Wizard asks for the principal and interest category and subcategory, enter them in the text boxes provided. (If you're creating new categories or subcategories, Money will ask you to confirm your choices after each entry.) Then click Next.

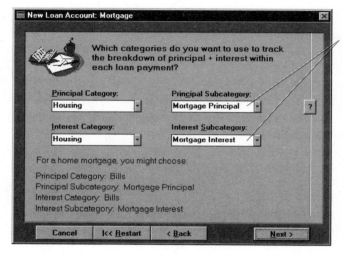

Money lets you categorize both the principal and interest portion of a loan payment.

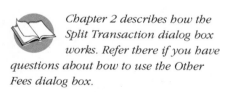

*Chapter 2 describes how the Split Transaction dialog box works. Refer there if you have questions about how to use the Other Fees dialog box.*

**23** The Wizard displays a dialog box that asks about any of the other charges or fees you'll pay with your regular loan payment. If you have to pay other charges, such as property taxes collected with a mortgage payment, insurance premiums, and so forth, click the Other Fees button. Money displays the Other Fees dialog box, which works just like the Split Transaction dialog box. Use this dialog box to describe the additional loan charges or fees.

**24** Click Next. The Wizard asks when and if you want to be reminded to make this loan payment.

**How Does Money Remind Me About Payments?** *You use Money's Payment Calendar to track payments you're supposed to make sometime in the future. To add a payment to the Payment Calendar, display the Account Register window, select the payment, and then choose the Edit Add To Payment Calendar command. To see the Payment Calendar, click the Contents window's Payment Calendar button. To record the payments shown on the Payment Calendar, click the payments you want to make (so they're marked with a check), and then click the Enter button.*

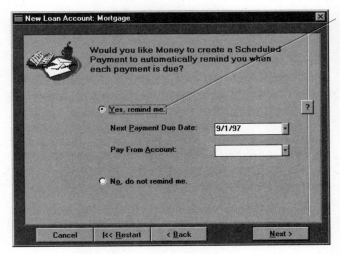

Answer the Wizard's question and provide any information it needs, including the date you want to be reminded and the bank account from which you'll make the payment. Then click Next.

**25** The Wizard displays a dialog box page that summarizes everything you've told Money about the loan and everything Money has figured out on its own.

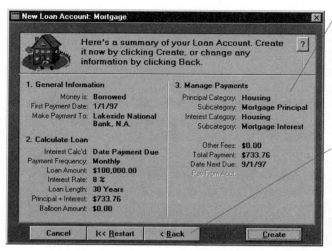

After you've entered all the loan account and payment information, and after Money makes all the loan calculations, Money summarizes the loan.

If you discover you've made a mistake, you can click Back to backtrack your way through the New Loan Account Wizard's dialog boxes. You can also click Restart to start over from scratch.

26 Click Create. Money creates the new loan account. When Money finishes, it displays the final New Loan Account Wizard dialog box.

27 Click Exit to return to the New Account window.

28 If you have no other loan accounts to create, click the I Have no Other Accounts At This Bank Option and click Finish.

## Recording Loan Payments

Once you've set up a loan account or liability account, it's easy to record payments. But how you record a payment depends on the type of account you've set up.

### Recording Liability Account Payments

If you set up a liability account, you record any check that pays interest or principal for the liability in the usual way. If you record a check that pays only interest, for example, you just write the check and categorize it under an interest expense category.

*Remember, a liability account is the one you use for a loan that isn't amortized.*

If you want to record a check that pays both interest and principal, you split the transaction. The figure here shows how the Split Transaction dialog box looks if you record a $1,100 payment that pays $1,000 of interest and also reduces the liability account balance by $100.

This $100 transfer to the Home Equity Loan account reduces the liability amount by $100.

## Recording Loan Account Payments

If you set up a loan account, you record your payment in a slightly different manner. First, you display the new loan account's account register. To do that, display the Account Manager window, select the new loan account, and then click the Go To Account button.

To record a loan payment, you click the New button and then describe the loan payment by filling in the blanks. Follow the steps on the next page.

*If Money already displays the Account Register window, you can use the triangle menu near the top-left corner of the window to display a list of accounts. To view the loan account, simply click the triangle and select the account from the list.*

## Recording a Loan Payment

**1** Click New.

**2** Enter the payment number. The first loan payment you make is number 1, the second is number 2, and so on. (If you told Money to go back and record old loan payments when you set up the loan account, these show up already.)

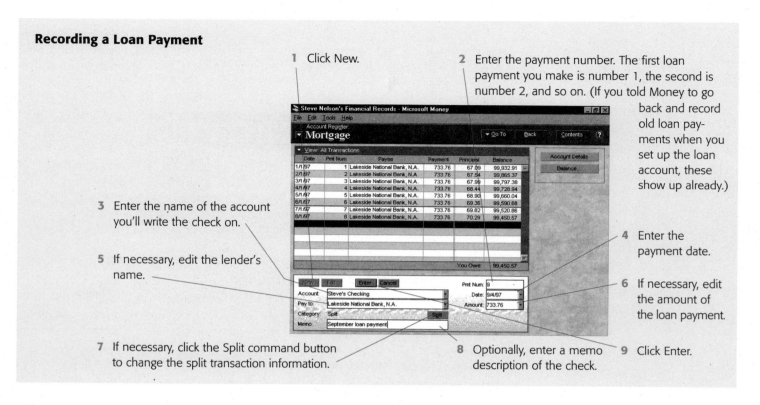

**3** Enter the name of the account you'll write the check on.

**4** Enter the payment date.

**5** If necessary, edit the lender's name.

**6** If necessary, edit the amount of the loan payment.

**7** If necessary, click the Split command button to change the split transaction information.

**8** Optionally, enter a memo description of the check.

**9** Click Enter.

Money records the loan payment and recalculates the account balance. It also adds the loan payment to the register and shows which portion of the loan payment represents interest and which portion of the loan payment represents principal.

## Fixing Loan Account Balance Errors

Even though Money calculates the interest and principal portions of the loan payments you make, Money's calculations may still be wrong. This is especially true if the interest calculation is based on the date the payment is received by the lender. In this case, a delay in the mail of just a few days can create a difference in Money's calculation of the interest and the lender's calculation of the interest.

Fortunately, it's easy to fix these kinds of errors. To do so, you simply balance the loan account by following these steps:

 *It's a good idea to balance your loan balance each time you get a monthly loan statement.*

1 Display the loan account in the Account Register window. You can do this, for example, by displaying the Account Manager window, clicking the loan account, and then clicking the Go To Account button.

2 Click Balance. Money displays the first Balance Account dialog box. (Money uses the name of your account in the title bar of the dialog box.)

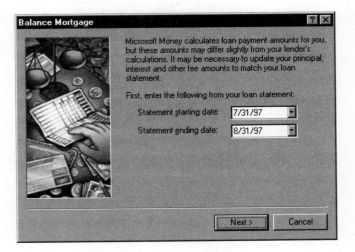

3 Enter the starting date and the ending date from the monthly statement and click Next.

4 Money displays a second Balance Account dialog box. Verify that what the second Balance Account dialog box shows as the Principal Paid and Interest Paid is correct. If it isn't, edit the contents of these two text boxes so they are correct.

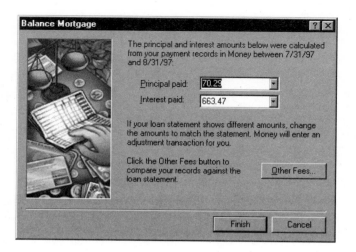

**5** If any fees are not accounted for in your records, click Other Fees. When Money displays the Other Fees dialog box, enter the missing information so it is correct.

**6** Click Finish. Money makes the necessary adjustments and returns you to the account register. It now shows the correct loan balance.

## How to Shop for a Loan

Shopping for a mortgage—or any other large loan—can be a daunting task. You often find yourself overwhelmed with data that's very difficult to compare. At the same time, you often have only a few days or weeks to select a lender and be approved for a loan. Fortunately, Money provides two tools to help you think about and shop for a loan:

➤ The Loan Calculator, which lets you calculate loan payment information

➤ The Mortgage Planner, which simplifies your search for the most inexpensive loan

**Should I Consider Using a Mortgage Broker?** *The answer is definitely "yes!" A mortgage broker usually represents several dozen lenders, so he or she can easily shop around for the lowest-priced mortgage. You won't pay anything for this service, either. The bank or mortgage company pays the mortgage broker out of its loan fees. Because anybody can advertise their services as a mortgage broker, however, you should pick a broker carefully. A good way to find someone honest and trustworthy is to ask for referrals from friends and family members, your professional advisors, and even your real estate agent.*

# Calculating a Loan Payment

Money's Loan Calculator lets you calculate a loan payment and any of the other variables that determine what a loan payment is: loan amount, interest rate, loan length, or ballon amount. Often, calculating a loan payment is the first step you make when you assess a loan. Before you even consider buying a new car or house, for example, you want to make sure that you can afford to make the payments.

To use the Loan Calculator, display the Money Contents window, click the Planning Wizards button, and click the Loan Calculator button. When Money displays the Loan Calculator dialog box, fill it in.

## Using the Loan Calculator

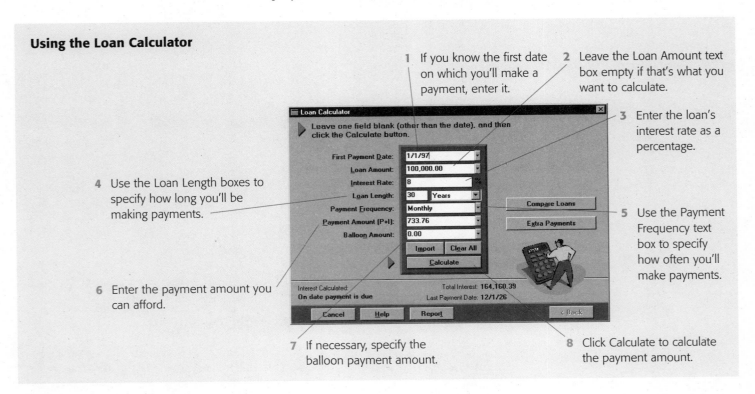

1 If you know the first date on which you'll make a payment, enter it.

2 Leave the Loan Amount text box empty if that's what you want to calculate.

3 Enter the loan's interest rate as a percentage.

4 Use the Loan Length boxes to specify how long you'll be making payments.

5 Use the Payment Frequency text box to specify how often you'll make payments.

6 Enter the payment amount you can afford.

7 If necessary, specify the balloon payment amount.

8 Click Calculate to calculate the payment amount.

# Making Extra Principal Payments

The Loan Calculator provides a couple of neat enhancements:

➤ An extra principal payment analyzer so you can see the effect of paying a little extra in principal each month

➤ A loan comparison analyzer so you can compare the effective interest costs of two different loans (this is discussed in the next part of the chapter, "Comparing Two Loans with the Loan Calculator")

To use the extra principal payment analyzer, first display the Loan Calculator and use it to calculate the loan payment. Then click the Extra Payments button on the right side of the dialog box. When you do, Money displays the Extra Payments page of the Loan Calculator dialog box.

## Calculating Extra Principal Payments

1 Use the Extra Amount text box to specify how much you'll pay in addition to the regular payment.

2 Use the Frequency drop-down list box to specify whether you'll make the extra payment once or many times.

3 Tell Money when you'll make the extra payment or when you'll start making the extra payments.

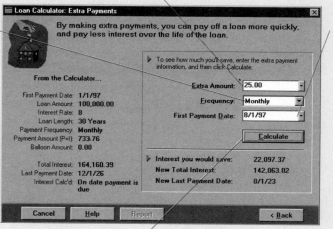

**Loan Calculator: Extra Payments**

By making extra payments, you can pay off a loan more quickly, and pay less interest over the life of the loan.

To see how much you'll save, enter the extra payment information, and then click Calculate.

From the Calculator...

First Payment Date: 1/1/97
Loan Amount: 100,000.00
Interest Rate: 8
Loan Length: 30 Years
Payment Frequency: Monthly
Payment Amount (P+I): 733.76
Balloon Amount: 0.00

Total Interest: 164,160.39
Last Payment Date: 12/1/26
Interest Calc'd: On date payment is due

Extra Amount: 25.00
Frequency: Monthly
First Payment Date: 8/1/97

Calculate

Interest you would save: 22,097.37
New Total Interest: 142,063.02
New Last Payment Date: 8/1/23

Cancel    Help    Report    < Back

4 Click Calculate. Money calculates the interest savings you'll realize because you've paid the extra amount or amounts.

Let me issue an important caution here. When you calculate how much you can save by making extra principal payments, the numbers quickly get breathtakingly large. On an 8-percent $100,000 mortgage, for example, paying an extra $25 a month (over the life of the mortgage) translates into more than $21,000 of interest savings and gets the mortgage paid off almost three years early.

Before you conclude that I've tipped you off to the true secret of financial success, however, you should know that anytime you compound interest over long periods of time, the numbers always get huge. So you can't focus on the interest savings.

## When It Makes Sense to Repay a Mortgage

To determine whether it makes sense to repay a mortgage (or any other debt) early, you need to compare the interest rate the loan charges with the interest rate or investment return that some other investment pays. The rule is simple: Your loan's interest rate needs to exceed the investment's interest rate or investment return in order for early loan repayment to make sense. If your mortgage charges 8-percent interest but you can buy a bond that pays 10 percent, for example, you shouldn't "invest" your money by repaying your mortgage early. You end up with more money by investing in the 10-percent bonds.

As a general rule, too, I should tell you that except in unusual situations (when your mortgage interest rate is in double-digits, for example), early mortgage repayment is probably not all that great a deal. If you can stick more money in your employer's 401(k) or 403(b) plan or in a tax-deductible individual retirement account (IRA), the 401(k), 403(b), or IRA always beats early mortgage repayment. In fact, it's not even a contest.

## What about Your Other Debt?

While you get truly awesome interest savings when you look at the effect of repaying a long-term loan like a mortgage early, it's really a better deal to get out from under your credit card debt and other consumer credit debt.

 **Which Is the Better Investment?** *If you pay an extra $25 a month on an 8-percent $100,000 mortgage over the life of the mortgage, you save about $21,000 in interest. That sounds pretty good, and it is pretty good, but if you put that same $25 plus any tax savings into a tax-deductible IRA, you end up with about $40,000. And if you put that $25 plus any tax savings into a 401(k) plan in which your employer matches 50 percent of your contributions, you end up with around $60,000. The reason you do better with an IRA or 401(k), of course, is because of the income tax benefits and, in the case of the 401(k), because of the employer's matching contribution.*

Interest on consumer credit such as credit cards and car loans isn't tax-deductible. So a credit card that charges, say, 16 percent, really does cost 16 percent, whereas an 8-percent mortgage doesn't really cost 8 percent. Depending on your income tax situation, you get a tax deduction that effectively lowers your 8-percent mortgage to something between 5 and 7 percent. In effect, by paying off a credit card that charges a 16-percent interest rate, you make a 16-percent profit on your investment. (Your investment is paying off the credit card early.) If you pay off a mortgage that charges an effective, after-income-taxes-are-figured, interest rate of 5 percent, you make a 5-percent profit on your investment.

There's one other point that I should make about early repayment of debts. The idea is sound, but it doesn't really pay off if you go out and replace your old debt with new debt. Okay, that sounds funny. But let me explain. Paying off your mortgage early sounds like a great deal—and it is a great deal, really. But if you pay your mortgage off early and then, because you don't have mortgage payments, go out and purchase a new, larger, more expensive home, you're not really getting ahead. And if you get that credit card paid off early, but then you go out and fill your closet with a dazzling new wardrobe, you're not getting ahead that way either.

## Comparing Two Loans with the Loan Calculator

The Loan Calculator also provides a special page for comparing two loans. If you click the Loan Calculator's Compare Loans button, Money displays a Loan Calculator page that shows two calculators. To compare two loans, you use one calculator for the first loan and the other calculator for the second loan.

## Creating an Amortization Schedule

An amortization schedule shows the principal and interest portions of a loan payment as well as the principal balance after each loan payment is made. You can tell Money to create an amortization schedule by using the input and output boxes on the Loan Calculator dialog box. To do this, click the Report button. Money creates an amortization report like the one shown here.

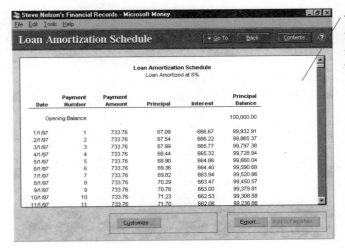

The Loan Amortization Schedule window showing an amortization report.

# Using the Mortgage Planner

Typically, a person's largest single financial commitment is a mortgage. When you add up the payments you're agreeing to make over 30 years on an 8-percent $100,000 mortgage, for example, you're agreeing to more than a quarter of a million dollars in payments. With numbers this large, you shouldn't be surprised to learn that small differences in interest rates and loan fees make big differences in the overall cost of a mortgage. Early in this chapter, I noted that a mere eighth of a percent difference in an interest rate can make a $10,000 difference in what a $100,000 mortgage costs.

The bottom line is you can save yourself money—sometimes lots and lots of money—by carefully considering all your options when you shop for a new mortgage. Thankfully, Money provides a very powerful, very sophisticated Planning Wizard called the Mortgage Planner. With it, you can compare two mortgages. You can also use the Mortgage Planner to determine whether or not it makes sense to refinance a mortgage.

**Should I Get a Loan that Requires a Balloon Payment?**

*A balloon payment is an extra payment you're required to make after you finish making all your regular payments. A balloon payment makes regular loan payments smaller. But balloon payments are dangerous because the amounts are often very large. On a $100,000 mortgage, for example, a balloon payment after ten years of regular monthly payments might equal $90,000! Not surprisingly, making a payment of this size often presents significant problems for the borrower. Often, the only way the borrower can come up with the balloon payment is to take out another loan.*

# Comparing Two Mortgages

To use the Mortgage Planner, first display the Money Contents window, click the Planning Wizards button, and then click the Mortgage Planner button. When you do, Money displays the first screen of the Mortgage Planner dialog box. To use the Mortgage Planner, click Next and follow these steps:

1 Money asks for the purchase price. Enter the total purchase price of the home. Don't worry about including closing costs, however. The Mortgage Planner addresses these costs later. Click Next when you're done.

2 Money asks for down payment information for the two loans. Use the Down Payment options and boxes to describe the down payment percentages required by both mortgages. (Very likely, both mortgages require the same down payment.) Click Next when you're done.

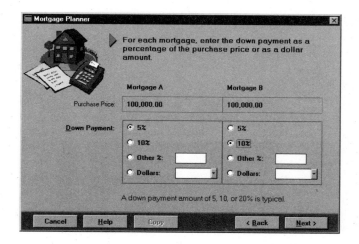

**3** Money displays another window of the Mortgage Planner. It shows the down payment and mortgage amounts for each mortgage. Click Next.

**4** Money asks for the **balloon payment** amount for the mortgages. Use the Balloon Amount text boxes to enter any balloon payments required for either mortgage and click Next.

**5** Money asks how long you would pay on the mortgages and what interest rates they charge. Click Next.

**Why Do I Have to Pay Discount Points and Loan Fees?** *Actually, you don't have to pay these fees. In many areas, however, it's common for borrowers to pay their lenders two ways: with an up-front fee that's paid as the loan money is provided and with regular interest charges. If you don't pay these up-front fees, the lender just charges you a higher interest rate. Note, too, that in some cases the loans that don't charge you up-front fees actually cost more in the long run. They cost more because their higher interest rates more than offset the absence of discount points and loan fees.*

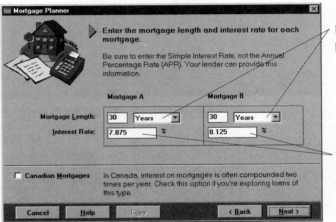

Describe how long you'd pay on the mortgages.

Give the interest rate for both mortgages. Click Next when you're done.

**6** Money asks what points you'll pay to secure the loan.

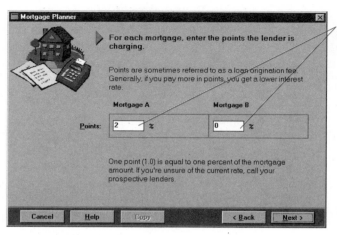

Specify the **discount points** that you'll pay by using the Points text boxes and click Next.

**7** Money asks about any **loan service fee** you'll pay. If there is one, specify the amount of the fee. Be careful, though, not to count the same cost twice. Don't, for example, enter a loan fee once in the discount points text boxes (the earlier page of the Mortgage Planner dialog box) and then enter the same loan fee again in the Loan Service Fee text boxes. Click Next when you're done.

**8** Money asks about the closing costs. Click Next.

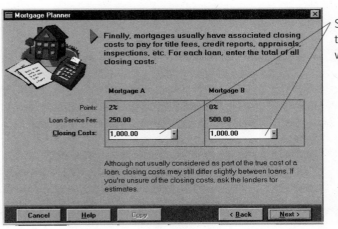

Specify the closing costs for the two loans. Click Next when you're done.

**Junk Fees.** *Although it seems odd, different mortgage lenders can offer very different total closing costs. Extra, add-on fees—often called "junk fees"—can make a mortgage with an attractive interest rate the more expensive mortgage. Many lenders charge a couple hundred dollars of junk fees for a mortgage, by the way. Watch out for really excessive junk fees.*

**9** Money displays a summary page that describes the total up-front costs of the two mortgage options you've been describing. Carefully review this information if it's important to minimize your out-of-pocket cash costs. Click Next when you're done.

**10** Money displays another summary page of information that describes the regular loan payments you'll make. Carefully review this information, too, since it shows the regular payments you commit to making in the years to come. Click Next when you're done.

**11** Money displays a page that gives the Annual Percentage Rates (APRs) for the two loans. Click Next when you've looked this page over.

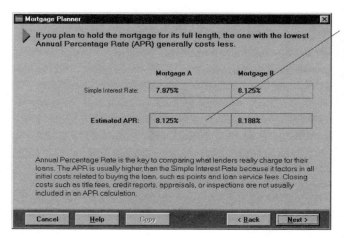

If you'll be paying on the loan for the entire scheduled loan length, the loan with the lower APR is the cheaper loan.

**Determining the Annual Percentage Rate.** *The Annual Percentage Rate (APR) adds up the discount points, loan service fees, and other closing costs you pay and treats these amounts like extra interest charges. For example, if you have $3,000 of these extra charges and you'll hold the loan for 30 years, the APR shows there's roughly $100 of extra interest every year (because 30 years x $100 = $3,000). If you'll hold a loan for a far shorter time period than the scheduled length, however, things change dramatically. For example, if you have $3,000 of extra charges and you'll hold the loan for only 5 years, the APR would show that there's really an extra $600 of interest every year (because 5 years x $600 = $3,000).*

**12** Money next asks how long you'll hold the loan. Enter the number of years or months until you expect to either move or refinance the loan.

**13** Click Calculate. Money calculates a revised APR based on how long you'll be in the home.

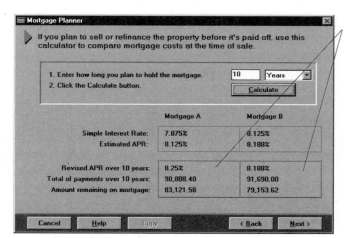

This is the APR you want to focus on because this APR takes into account how long you'll actually live in the home. The one in step 11 showed the entire scheduled loan length. When you're done looking at this screen, click Next.

**14** Money displays a final summary page that compares the two loans.

The key numbers to focus on here are the last four rows of the schedule: the Total Initial Costs, Monthly Payment, Total of Payments, and Estimated APR.

 *Notice that which loan is better, Mortgage A or B, depends on how long the loan will be held.*

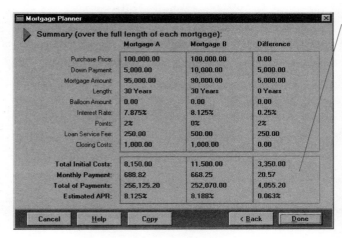

Make sure that you carefully consider the Total Initial Costs and Monthly Payment values. If you can't afford one of these figures, then you can't afford the loan. Note, however, that the APR shown here is based on the scheduled length of the loan, not on how long you'll be in the home. So it's really better to focus not on this APR, but on the one described in step 13.

**15** Click Done. Money returns you to the Planning Wizards window.

## Refinancing a Mortgage

If you're paying a mortgage, it's easy to wonder whether you should refinance when interest rates drop. The logic seems straightforward enough: Replace an expensive mortgage with a cheap mortgage and save money. Unfortunately, figuring out whether you'll actually save by refinancing a mortgage is very difficult.

### Refinancing in a Nutshell

*Misconceptions about Refinancing. The usual refinancing rules of thumb are wrong. For example, you actually don't know whether you'll save money if you refinance when interest rates drop by, say, more than 2 percent. (One rule of thumb.) And you actually don't know whether or not you're saving money just because you can pay back your refinancing costs in two years through lower payments. (Another rule of thumb.)*

The trick to refinancing a mortgage is to make sure that you pay less for the new mortgage—taking into account both the interest charges and any refinancing costs—than you pay for your existing mortgage. To see if you pay less, you need to consider the interest rate and the refinancing costs, of course, but you also need to think about how long you'll be paying interest.

**What's Wrong with the 2 Percent Rule.** *One problem with the first refinancing rule of thumb, the one about interest rates dropping by 2 percent, is that anyone who originally purchased a home in 1980 and then religiously applied this rule would have refinanced four or five times in the last 15 years, most recently in the summer of 1995. And this person would still be 30 years away from paying off the mortgage—even though he or she would already have been paying on it for the last 15 years. Sadly, if this person instead would have refinanced only once and then used all the other money spent on fees toward paying the mortgage too, he or she would probably have paid off the mortgage by now.*

*For purposes of making this analysis, you need to compare two mortgages of equal size. You can't, for example, use the Mortgage Planner to figure out whether a new, 8-percent $100,000 mortgage makes more sense than a 10-percent $80,000 mortgage.*

Fortunately, you can use the Mortgage Planner to perform this analysis. You use the Mortgage Planner as described in the preceding section, but with several minor twists.

When you describe your existing mortgage as the first mortgage (Mortgage A), don't worry about the loan fees and payments you've already made. For your existing mortgage, then, there aren't discount points, loan service fees, or closing costs. And for your existing mortgage, the loan balance and the scheduled loan length equal what is left for you to pay, not what you originally had to pay.

Does all that make sense? Think about it for a minute and it should. When you consider refinancing a loan, you basically compare two loans: your existing loan, for which you'll pay no extra discount points, no loan service fees, and no closing costs, and a new mortgage, for which you'll pay all these extra charges.

## The Complicating Factor

Unfortunately, there's also a complicating factor when it comes to mortgage refinancing. If you want to refinance as a way to save money over the long haul, you shouldn't do it as a way to stretch out your payments. In other words, you're very unlikely to save money by replacing an existing mortgage that has 15 years of payments left with a new, refinanced mortgage that requires 30 years of payments. Even if the new mortgage's interest rate is much lower, you'll be borrowing the money for a lot longer with the new mortgage.

# In Conclusion

This is a long chapter, but if you're serious about succeeding financially, it's well worth understanding. If you're smart and sophisticated in the way you acquire and manage your debts, you can quite easily adds tens of thousands of dollars to your net worth. What's more, if you are smart about all this stuff, you're much less likely to make the easy mistakes that can undermine your financial success—and create a lot of personal stress.

# Homes, Boats, and Cars

**M**oney's strength lies in keeping records of financial assets like bank accounts, money-market funds, and investments, as well as in tracking liabilities such as mortgages and credit cards. But besides tracking these sorts of assets and liabilities, you can also use Money to track whatever else you own. By doing so, you can produce net worth reports. If you're a homeowner, you can even keep a record of the improvements you've made to your home—and that can save on taxes later on.

## Setting Up an Asset Account

To track your net worth, you set up asset accounts for each major asset you own: your house, the car or cars you drive, and any other large, valuable items. You may also want to set up a catchall account for tracking the items that perhaps aren't valuable individually but collectively add up to a significant value, things like baseball cards or nineteenth-century lingerie.

To set up an asset account, follow these steps:

1 With the Money Contents window displayed, click the Account Manager button. Money displays the Account Manager window.

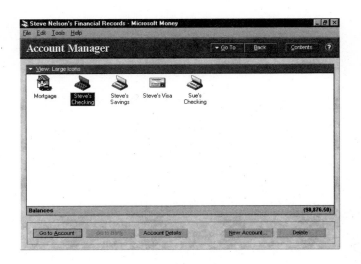

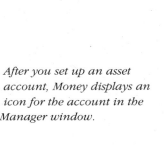

*After you set up an asset account, Money displays an icon for the account in the Account Manager window.*

2 Click the New Account button. This tells Money to start the New Account Wizard.

3 The Wizard asks for the name of the bank or institution at which the Account is held. You can just leave the box blank and click Next.

4 When the Wizard asks what kind of account you want to set up, click Asset.

5 Click Next. When the Wizard asks what name you want to give your asset account, enter a name.

*If, in step 3 of setting up an Asset account, you enter the name of a bank or financial institution, the Wizard will ask you if you have other accounts there, and if you want information about online banking.*

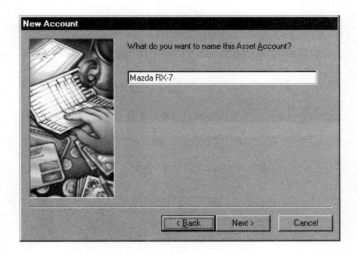

6  Click Next. When the Wizard asks for the account's opening balance, enter either the current value of the asset or its original cost. (If you're setting up an asset account for a house, enter the house's original cost.)

7  Click Finish. If you need to set up additional accounts, repeat steps 2 through 6.

When you finish working with the Account Manager, you can return to the Money Contents window by clicking the Back button. Or, if you want to describe an account in more detail, select an account, click the Account Details button, and use the dialog box that Money displays to enter additional information about the account.

**How Can I Describe an Asset Account in More Detail?**
*When Money displays the Account Details dialog box, you can use it to rename an asset account, jot down comments about the asset, and view a chart that shows an asset's account balance over the previous year.*

# Tracking an Asset with Money

Once you've set up an asset account, it isn't difficult to keep a record of the asset and track the changes in its value. As with recording a check in a bank account register, you use the data-input area at the bottom of the Account Register window to track changes to the value of an asset. In a nutshell, what you do is click the Decrease or Increase tab and then describe the change in the asset's value by filling in the blanks.

**Tracking an Asset**

**1** Click the Decrease or Increase tab, depending on whether you're describing a positive or negative change in the asset's value.

**3** Optionally, enter the name of the person or business you're paying.

**2** Enter the date of the change.

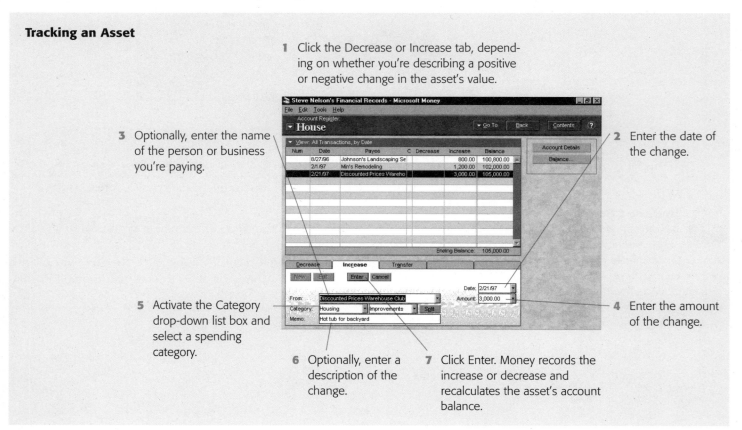

**5** Activate the Category drop-down list box and select a spending category.

**4** Enter the amount of the change.

**6** Optionally, enter a description of the change.

**7** Click Enter. Money records the increase or decrease and recalculates the asset's account balance.

# Tips for Tracking Assets

Asset accounts work very much like bank accounts, and the mechanics of keeping track of an asset with Money are straightforward. Asset record-keeping, however, can be a little tricky. So, in the rest of this chapter, I'll give you ideas about how to make the whole process easier.

## Your Home

A home is usually a person's single largest asset. If you own a home and have decided to track your net worth with Money, you'll want to set up a home, or personal residence, account and use it to track the value of your home.

The historical appreciation of real estate makes it tempting to track the fair market value of a home. However, it makes more sense to track the original cost of the home as well as the cost of any home improvements. The reason for this is that in general, the gains you realize when you sell a house are taxed as income.

Even if you think that one of the two capital gains exceptions might apply to you, it makes sense to keep a record of your home's cost as well as the cost of improvements you make to it. There's no harm in doing so, the work is extremely minimal, and you might someday save a lot of money (because the two exceptions mentioned earlier might not apply).

To keep a record of a home's cost and the cost of improvements, you first set up an asset account named something like "Home" or "Residence." (I described how to do this at the start of this chapter.) In this account, you record as transactions the original cost of the home as well as associated purchase costs such as escrow fees and title insurance. In the future, whenever you spend money to improve your home, you transfer the money from your checking account to the asset account set up for your home.

What qualifies as an improvement? Anything that adds value to a home or to its useful life. For example, adding a swimming pool, finishing the basement, and landscaping the site all qualify as improvements. However, maintenance costs such as those for painting the exterior or interior, repairing a leaky roof, or fixing faulty electrical wiring don't qualify as improvements.

**Two Exceptions to the Capital Gains Tax.** *There are instances when the capital gains on the sale of a house are not taxed as income. You don't have to pay income tax on a gain if you purchase another home of equal or greater value within 24 months of selling the home. Also, taxpayers age 55 or older are allowed to ignore, once, up to $125,000 of gain on the sale of a primary residence.*

**Tracking a Home's Market Value.** *One problem with the approach I've described here is that your financial records don't show the value of your home—only the total of its cost and any improvements. If you want to also show the home's value, you can add a transaction to your asset register that adjusts the account's total to the home's market value. Just be sure to delete this transaction before you calculate the capital gain stemming from the sale of the home.*

## Cars, Boats, and Other Personal Property

Cars, boats, and other valuable personal property can usually be handled nicely with individual accounts. In general, you don't need to make a lot of adjustments to the value of these assets. And you probably won't make improvements that increase their value, anyway. So you may just want to periodically—say, at the end of each year—update the account balances so that the asset's ending balance approximates its fair market value.

## Asset Lists for Property and Casualty Insurance

It's not a bad idea to maintain records of the assets you've insured with a property insurance policy. The reason for this is probably clear: If disaster strikes, a list of the insured items can make claim reports and collections easier and more complete.

To create such a list, set up another asset account called something like "Personal Property" and carefully list all assets you've insured. When you purchase a major new item in the future, remember to add it to the list. The more information on your list, the better. If possible, include information like model numbers and original costs. Remember that you can use the Split Transaction dialog box to store additional data.

One other point. Your asset list won't do much good if your computer and all your backup disks are lost in a fire or flood (or whatever casualty destroys or damages the property you've insured). For this reason, you should probably keep an up-to-date copy of your asset list in a secure place such as a safe-deposit box.

## In Conclusion

Because Money provides an asset account, you can use Money to keep records of all your major assets: your home, the cars you drive, and any other valuable items you own. To be quite frank, most people probably won't want to—and shouldn't—go to the work of keeping records of their nonfinancial assets. The work required can be rather significant in light of the benefits. But those people who do will be able to produce net worth reports easily. And homeowners can probably save capital gains taxes in the future when they sell their homes.

# Getting Wired

**I**'m sure you've heard plenty about the Information Superhighway and all the spectacular things people are doing on it. But as they do with many newer technologies, a lot of people encounter frustration, confusion, and teeth gnashing when they try to explore cyberspace.

Fortunately, in the area of personal finance, cyberspace is actually one of the best places for collecting information and even for buying and selling investments. The investment world moves quickly and that makes cyberspace a great place for finding up-to-the-minute information. I'll talk about this more in Chapters 20 and 21.

## Overview of Money's Online Services

One way to take advantage of the power of emerging online technologies is by using any or all of Money's online services:

➤ Online Bill Payment

➤ Online Banking

➤ Online Quotes

You might have read an article or two about home banking and how it will revolutionize the way people interact with their banks. Well, these sorts of services are what much of the hullabaloo is about. But actually, these services are not completely new. (They existed in the previous version of Money, for example.) It's just that no one seemed to take much notice of them earlier.

*You need to belong to a participating bank if you want to use the Online Banking service. You can use the Online Bill Payment and Online Quotes services with any checking account in the United States. For a list of participating banks, see Chapter 11.*

Things have changed a lot in the past couple years. One reason is that the number of home PCs has increased dramatically. This has led to more banks offering online services. Users of version 3 of Microsoft Money had only three banks to choose from if they wanted to bank online. By the time version 4 came out, twenty banks participated, including some of the largest in the country.

As I said, you can sign up for one, two, or all three of Money's online services. You need only meet the following requirements to use the Online Bill Payment and Online Quotes services: you need a modem, and you must have opened a checking account somewhere in the United States. The services are tightly integrated into the program and require no additional software.

I'll go into more detail about what you can do with the services and how to get signed up later in this chapter, the following two chapters, and in Chapter 20. For now, lets talk a little about modems.

## Modems

A *modem* is an automobile that drives you along the information superhighway. (What is it about cyberspace that encourages such bad metaphors?)

Basically, a modem is a communications tool that acts as the intermediary between your computer and cyberspace. Modems communicate through standard telephone lines. They aren't half as scary as they seem, once you get to know them. By learning a few basics, you and your modem can establish a healthy, mutually respectful working relationship with little effort.

If you bought your computer in the past couple years, chances are a modem was included with it. Most of the modems that come pre-installed on computers are internal modems, so you may not know if your computer has one or not. To find out if your computer has a modem, you can check the piles of paper that came with your computer or you can look in the Windows 95 Control Panel under Modems. Just click the Windows 95 Start menu, point to Settings, click Control Panel, and then double-click Modems to see if any modems are listed.

**Which Modem Should I Purchase?** *If you need to purchase a modem, you'll probably want to buy one that operates at a speed of at least 14,400 bps. If you can afford it, you won't be sorry buying one that operates at a speed of 28,800 bps. At the time I'm writing this, you can purchase a 14,400 bps modem for less than $100. You can purchase a 28,800 bps modem for under $200.*

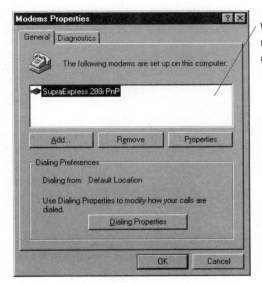

Windows 95 shows the modems connected to your computer here.

## Modem Speed

If you do have a modem, the next step is to find out what speed it runs at. Modem speed is measured in what's called *bps*, which stands for "bits per second." Knowing your modem's speed is necessary as you consider how to use your modem.

If you'll use your modem only to access Money's online services, an old 2400 bps standby probably works fine. But if you plan to surf the Internet or use an online service such as MSN (The Microsoft Network), a 2400 bps modem won't do the job. Using one would be like cruising the information superhighway in a '76 Ford Pinto with only three cylinders running. (Okay, I said I wouldn't use any more bad metaphors. I said nothing about bad similes.)

In the past couple of years, the industry standard for modem speeds has risen from 9600 to 14,400 to 28,800 bps, the current Lamborghini of modems. Before last year, 14,400 bps modems (often referred to as "fourteen four" modems) were the biggest sellers. These modems are pretty speedy and are reasonably priced. But by the end of 1996, the 28,800 bps modem (also known as the V.34) will be the biggest seller.

Either way, the upgrade question is a matter of what you use your modem for and how much you want to spend to upgrade. If you're curious about pricing, check the ads in the Sunday edition of your local paper. It is almost sure to have advertisements for modems.

 **Upgrading an Internal Modem.** *If you want to upgrade an internal modem, the installation process is a bit more tricky, if only because you need to remove the cover from your computer and hope that the right size slot is available. For novice users, I recommend sticking with an external modem.*

## Installing a Modem

If you have an external modem, installing it is as simple as can be under Windows 95. You're probably thinking, "I've heard that before." But in this case, it really is true. Just follow these steps:

1 If necessary, disconnect the old modem from the cable that connects it to your computer and switch it to your new modem.

   If the connections are not the same size, mix and match the jumble of cables and adapters that came with your new modem until you find a combination that works.

   If this is your computer's first modem, no problem. Just find an empty communications port in the back of your computer and find the right combination of 9-pin or 25-pin, male or female cables and adapters that allow you to make the connection.

2 Once your computer and modem have been connected, make sure all the cables are securely attached and plug the modem's AC adapter into the modem. Plug the other end into a power source.

**3** Plug a regular phone line into the phone jack on the modem labeled "Line." Take another phone line (one came with your modem, I hope) and plug one end into your phone and the other into the jack on the back of the modem labeled "Phone."

## Making Your Modem and System Work Together

By installing the modem, you force your modem and computer into an "arranged marriage." Now it's time to introduce them to each other. Saying, "Modem, this is computer; computer, this is modem" is where Windows 95 really comes in handy. It's all taken care of with "plug and play" technology. You've probably heard the term "plug and play" before. Basically, once you've plugged the modem into the computer, it's up to Windows 95 to make sure that they work and play well together and don't end up in a nasty custody battle over the mouse.

To start the introductions, make sure the modem is turned on, and then follow these steps:

**1** Click the Windows 95 Start button, point to Settings, and click Control Panel. The Control Panel window opens.

**2** Double-click the Modems icon.

**3** Click the Add button. You'll see the Install New Modem dialog box.

**4** If you want to direct Windows 95 to the modem yourself, click the Don't Detect My Modem; I Will Select It From A List check box and then click Next. Otherwise, just click the Next button. Windows 95 starts sniffing around for the new modem.

With even the slightest amount of luck, Windows 95 magically detects the modem's make and model.

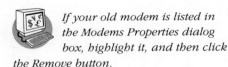

*If your old modem is listed in the Modems Properties dialog box, highlight it, and then click the Remove button.*

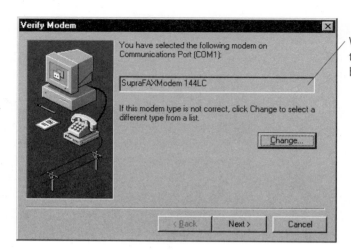

Windows 95 identifies the name of your modem here.

**What Should I Do If Windows 95 Selects the Wrong Modem?**

*If Windows 95 selects the wrong modem, click the Change button. Then select your modem from the list that Windows 95 displays.*

5 If Windows 95 found the correct modem, click the Next button.

6 If it isn't the correct one, click the Change button and Windows 95 will let you manually select the modem type.

7 When you're done, click the Next button. Windows gives you a confirmation message telling you that your new modem is now set up and ready to go!

## Online Services

Money's Online Services are built into the Money program, so you don't need to get additional software to use the services. You don't need to know much about the Internet or electronic commerce, either. In other words, you don't have to be a nerd to use this stuff. It's all very simple.

Money offers three services for performing tasks electronically:

> **Online Bill Payment**: Lets you pay all your bills from your computer. Yes, this means you can even send a payment directly from your computer to your mom in Indio, California. For more information on using this service, see Chapter 10.

> **Online Banking**: Lets you download bank statements and account balances, transfer money between accounts electronically, and e-mail your bank to inquire about a payment, order new checks, or just say "Hi." To use this service, you must have an account at a participating bank. For more information on using this service and to see a list of participating banks, see Chapter 11.

> **Online Quotes**: Lets you download the latest prices of stocks and major mutual funds. For more information on using this service, see Chapter 20.

 *You can learn more about online services by clicking the Home Banking button on the Contents screen. Click Set Up Online Services and then, in the first Online Services Setup dialog box, click The Frequently Asked Questions button.*

## Is It Safe to Use Online Banking Services?

Whether it is safe to use these services seems to be one of the biggest concerns people have about online banking services. But there's really not much to worry about. In order to make a connection to online services, the user must enter a Personal Identification Number (PIN). Users get to assign their own PIN numbers. You can provide an additional layer of security by assigning a password to the Money program.

If you're concerned about an out-of-control, evil genius hacker breaking into your system and directing a little cash his or her way, don't worry, because there isn't much chance of this happening. Money's online systems use basically the same security technology as ATM machines. (And you can't withdraw cash from a computer—yet.)

*To protect a Money file with a password, click Password on the File menu, and then follow the directions on the screen.*

**How Do I Choose a Password?**
*There are a few rules about choosing a password that might come in handy. First, use a combination of letters and numbers if you can. Don't use anything that might be common knowledge or easily acquired, like your social security number or birthday. The best would be combining two disparate facts, say, your dog's name and your spouse's birthday, for instance—ROVR0912. (Of course, you wouldn't tell your spouse you combined his or her birthday with your dog's name, even if you left off the year.) Second, change your password periodically.*

The first time you connect to the online services, you are prompted to change your PIN from the one assigned to you in your start-up kit. Be sure you don't change it to something that can easily be guessed—such as the name of your spouse or your dog. And be sure you don't write the number down and leave it near your computer if you're concerned about unauthorized use.

Nothing is secure 100 percent of the time, but if you follow these fundamental safety measures, the security of this system should not be something you need to worry about.

## Setting Up Online Services

Now that your modem is ready and you know a little about Money's online services, you can start the process of getting set up.

1 From Money's Contents screen, click Home Banking. Then click the Set Up Online Services button on the Accounts tab.

2 Read the contents of each wizard screen and click Next when you're ready to go on.

*In order to use Online Banking, you must have an account at a participating bank. To find out what services your bank offers, give it a call or call Microsoft at (800) 200-7622.*

*Your bank bills you monthly for using the online services. Payments are taken directly from your checking account. A record of the payment appears on your monthly statement along with the other transactions.*

*You can also find your bank's routing number in your start-up kit.*

**3** When you're asked for your bank's identification number, enter the nine-digit electronic code. You can find it in the lower left corner of a check from the account. Then click Next.

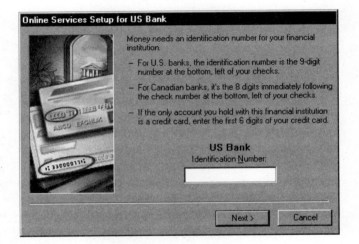

**4** In the next dialog box, Money gives some basic information about your bank's online services program.

If you click the More Information button, Money opens a Word Document containing information about your bank and an online application.

**5** Call the phone number, or fax in the application. When you've received setup information from your bank, continue the setup procedure. Click Next.

**6** In the next dialog box, click Yes, I Have This Information.

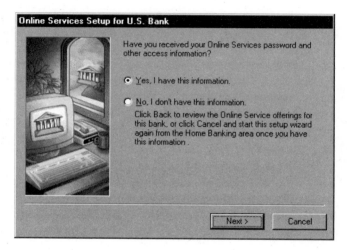

Then click Next.

**7** Money displays an information screen. Click Next again.

**8** When you're asked for personal information such as your address, phone number, and social security number, enter the information for the primary user of the services. In the phone number section, enter your own phone number. You'll be asked later for the number you've been assigned for calling the online services.

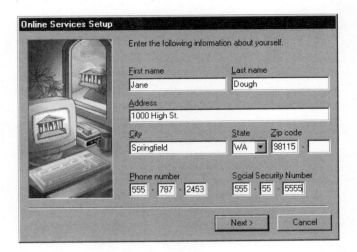

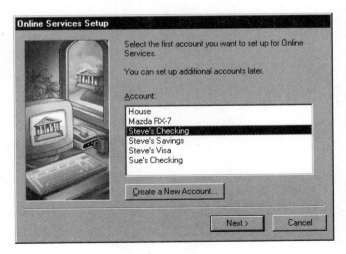

**Where Do I Find the Telephone Number for Online Services?** *You can find the telephone number for Online Services in your start-up kit.*

**9** Click Next. In the Account box, highlight the first account listed in your start-up kit.

If you haven't yet created the account in Money, you can do so now by clicking the Create A New Account button.

**10** Click Next. In the next Wizard dialog box, click the check box next to the service(s) the account is approved for. The services you selected should have a check mark next to their names. You cannot set up an online account with one of the services unless you've made prior arrangements with your bank.

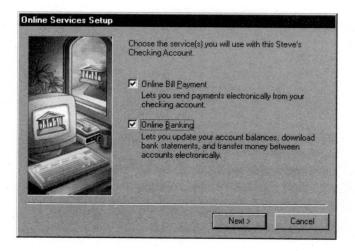

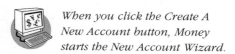

*When you click the Create A New Account button, Money starts the New Account Wizard.*

**11** Click Next. Enter your account number and the bank routing and ID numbers.

*Chapter 10 describes Money's Online Bill Payment feature.*

*Chapter 11 describes Money's Online Banking feature.*

*Chapter 20 describes another online service: Online Quotes. Online Quotes allow you to retrieve up-to-date prices for the securities you own.*

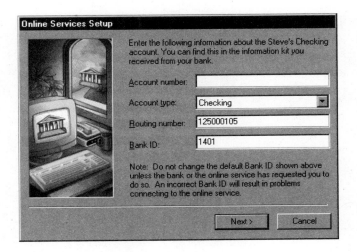

**12** Click Next. If you want to set up additional accounts, you can do so in this Wizard dialog box. If you have more than one account, you should probably set all of them up at once. If you have no more accounts to set up, choose the option that says No, I'm Finished With Online Services Setup and then click the Next button.

**Lightning Strikes.** *Once you set up an account with the online services, a lightning bolt appears next to the account in the list of accounts.*

If you chose to set up additional accounts, you are sent back to an earlier Wizard dialog box so you can select another account and go through the process again. Return to step 9 of this procedure if you need help setting up any additional accounts.

If you indicated that you were finished, Money displays a screen that gives you some cursory instructions on using the online services with your account. Click Finish.

Now you're ready to use the online services. I explain how to use online bill paying and online banking in the following two chapters.

## What If I Want to Set Up More Accounts Later?

No problem. To set up another account—or to disable an account that's currently set up:

*If you haven't already setup online banking, the Select Online Services button will be called Setup Online Services.*

1 Go to the Account Manager.

2 Highlight the account in the list.

3 Click the Account Details button.

4 Click the Select Online Services button.

5 Follow the instructions in the Online Services Setup Wizard, which follow the same pattern as described in the previous section.

### Sending E-Mail to Your Bank

*If you send a payment investigation letter, it will be answered within two business days. Don't forget to connect again in order to get the response.*

You can send electronic mail to your bank to inquire about a payment, request a copy of a check, order new paper checks, or send a general-purpose letter. Click the Home Banking button in your Contents window, and you'll see the Home Banking window, which now displays the name of your online bank. Just click the Write Letter button. When Money displays the Write Letter dialog box, you can use its options to choose which type of letter you want to send. To learn more about each option, click it with the right mouse button. When the What's This button appears, click it.

## In Conclusion

You know what surprises most people about using Money's online services? The fact that it just isn't very complicated to get started. You get a modem. You tell Windows 95 to set it up for you. You tell Money you want to use its online services. And then you're done.

# 10

# Paying Bills Online

**W**ith Money's Online Bill Payment service, you can pay any business or individual in the United States from your computer. The service works with any checking account in the United States. Yes, even the one you're using right now. The suggested retail price is $4.95 per month for 20 payments. Additional payments are $.50 each.

*If Money's $.35 per transaction charge sounds expensive, remember that you'll save a $.32 stamp every time you pay a bill electronically.*

The service lets you drastically reduce the time you spend paying bills. You no longer have to write out checks by hand, address envelopes, or lick stamps. You just enter all the payment information in Money and send off the payment through your modem.

## How It Works

Basically, the Online Bill Payment service is a convenience and a good way to impress your friends. You enter all the payment information in Money as you normally would, except you enter "Epay" in the Number field and the date you want the payment to be made in the Date field. Once all your payments are entered, you click the Home Banking button, which appears on the Money Contents window, and then click the Connect button to send the payment information on its way. On the scheduled day, the payment magically appears in the mail box of the payee.

Actually, there's nothing magical about it. The payment information is sent to a central processing center. From there, the payment is either forwarded electronically to the payee (only a limited number of payees can receive payments this way) or else a check is cut and sent through the good old U.S. Postal Service to the payee at an address you specify.

**How Long Should I Allow for Payment?** *I usually do not enter a payment date at all and let Money propose a delivery date when I enter the transaction. This way, I don't have to look at the calendar to see what the earliest payment date is. For most payees, you need to allow four business days for the payment to be processed and sent. When you enter the date, Money checks its calendar to see if you've allowed enough time for delivery. If the date you entered is too soon and the payment can't be delivered on time, you see a message that tells you the earliest date the payment can be made.*

Payments you send through the Online Bill Payment service show up on your monthly bank statement in the same way as the checks you write now. You can keep writing regular checks the usual way at the same time as you make payments electronically. Don't worry—when you're out at a restaurant or monster truck show, you can still write as many checks as you like by hand.

The payments you make electronically are given special check numbers so that they don't conflict with the numbers on the checks you write by hand. You can also use the Online Bill Payment service with as many as ten different accounts.

In order to use the service, you must go through the setup process explained in Chapter 9. If you haven't done that yet, go do it. I'll wait here until you get back.

## Entering an Electronic Payment

Once you've subscribed to the service and set up your accounts, you're ready to enter your first payment. If you're at all apprehensive, you might want to give it a test run by sending a check for $1 to yourself. To enter a payment:

1 Go to the Account Register and switch to the checking account that you've set up. I'm sure you know how to switch accounts by now, but just to be sure, click the triangle menu next to the account name at the upper left of the screen, and then click the account you want. (Remember, all online banking accounts have a lightning bolt next to their names.)

2 Click the Check tab in the input area below the register.

3 Enter the payment information.

## Recording an Electronic Payment

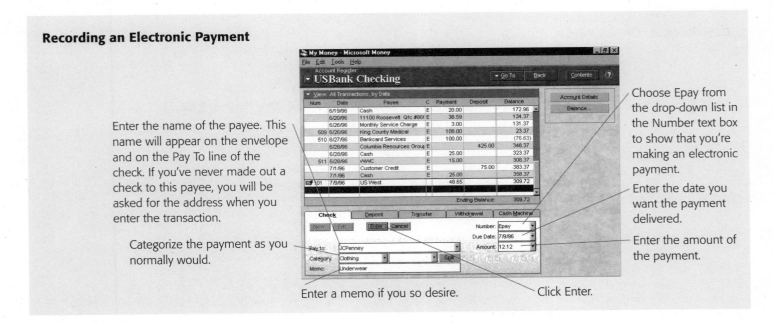

Enter the name of the payee. This name will appear on the envelope and on the Pay To line of the check. If you've never made out a check to this payee, you will be asked for the address when you enter the transaction.

Categorize the payment as you normally would.

Enter a memo if you so desire.

Choose Epay from the drop-down list in the Number text box to show that you're making an electronic payment.

Enter the date you want the payment delivered.

Enter the amount of the payment.

Click Enter.

If Money can't make the payment by the date you entered, you'll see a message that lets you know when Money can make the payment. After that, you can choose if you want to use Money's suggested date instead.

If you haven't used this payee before, you'll then be prompted to enter the payee's address.

## Describing an Online Payee

Make sure this is the way you want the payee's name to appear on the check and on the envelope.

If you want, enter the phone number of the payee. This is not required and is used only if there is a problem with the payment.

If this payment is going to a business with which you have an account, such as the phone company, enter your account number here. If this is a payment to your mom, just type "Hi Mom!"

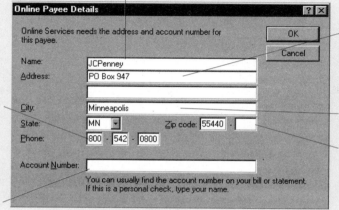

**Online Payee Details**

Online Services needs the address and account number for this payee.

Name: JCPenney
Address: PO Box 947

City: Minneapolis
State: MN
Zip code: 55440 -
Phone: 800 - 542 - 0800

Account Number:

You can usually find the account number on your bill or statement. If this is a personal check, type your name.

OK
Cancel

Enter the street address of the payee. Use the second line if you need more space.

Enter the city name in the address.

Enter the 5- or 9-digit zip code.

Click OK when you're done.

*If you have an electronic payment but have not yet sent it to the Online Bill Payment service, you see a reminder on the Money Contents screen and in the account register.*

You only have to enter information once for each payee. After Money knows the address of the payee, it doesn't ask you for it anymore. Thanks to SmartFill and SuperSmartFill, entering a transaction is as easy as typing the first few letters of the payee's name.

Once you enter a transaction, an open envelope icon and a lightning bolt appear in the Number field of the account register. The lightning bolt, of course, means it's an electronic payment. The open envelope means you haven't sent the payment yet.

Even though the payment information is now entered in Money, you're not finished until you send it through your modem.

# Sending Electronic Payments

*Payments sent electronically don't debit your account until the payee actually cashes the check—just like with the checks you write manually.*

Once you enter all your electronic payments, the next step is to send them to the online services. You make a connection through your modem to the online services, they speak their funny little modem speak, and the payment information is transferred. Then the check is cut so it can be sent through the mail to the payee.

To send an electronic payment, follow these steps:

1 If you're in the account register, there should be a reminder to the right of the screen. If that's the case, click the Home Banking button. Otherwise, go to the Contents window, and click the Home Banking button.

2 Click the Connect tab. Review the payment information to make sure the amounts, payees, and payment dates are correct.

If you also subscribe to the Online Banking service, you'll see instructions for updating the statement and balance of your Online Banking accounts.

*If you decide you don't want to send one of the payments now, just click it with the right mouse button and then click Don't Send On Next Call.*

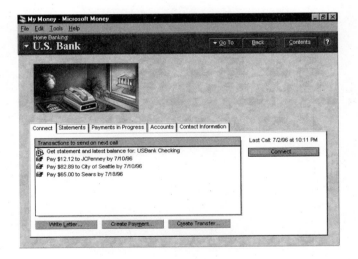

**3** When all the payments are ready to send, click the Connect button. Money displays the Call Online Services dialog box.

**4** Optionally, click the Dialing Properties button to customize how Windows 95 handles your calls. (This button appears on the Call Online Services dialog box.)

If you have to dial a special number in order to access an outside line (which you might have to do if you're dialing from an office), enter the number(s) here.

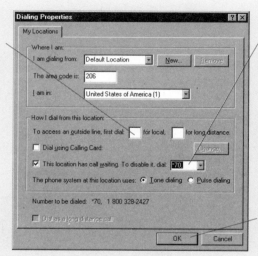

If you have call waiting, you should check this box and then choose a disable code from the drop-down list. Call your local phone company to find out which code you need to disable call waiting. If you don't do this, your connection could be disrupted if someone calls while you're connected to the online services.

Click OK.

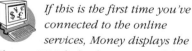

*If this is the first time you've connected to the online services, Money displays the Change PIN dialog box on top of the Call Online Services dialog box. It asks you to enter and change your Personal Identification Number (PIN). Enter the PIN information requested and then click OK to return to the Call Online Services dialog box.*

**5** Now you're ready to send the payment instructions. Click the Connect button. You'll then see a progression of messages that read "Initializing...," "Dialing...," "Establishing a Secure Connection...," "Sending...," and, finally (and thankfully), "Receiving...."

**6** The Call Summary dialog box appears. Review the list of transactions to make sure everything looks okay.

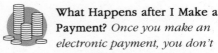 **What Happens after I Make a Payment?** *Once you make an electronic payment, you don't see it again until the payee cashes the check and a record of the transaction appears on your bank statement.*

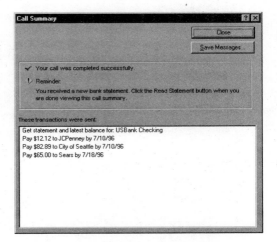

**7** When you're ready, click the Close button.

That's it! You've sent your first electronic payment. Do you feel like a rebel, a cyberpunk, an Internet-surfing pioneer of the electronic frontier? No? Oh well. At least you know the bills are being paid on time.

## What If I Need to Cancel a Payment after It's Sent?

What if you realize later in the day that you've made a horrible mistake. You don't like your Aunt Enid as much as you thought, and you don't want to send her quite that much birthday money? You can cancel the payment after it's been sent as long as the Online Bill Payment service hasn't sent the payment to dear old Aunt Enid. Just follow these steps:

**1** In the account register, click the transaction with the right mouse button, and then point to Mark As and click Void.

**2** A message appears asking if you want to create an instruction to cancel the payment. Click Yes.

**3** Click the Home Banking button on the right side of the screen.

**4** On the Connect tab, make sure that the cancel payment instruction is there.

**5** When all your instructions are ready, click the Connect button.

**6** From here, I think you know the routine.

If you haven't yet sent the transaction (if it still says "Epay" next to the open envelope icon in the Number field of the account register), you can cancel it by highlighting it in the account register and pressing the Delete key.

**How Do I Stop a Payment?** *To cancel or stop a payment that has already been sent to the payee, contact your local bank or financial institution for a Stop Payment order.*

## What If the Payee Doesn't Receive the Check?

I've been using the Online Bill Payment service for well over two years now and have yet to have a payment not show up on the payee's doorstep. This doesn't mean it won't ever happen, though, if for no other reason than the U.S. Postal Service can't be 100-percent effective all the time. So, if Aunt Enid cuts you out of her will for failing to send a birthday check, here's what to do:

**1** Go to the Home Banking area.

**2** Click the Write Letter button.

**3** Click the A Letter Inquiring About A Specific Payment option button and then click Continue.

**4** In the Payment Investigation dialog box, highlight the payment in the list and then click OK.

**5** Review the information in the Letter dialog box and then click OK.

**6** Review the instructions in the list on your screen and then click the Connect button.

You will receive a response within two business days. But remember, you need to connect to the online services again to receive the response.

# Creating Automatic Payments

If you want to take this convenience thing one step further, you can also tell the Online Bill Payment service to make payments for you automatically. This only works for recurring payments of a fixed amount, such as rent, car, and mortgage payments. When you authorize an automatic payment, the checks are sent weekly, monthly, bi-monthly, or at whatever frequency you specify.

When you connect to the Online Bill Payment service within a month of the date that an automatic payment is scheduled to be sent, the payment is sent to the Online Bill Payment service and recorded in your account register. This way, you have a whole month to cancel or make changes to the automatic payment before it is actually sent to the payee.

To set up an automatic payment, follow these steps:

1 Go to the Payment Calendar and click the New button.

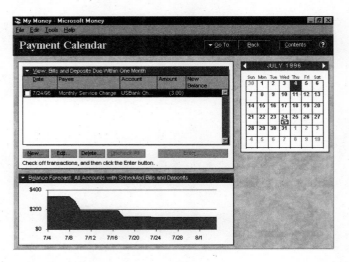

2 In the Create New Recurring Payment dialog box, choose Bill, and then click the Next button. Fill out everything as you normally would, with these differences:

From the drop-down list, choose the account from which you want the payments to be made. The account must be set up with the Online Bill Payment service. All accounts that are set up for online services have a lightning bolt next to their names.

Choose the frequency of the payment.

From the drop-down list, choose Automatic Payment (Apay).

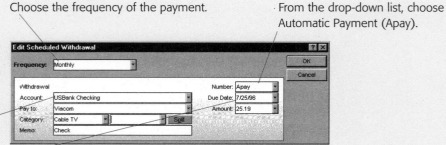

Enter the date you want the first payment to be made. If this is a monthly payment, such as a loan payment, the date you enter is the date the payment will be made every month. For example, if you enter 3/1/97, the payment will be delivered on the first of each month.

3 When you're done, click OK.

4 In the Set Up Automatic Payment dialog box, read all the text and enter the number of payments or the date of the final payment. If you want payments to be made until you cancel them, leave both fields blank.

5 Click the OK button. If this is a new payee, fill in the boxes of the Online Payee Details dialog box. Then click OK.

 *You have to be careful with automatic payments because once you set them up, the payments are made whether or not you connect to the online services. Therefore, it's important to remain aware of your account balance and keep enough money in your account to cover automatic payments.*

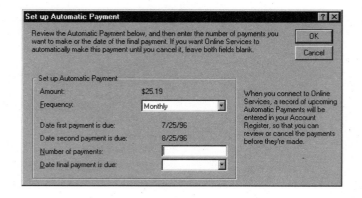

6 Go to the Home Banking area by clicking the Go To button and choosing Home Banking.

7 On the Connect tab, scan the Automatic Payment information to make sure everything is correct.

8 When all your instructions are ready to send, click the Connect button to send the payment just like you would any other payment.

From now on, one month before each automatic payment is due, it will be downloaded to your account register as a reminder that it's coming up. Once it has been downloaded, you can make any changes you want (including canceling the payment).

## Canceling an Individual Automatic Payment

If you want to continue with the automatic payments you've set up but you want to cancel a single payment—for example, if you need more excitement in your life and decide to not pay the rent for a month—follow these steps:

1 Go to the account register. In the register above the check forms, click the transaction you want to cancel with the right mouse button.

2 Point to Mark As and then click Void.

3 Go to the Home Banking area and review the cancel payment instruction on the Connect tab on your screen.

4 Click the Connect button to send the instruction just like all the others.

## Permanently Canceling an Automatic Payment

If you didn't set an end date for the automatic payment, or if you just decide to join a cult and want to stop making your loan payments, follow these steps:

1 Go to the Payment Calendar.

2 Click with the right mouse button on the automatic payment you want to cancel and then click Cancel Automatic Payment.

3 Go to the Home Banking area. Look at the instruction to cancel the automatic payment on the Connect tab to make sure it's there. Then click the Connect button. You know the rest.

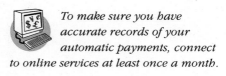

*To make sure you have accurate records of your automatic payments, connect to online services at least once a month.*

# Checking on the Status of a Payment

You can quickly see the status of an electronic payment you've made in the last sixty days. Just go to the Home Banking area and click the Payments in Progress tab. In the status column you can see if the payment status is Scheduled, Transmitted, Canceled, or Cleared. You can also highlight any of the transactions and click the Payment Status button to see what its status is.

The Payment Status dialog box shows you the date the payment was transmitted and whether or not you marked the transaction as cleared. If the payment has not yet been cleared, the dialog box tells you the date the payment was scheduled to be sent to the payee.

# In Conclusion

A good way to go about using Money's Online Bill Payment service is to schedule a regular bill-paying session—perhaps Saturday morning—when you enter and then send your electronic payments. You'll find that electronic bill-paying saves you both time and trouble.

# Banking Online

**W**ith Microsoft Money's Online Banking service, you can download your bank statements and latest account balances directly from your bank, transfer money electronically between accounts, and send e-mail to your bank to ask questions or to order new paper checks, for example. The prices for these services vary, since they're set by the bank. Contact your bank directly for more information.

What can the service do for you? Well, as it is now, if you want to track your finances by computer, every couple of days you have to type in all your day-to-day transactions, or you have to enter all your transactions on the computer when the statement comes from the bank at the end of the month. Not exactly my idea of fun. With the Online Banking service, all your transactions are entered electronically, which means no more typing.

The only catch with this service is that you have to have an account at a participating bank in order to use it. As I write this, the twenty banks listed in the table on the next page are participating. If your bank isn't on this list, call your bank and ask about it, or call (800) 200-7622 to check service availability.

## How It Works

Basically, with the Online Banking service, you get the convenience of being able to download all transactions that affect your checking accounts, savings accounts, and sometimes even your credit card and line of credit accounts. The data is downloaded directly into Money so you don't have to enter the transactions yourself.

**Participating Banks**

| Bank | Phone Number |
| --- | --- |
| Bank of Boston | (800) 476-6262 |
| Centura Bank | (800) 721-0501 |
| Chase Manhattan Bank | (800) 242-7324 |
| Chemical Bank | (800) 243-6226 |
| Compass Bank | (800) 266-7277 |
| CoreStates | (800) 562-6382 |
| Crestar Bank | (800) 273-7827 |
| E-Direct | (800) 708-8768 |
| First Chicago Bank | (800) 800-8435 |
| First Interstate Bank | (800) 968-2634 |
| Home Savings of America | (800) 310-4932 |
| M&T Bank | (800) 790-9130 |
| Marquette Banks | (800) 708-8768 |
| Michigan National Bank | (800) 225-5662 |
| Sanwa Bank California | (800) 237-2692 |
| Savings Bank of America | (800) 317-4932 |
| Smith Barney | (800) 221-3636 |
| Texas Commerce Bank | (800) 235-8522 |
| Union Bank | (800) 796-5656 |
| US Bank | (800) 422-8762 |
| Wells Fargo | (800) 423-3362, ext. Q |

Online Banking also puts you in closer contact with what's happening to your accounts. Instead of waiting until the end of the month to see all the transactions, you can connect to the service whenever you wish. This way, if you notice any anomalies, like a $2,000 check to Nordstrom that magically appears out of nowhere, you can track it down to its source while the trail is still fresh. You don't have to wait until the end of the month when the bank statement arrives. You also get the benefit of seeing the latest balance in all your accounts when you download the statement.

I usually connect every third or fourth day. I also use my debit card from my bank account—which is one of my Bank Online accounts—instead of cash for most purchases so that most of my expenses are accounted for. When I get cash from an ATM and spend it at the grocery store, all I get in Money is a huge category of ATM expenses labeled "Miscellaneous." But if I use my debit card at the grocery store, the amount I spend there is appropriately tracked as "Food: Groceries," which makes for much more useful spending reports and charts.

I usually have about five to ten transactions to download every few days. Since the payee name is usually downloaded with the transaction, it's easy to add the appropriate category to each transaction before it's entered. This way, nearly all my expenses are accounted for with little work on my part. I know many people enjoy putting a lot of time and effort into tracking their finances. I don't happen to be one of them. I have more important things to do with my time—like watching "Seinfeld" and "Hard Copy." (I like to stay informed.)

# Should You Keep Entering Transactions Manually?

When you start using the Online Banking service, you have to decide whether to keep entering transactions manually as a backup or verification of the bank's records. If you've entered transactions manually, Money searches your account register to find matching transactions when it downloads records from your bank. When it thinks it has found a match, Money presents it to you so you can make sure the transaction you recorded and the one from the bank do, in fact, match. This way, you can be certain that your transactions are not entered twice.

As for me, I subscribe to the Online Banking service specifically to keep from manually entering my transactions. Why create more work for yourself? As I mentioned, I use my debit card for all ATM withdrawals and for most purchases, including gas, groceries, and dining out. Then, a couple of days after I make a purchase, I download the transaction to Money, which means I don't have to enter the transaction myself. I check each transaction before it's downloaded to make sure it's correct. And that's it.

For maximum control with minimal effort, it's pretty tough to beat using debit cards along with the Online Banking service. If you don't want to manually enter your transactions but you still want to be extra careful, you can save the receipt you receive with each debit card purchase or withdrawal and check your receipts against your downloaded transactions.

I know that even with this endorsement of convenience, some of you are going to insist on entering your transactions manually, which is fine. As I said, Money accommodates this tracking method too.

 **Online Banking Makes Balancing Easy.** *Balancing your accounts is also much easier if you use the Online Banking service. Because the transactions are downloaded directly from your bank's records, your Money records match your monthly bank statement exactly. Also, when a transaction is downloaded to Money, it is cleared automatically, and Money puts an E in the cleared field of your account register.*

## Downloading Your Bank Account Records

Once you're set up to use the Online Banking service, downloading your statements is a cinch (as they say). It involves two steps, as a glance at the Online Services area screen will show you. First, you make the connection and download the transactions and account balances. Then, you click another button to enter the transactions into your account register. This way, if you want to check your current balances but not add the new transactions to the account register, you can do that.

## Making the Connection and Downloading

To start the process, follow these steps:

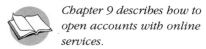

*Chapter 9 describes how to open accounts with online services.*

1 From the Money Contents window, click the Home Banking button. Each account you've set up with the Online Banking service should automatically show up on your screen.

If any of the accounts that your start-up kit says are available for online banking don't appear here, go to the Account Manager, highlight the account, and click Account Details. Then click Setup Online Services, click the Next button, and follow the instructions on your screen.

**2** When all the instructions are ready to send, click the Connect button. Money displays the Call Online Services dialog box.

**3** Optionally, click the Dialing Properties button to customize how Windows 95 handles your calls.

If you have to dial a special number in order to access an outside line (which you might have to do if you're dialing from an office), enter the number(s) here.

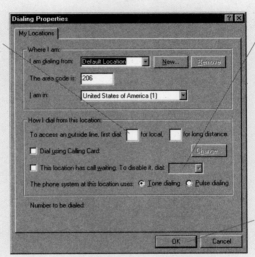

If you have call waiting, you should check this box and then choose a disable code from the drop-down list. Call your local phone company to find out which code you need to disable call waiting. If you don't do this, your connection could be disrupted if someone calls while you're connected to the online services.

Click OK.

 *If this is the first time you've connected to the online services, Money displays the Change PIN dialog box on top of the Call Online Services dialog box. It asks you to enter and change your Personal Identification Number (PIN). Once you enter this information, click OK to close the Change PIN dialog box.*

**4** Now you're ready to receive the transactions. Click the Connect button. You'll then see a progression of messages that read "Initializing...," "Dialing...," "Establishing a secure connection...," "Sending...," and, finally, "Receiving...."

**5** The Call Summary dialog box appears. Review the list of transactions to make sure everything looks okay.

*If you downloaded your statement information but have not yet entered it in your account register, you see a re-minder to do so in Money's Contents screen and in the account register.*

**6** When you're ready, click the Close button.

As I said, this is a two-step process. That takes care of the first part. Now on to the second.

## Adding the Transactions to the Account Register

If you look carefully at the Home Banking window you can now see how many transactions were downloaded. You're ready to add them to your account register. You can also see the current balance of each account under the column labeled "Bank Balance." When you're ready to add the downloaded transactions to your account register, follow these steps:

**Your Balance and the Bank's Balance.** *The downloaded account balance you see on the screen has nothing to do with the balance you see in the account register or the Account Manager. The amounts may differ because the balance shown in Money reflects all transactions, even transactions scheduled to take place in the future, whereas the balance from your bank does not. If you want, you can enter an adjustment transaction to make your balance in Money jibe with your actual bank balance.*

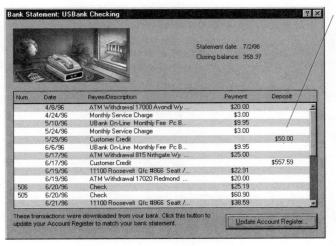

These transactions are the ones you've just downloaded from the bank.

**1** Click the statements tab. Highlight an account in the list on your screen and click the Read Statement button.

**2** In the Bank Statement dialog box, you see a list of all the transactions that have affected the account since the last time you downloaded transactions from your bank. Review the list if you like, and when you're ready, click Update Account Register.

**3** For each transaction, Money tries to find a matching transaction in your account register. When it finds one that appears to match, it asks you to confirm the match. You can then choose whether this is, in fact, the same transaction, or whether you want Money to keep looking.

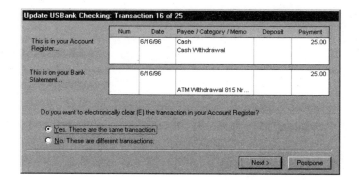

**Entering All Downloaded Transactions Automatically.**
*You can tell Money to auto-matically enter all downloaded transactions without a confirmation. To exercise this option, click Options on the Tools menu, and then click Online Services. To turn off the confirmation, clear the Show Me Each Downloaded Transaction check box. This way, when you click Add To Account Register, Money will add all your transactions without showing them to you first.*

If Money doesn't find a match (which is always the case if you don't also manually enter your transactions), it displays the transaction and gives you a chance to make any changes. At this point, you might want to change the payee name or add a category or subcategory.

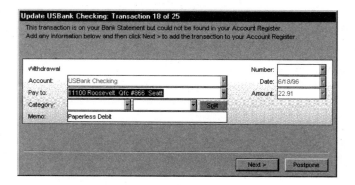

*For credit and debit card transactions, Money suggests a category based on the type of business.*

4 Go through each transaction and make any changes you want. Click the Finish button when you're ready to move to another transaction. You've downloaded your first electronic bank statement.

# Transferring Money between Accounts

As long as two accounts are at the same bank and both are registered for the Online Banking service, you can electronically transfer money between them. For example, if you want to transfer money from your checking account to your VISA account, you can do it electronically. Here's how:

1 Go to the Account Register and switch to the account you want to transfer money from. To do this, click that little triangle menu button next to the account name in the upper left corner of the window and then click the account.

2 Click the Transfer tab in the input area below the register.

*For electronic transfers, you must use today's date. The transfer takes place at the end of the day. If it's sent after the cut-off time, it is processed at the end of the following business day. Transfers to and from credit card accounts have an additional one-day delay.*

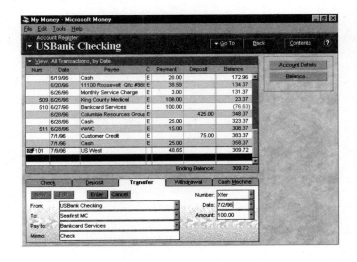

3 Choose Xfer, or Electronic Transfer, from the drop-down list.

4 Enter the account you're transferring money from.

5 Enter the transfer date.

6 Enter the account you're transferring money to.

7 Enter the amount you want transferred between the accounts.

8 When you're ready, click the Enter button.

9 Go to your bank's Home banking area by way of the Go To button.

10 Under step 1 on your screen, scan the list of instructions to make sure the transfer is there and that everything is correct.

11 When all your instructions are ready, make sure your modem is turned on and click the Call button.

That's it! If you want, you can check your statement the next day to make sure the money was transferred.

*It's best to choose an account from the drop-down list. That way, you won't make a mistake when typing it. Accounts involved in money transfers must have lightning bolts next to their names to indicate they're registered for online banking.*

## In Conclusion

Online banking sounds pretty nice, doesn't it? With no real additional effort, you can electronically download your bank statements and transfer money between accounts. The one thing that's a little bit awkward about it is that you need to bank someplace that provides the service. And this raises the question: Is Online Banking worth switching banks for?

If your bank provides you with only a checking or savings account and you do most or all of your banking by mail or telephone, you might as well switch banks. You're not going to lose much of anything by switching banks—and you'll gain Online Banking. However, if your bank provides you with many different services—bank accounts, loans, safe deposit boxes, convenient branches and ATM machines, and so on—it might not make sense to switch.

# Part 2

# Personal Finance and Money

# Personal Financial Planning

**P**ersonal financial planning might sound sophisticated, but it's really not. When you boil it down, personal financial planning covers three commonsense activities:

➤ Arranging your day-to-day financial affairs so you get to live in a joyful and fulfilling way

➤ Picking and then plotting a course toward major, long-term financial goals, such as buying a house or retiring

➤ Creating a financial safety net so that a personal tragedy doesn't mean financial disaster

These three activities sound straightforward, don't they? They really are.

## Arranging Your Day-to-Day Financial Affairs

The best way to arrange your day-to-day financial affairs is to summarize how you spend your income and then create guidelines for your spending. Most people call this "budgeting." But before I get into the mechanics of how to budget using Money, let me spend a few paragraphs describing how you can make budgeting easier and find extra money in your budget.

# Five Budgeting Tips

The word "budget" has some pretty ugly connotations in most people's minds. It's easy to think of a budget as the equivalent of financial handcuffs. It's also easy to connect the term with the sometimes disappointing realities that a budget uncovers—such as the fact that you don't have the money for everything you want. The other awkward thing to bring up—but I'll say it anyway—is that creating a budget often forces you to discuss spending and life-style compromises with the people you love.

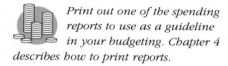 *Print out one of the spending reports to use as a guideline in your budgeting. Chapter 4 describes how to print reports.*

Yet, in spite of all the negative vibrations that the word "budget" sends out to people, budgeting is really the only way you can achieve financial success. As you arrange your day-to-day financial affairs, you must do so in the context of what you earn and how you (and your loved ones, if you're a member of a family) want to spend that money. So what you need are some ideas you can use to budget more successfully.

## Don't Start with a Wish List

Most people start the budgeting process with a wish list of the things they want to buy. I think that's a mistake—at least for anybody reading a book like this. A far better place to start is with a list of the things you're thankful for. I know this sounds like a philosophical digression—especially in a computer book. But you know what? It's way too easy for affluent, middle-class people to turn the budgeting process into a materialistic fantasy session: "I'd like to get that new piece of furniture, then go on a camping trip, then get a CD player for my car...."

If you instead start the budgeting process by making a list of things you're thankful for, you'll find that budgeting is easier, more enjoyable, and less taxing. Got a job you like most of the time? Are you proud of your kids? Do you have a decent place to live, a way to get around, and good food to eat? Is your health good? Start the budgeting process by putting this stuff on your list!

Just for the record, I have no particular philosophical problem with getting everything you want. I'd actually be quite happy for you. But if you start the budgeting process by building a huge wish list, you'll find yourself chronically

**How to Survive in the Desert.** *There's a curious game called "Desert Survival" that the U.S. Air Force used to play at one of its training camps. In the game, a class is broken into small groups and presented with this scenario: You're a passenger on a plane that's just crashed in the desert. You need to decide which items to salvage from the wreckage and whether to wait to be rescued or try to find help on your own. You make these two decisions first as an individual and second as a group. The really interesting part of the game—at least in terms of decision making—is that people usually make smarter decisions as a group than they do as individuals. In the desert, of course, smarter decisions mean you increase your chances of survival. The stakes aren't quite as high when it comes to budgeting, but the basic lesson of the Desert Survival game still applies: People tend to make better decisions when they make the decisions as a group.*

frustrated in your planning. Building a wish list focuses your attention on the things you don't have, rather than on the stuff you really need (and that you may already have). If you start the budgeting process by building a list of the things you're thankful for, you'll find it much, much easier to focus on your true needs and to make any necessary compromises.

## Get the Whole Family Involved

Here's another idea for you: Get the whole family involved. Or, at the very least, make sure that you and your spouse or partner budget together. If you and the members of your family build a budget together, you'll build a better budget. (You might learn that no one cares about getting a new car, for example, or that the most important thing in the world to your daughter is her dance lessons.) And if you build a budget together, you'll also find it easier to get and keep everyone committed to following the plan.

## Focus on the Big Picture

*Creator* is one of my favorite movies. In it, Peter O'Toole plays an eccentric biology professor. At one point in the movie, O'Toole's character attempts to talk a young student into taking a job as a research assistant. But the student balks at the offer and explains that he needs to get at least 15 credits that quarter. O'Toole's character pauses for just a split second, and then, before the student has a chance to protest, he registers the student for a brand-new, upper-division, 15-credit course called "Introduction to the Big Picture." While the student looks on with shock, O'Toole's character explains that only the big picture matters.

Now this "big picture" stuff may seem irrelevant to our discussion of budgeting, but it's really not. I cannot emphasize enough that it is the big decisions you make that determine where you end up in life financially. The size of the apartment you rent or the house you buy. Cars. Getting married...or divorced. Deciding to have another child. For this reason, you need to pay most attention to the big decisions you make. Don't sweat the small stuff. If you make good decisions concerning the big stuff, you almost can't help but succeed—and that is true even if you just ignore everything else.

## Leave Some Money on the Table

Don't plan to spend everything you make. If you do, and you have one tiny surprise, you'll blow your plan. And that means either you can't do something that you said you wanted to do at the beginning of the year, or—even worse—you are forced to borrow money on a credit card. If you don't leave some money on the table, you postpone solving a small problem today and have to wrestle with a much larger problem in the future.

## Keep Your Financial Affairs Simple

Let me say one more thing related to arranging your day-to-day financial affairs: Keep your financial affairs as simple as possible. You don't want to complicate your finances with complex budgets or sophisticated investments or high-powered financial services. That kind of stuff usually doesn't deliver what it promises (financial success), and it distracts you from the basics.

# Seven Ways to Stretch Your Budget Dollars Farther

I can't tell you how to live as if you make, say, $50,000 a year if you make $25,000. You just can't do it. But I do have some tips for how to stretch your dollars farther.

## Take Aim at Your Biggest Expenses

If you've been working with Money for any length of time, produce a spending habits report and look at your three largest spending categories. (These spending categories probably constitute most of your spending.) Next, sit down with your family and brainstorm about ways to reduce these expenses.

What you're doing here is only rational. It's much easier to carve out $25 a month of savings in a category in which you're spending $500 a month than it is in a category in which you're spending $50 a month. To save $25 in a $500-a-month expense, you need to figure out how to shave off only 5 percent. To save $25 in a $50-a-month expense, you need to figure out how to chop off 50 percent.

I know what you're thinking: "But Steve, my three biggest categories are housing, my car, and my grocery bills. I can't really cut those."

I understand your reaction. But I want to repeat the point again. If you want to find extra money, you're more likely to succeed by looking wherever you're currently spending the most money. Moving from a 3-bedroom apartment to a 2-bedroom apartment, for example, will save probably 10 percent or more on your housing expenses. So will moving into a smaller house.

If a housing change is too traumatic, consider driving a less expensive car or taking the bus. Try to arrange a car pool. If your family uses two cars, consider getting rid of one. You could also replace one of the cars with an inexpensive subcompact and use it for commuting or short trips around town.

## Live Healthier

Here's a strange coincidence. If you make healthy life-style choices, you usually save money. Quit smoking, for example, and you easily add $30 or $40 to the monthly cash flow. If you're a heavy smoker, you could add even more. Moderate your alcohol consumption or quit drinking alcohol and you can save just as much money each month. And there are the less obvious healthy choices: lowering your coffee consumption, eating less meat, cutting down on the sweets in your diet, walking whenever you can rather than driving a car.

To find out where you are spending money on bad habits, keep a record of where you spend each and every dollar for a few days. Then look at the list. The following table shows a sample list along with the annual cost of the habit.

| Item | Cost | Possible Yearly Savings |
|------|------|-------------------------|
| Morning coffee | $1.25 | $312.50 (if every working day of year) |
| Cookie after lunch | $0.75 | $187.50 (if every working day of year) |
| Cigarettes | $3.00 | $547.50 (if half-a-pack a day smoker) |
| Six-pack after work | $4.00 | $416.00 (if two six-packs a week) |

**How Much Does It Cost to Drive a Car?** *While the IRS says it costs around $.30 a mile to drive a car, driving a car very likely costs more than that when you consider not just the gasoline and maintenance costs but also the wear and tear on your car, insurance, car loan interest, and taxes. A better estimate for most middle-class drivers is $.50 a mile. And if you're driving an expensive import, it's easy for the per-mile cost to approach $1.00. This means that someone with a round-trip, 50-mile commute—common in the western United States—probably spends $20 or $25 a day on commuting.*

None of the preceding numbers are all that large, but they add up. A few hundred bucks here. A few hundred bucks there. Pretty soon, you're talking more than enough money to fix the car and take the trip to Yellowstone.

## Think Green

If you're environmentally conscious, you can also save money. And probably quite a lot. Think about how to participate more fully in recycling, for example. If you take good care of your car and make the necessary repairs, you may be able to drive it for 200,000 miles and keep it out of the junk yard for an extra ten years. If you don't have prejudices about second-hand stuff, you can purchase just about anything—clothing, furniture, cars—at great savings.

By becoming less of a consumer, you save money and help Spaceship Earth at the same time. Don't drive if you can walk. Turn your thermostat down a few degrees. Turn lights and appliances off when you're not using them.

## Identify Your Gazingus Pin

In their wonderful book, *Your Money or Your Life* (Penguin Books, 1992), Joe Dominquez and Vicki Robin talk about the pathology of gazingus pins. Their hypothesis, with which I agree, is that many people habitually collect items they don't need—gazingus pins. If you happen to have a personal gazingus pin (and you probably do), another easy way to put more slack into your budget is by simply saying, "Enough."

*One curious feature of gazingus pin collectors is that they often camouflage their mania for collecting gazingus pins by giving away their gazingus pins to friends and charities.*

Identifying someone else's gazingus pin is usually pretty easy. Typically, you only have to look in their closet or through their kitchen drawers. If you could have looked in Imelda Marcos's closet, for example, the hundreds of pairs of shoes would have identified shoes as her gazingus pin. It's tougher to spot your own gazingus pin, but take a look in your closet, kitchen, and garage, and look for items you haven't used or haven't worn in, say, a month. If you have multiple items falling into the same category—turtleneck sweaters, crystal stemware, or garden tools—there's a good chance you've spotted your own personal gazingus pin.

## Stop Using Your Credit Card

In Chapter 6, I noted that research suggests that people spend about 23 percent more on stuff when they shop with a credit card. If you then pay 15- or 20-percent interest on the money you've borrowed with your credit card, you end up paying almost 50 percent more for everything.

Given the propensity to spend more with credit cards, one thing you can probably do to save money is stop using your credit card. If you're skeptical about this gambit, by the way, just try it for a week or two. You may find yourself buying less expensive lunches or gasoline, or not purchasing certain items.

## Find One Expense That Wastes Money

One year when I went on vacation, someone broke into my house. In my emotional reaction to the burglary, I had a burglar alarm installed. And then I forgot about the burglar alarm system for two or three years. While I don't think there's anything wrong with burglar alarms in principal, it was a waste of money to pay $20 every month for an alarm monitoring service I wasn't using.

I mention this example of waste not to embarrass myself but to make a point. Often there are areas in our spending where we waste money, usually for emotional reasons. Without knowing the specifics of your situation, I am almost sure you have one or two expenses that, if you didn't make them, would not affect your life at all. For example, do you get a daily newspaper but have time to read only the weekend edition? Do you subscribe to magazines that you never get around to reading? Do you have an expensive toy or possession that you never use but still spend money to maintain? Consider pulling the plug on the expense. While there probably is some emotional reason for making the expenditure (as there was in my case), cutting these kinds of expenses doesn't affect your standard of living one iota.

## Find One Expense That You're Willing to Compromise

Another tactic that makes sense is to compromise some area of your spending. Decide right now that you're going to find an area where you will make do with less by living frugally or by making small sacrifices. Then go out and pick the

**An Interesting Fact.** *According to Carolyn Wesson, author of* Women Who Shop Too Much, *roughly 60 million people are addicted to shopping or spending.*

one expenditure in your budget that means the very least to you. Maybe it's athletic club dues. Or the premium cable television stations. Or your morning espresso. This sounds silly, but it usually works. It's often difficult to decide to save, say, $1.00 a day, but it's easy to decide to save a dollar a day by not stopping for coffee on the way to work any more.

If you're a member of a family, let me caution you about one thing: Compromising makes sense only if you pick out the areas where you can live more frugally or make sacrifices. Let your family members pick the compromises they must make to save money.

## Budgeting with Money

Once you've decided how you will budget your income and expenses, recording that budget with Money is simple. All you do is describe, for each income category and for each expense category, how much you'll earn or spend. To do this, choose the Budget command from the Tools menu. Click OK in the message box. When Money displays the Budget dialog box, you summarize your expected income and describe your planned expenses.

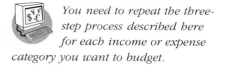

*You need to repeat the three-step process described here for each income or expense category you want to budget.*

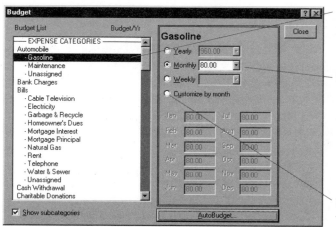

1 Select the income or expense category you want to budget by clicking it in the list.

2 Specify the amount you'll earn or spend in the selected category by clicking the Yearly, Monthly, or Weekly option buttons, and then entering the amount.

3 Click the Customize by Month option button if you want to specify different amounts for each month, and then enter a budgeted amount in the month text boxes.

If you don't want to enter each of your income and expense budget amounts individually, you can use Money's AutoBudget feature. AutoBudget takes your income and spending records from the previous year, previous month, or some other previous time period and uses this information to build a budget. To use AutoBudget, click the AutoBudget button at the bottom of the Budget dialog box, and then follow these steps:

**Investment Advice to Teen Smokers.** *If a 20-year-old pack-a-day smoker quits smoking, saves the cigarette money in an employer's 401(k) plan with 50-percent matching, and invests the money in the small company stock market, the ex-smoker could end up with more than $2 million by the time he or she retires at age 65. That amount equals roughly $500,000 dollars in present-day, uninflated dollars.*

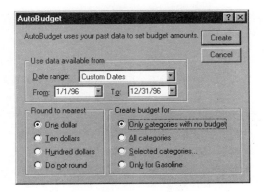

1 Identify which old income and spending data you want to use with the Use Data Available From boxes. You can choose a standard time period—Current Month, Current Year, Month to Date, Year to Date, and so on—by clicking the Date Range drop-down list box. If you don't see the time period you want in the Date Range drop-down list box, choose Custom Dates and then specify the other time period in the From and To boxes.

2 Use the Round To Nearest options to specify whether and how you want Money to round actual income and spending amounts.

**3** Use the Create Budget For options to specify for which categories you want Money to create a budget.

**4** When you're done, click create.

AutoBudget sounds good in theory. A lot of large businesses and government organizations use the same basic logic as the AutoBudget feature to build their budgets. In practice, however, AutoBudget isn't all that useful for families and small businesses. The problem with AutoBudget is simple: AutoBudget assumes you can plan or predict this year's income or spending by looking at last year's or last month's. While that sounds reasonable, it usually isn't. The income and expense categories of families and even small businesses change from year to year—and that makes it hard to use last year's categories and amounts for this year's budget. Another factor that makes AutoBudget impractical is **inflation:** Inflation, presumably, pushes up income and spending most years.

# Plotting a Course Toward Your Long-Term Financial Goals

Arranging your day-to-day financial affairs in a way that best suits you is the first part of personal financial planning. The second part is picking out and plotting a course toward your long-term financial objectives—things like retirement, sending your kids to college, buying a home, and so on.

Because many, many people choose retirement and sending a child to college as long-term financial goals, I have included chapters that discuss planning for these specific goals.

Unfortunately, I can't give you much specific advice about achieving your other long-term financial goals. I can't know, for example, whether your dream is to sail around the world in a 40-foot ketch or operate an orphanage in some third-world country. Nevertheless, I can provide you with three general tips: First and most importantly, do set a goal or two! Setting goals focuses your energies and assists you in setting your life's priorities.

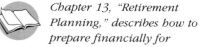

*Chapter 13, "Retirement Planning," describes how to prepare financially for retirement and includes tips on how to use Money's Retirement Planner Wizard to make these plans.*

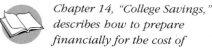

*Chapter 14, "College Savings," describes how to prepare financially for the cost of sending a child to college. While Money doesn't provide a special college savings calculator, I describe how you can trick the Retirement Planner into making this calculation for you.*

Second, keep your goal descriptions as general as possible. General goals don't preclude creative and daring solutions and, therefore, are much easier to achieve. (For example, with the goal, "retire early on a sunny beach location," you might choose to move to Central America, where you can live well for a few hundred bucks a month!)

Third, start early and be patient. The magic of compound interest—earning interest on reinvested interest—means that given enough time, just about any financial goal is achievable.

## Creating a Financial Safety Net

We've talked about the first two personal financial planning activities—arranging your day-to-day financial affairs in the way you want and plotting a course toward your long-term financial goals. Those two activities are really the most important things you need to do. But you'll also want to take care of a third activity: creating a financial safety net for you and your family so that a personal tragedy like a death, a severe illness, or an injury doesn't turn into a financial disaster.

People have written entire books on this subject, but if you're willing to keep your financial affairs pretty simple, you need to know only half a dozen points to create a financial safety net.

### Make a Will

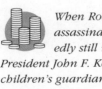

*When Robert Kennedy was assassinated, his will reportedly still named his brother, President John F. Kennedy, as his children's guardian, even though John Kennedy had been killed five years earlier.*

Nobody likes contemplating their own mortality, but if you've got kids or want to specify what happens to your **estate** when you die, you need a will. Plain and simple. As long as you don't do anything fancy, it shouldn't cost more than a couple hundred bucks to have an attorney prepare one for you. In your will, all you do is tell the probate court who you want to become guardians of your children and who you want to get your stuff should you die.

If you already have a will, get it out and read it again. Make sure it still accurately describes what you want to happen if you die.

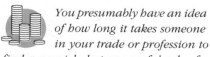

*You presumably have an idea of how long it takes someone in your trade or profession to find a new job, but one useful rule of thumb is one month for every $10,000 of salary.*

# Create a Rainy-Day Fund

You need a rainy-day fund for two simple reasons: First, having one means you don't need to get stressed out because you lose your job—for whatever reason. Also, having a rainy-day fund allows you to save money by buying insurance policies with higher deductibles so you pay less in premiums.

People throw around a bunch of different rules of thumb when it comes to rainy-day funds, and most of them are pretty good. When people ask me how big a rainy-day fund should be, I suggest having enough money to pay the deductibles on your medical insurance plus enough money to live on for the time it takes to find a job.

# Get Earnings Insurance

For many people, their major financial asset is their ability to earn a living. Someone who won't retire for twenty-five years very likely has a million dollars of income left to earn, for example. So you want to do two things to protect your best asset—your ability to earn a living.

### Do You Need Disability Insurance?

*In terms of lost income, being disabled for three months is the same as being unemployed for three months.*

Even if you're the only person who depends on your income to live, you probably need to get disability insurance. Don't worry about short-term disability coverage. It's very expensive. It's also unnecessary if you've got an adequate rainy-day fund.

What you do want to protect yourself against is the risk of getting a debilitating illness or injury that makes you incapable of earning a living. You need to talk to a good insurance agent for information and advice on finding and picking a disability policy. If you belong to a trade or professional organization, you also want to check with it to see if it offers inexpensive, group disability policies.

## Do You Need Life Insurance?

If you're not the only person who depends on your income to live—say, because you have kids or a spouse who depends on your income—you also need life insurance to replace your income in case you die. With a little bit of trickery with the Money Retirement Planner, you can easily and precisely estimate how much life insurance you need. (If you think using the Retirement Planner in this way is rather odd, think about a wage-earner's death as an untimely and early retirement.) To do this, follow these steps:

1 Click the Planning Wizards button in the Money Contents window. Money displays the Planning Wizards window.

2 Click the Retirement Planner button. Money displays the first Retirement Planner dialog box. It asks about your age and when you want to retire.

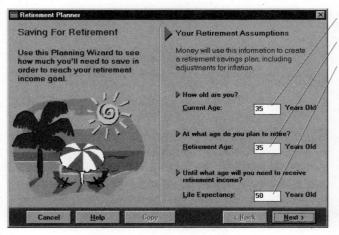

Enter your current age.

Enter your current age again.

Use the Life Expectancy text box to specify the age through which you would have needed to work to provide income to your family. This might not be until you would have retired, by the way, if, for example, your spouse will go back to work after completing additional schooling or raising the kids.

**My Disability Policy.** *Through the American Institute of Certified Public Accountants, one professional group I belong to, I have a $5,000 a month disability policy that costs about $200 a year. If I'm disabled in a way that prevents me from performing my usual job, after three months of disability, I get $5,000 a month for the rest of my life.*

**3** Click Next. Money displays the second Retirement Planner dialog box. It asks how much retirement income you want your savings to produce and whether you've already started saving.

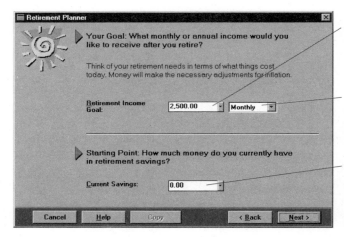

Enter the income you want your life insurance to produce in the Retirement Income Goal box.

Indicate whether you've specified your replacement income as a monthly or annual amount.

Enter any savings you've already accumulated that can be used to produce replacement income. Most people, by the way, won't enter anything here.

**How Do I Handle Inflation?**
*Don't worry about inflation when you enter your replacement income goal. Money adjusts your input for the inflation that will occur over the years that you're replacing income with life insurance. For example, if you want $25,000 of replacement income in twenty-five years, Money assumes that you want a replacement income figure equivalent to $25,000 in today's dollars. If inflation runs 3 percent annually over the next twenty-five years, for example, Money inflates the $25,000 figure to roughly $61,000 by the end of the twenty-five years.*

**4** Click Next. Money displays a dialog box that asks what rate of return you'll earn over the years you work and save and over the years you're retired.

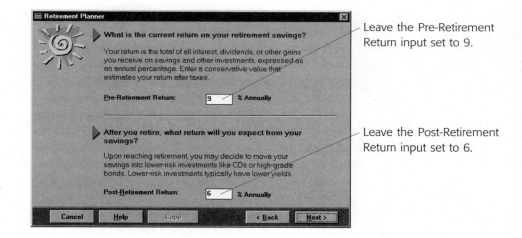

Leave the Pre-Retirement Return input set to 9.

Leave the Post-Retirement Return input set to 6.

*Since 1926, the stock market has produced an average annual return of 10 percent and long-term bonds have produced an average annual return of 5 percent.*

**5** Click Next. Money displays a dialog box that asks what inflation you expect over the years you work and save. (The dialog box also calculates the effect of inflation on your desired replacement income and the savings you'll need to accumulate.) Money initially uses 3 percent as the expected annual inflation, which is probably a good guess. If you want to enter a different inflation rate, however, you can enter it. Then click Calculate. Note the amount that Money shows as the total savings you need under the Revised Goal (Assuming [Inflation Rate] Inflation) box—you'll need it for the next step.

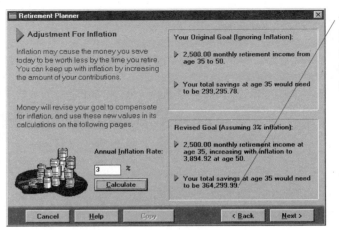

This is the amount of life insurance you need to replace your income over the specified number of years.

*Over the last sixty years, inflation has run at slightly more than 3 percent.*

6 Click Back twice. This returns you to the third Retirement Planner dialog box. Add the amount of life insurance you now know you need to whatever already shows in the Current Savings text box.

7 Click Next three times. Money displays a schedule that shows how your life insurance proceeds will produce income and decrease over time as they replace the income you would have earned had you lived.

8 Click Done. Money returns you to the Planning Wizards window, but it saves all your information.

## A Few More Words on Life Insurance

Before I conclude this discussion of earnings insurance, let me tell you just a couple more quick things about life insurance. First of all, as you get older, you should need less and less life insurance. In fact, at the point you retire, you shouldn't need any life insurance to replace your earnings because you won't be earning anymore. For this reason, you'll find it useful to periodically recalculate your life insurance. Maybe you don't need to do this every year, but it's not a bad idea to do it every other year or so. As you find yourself needing less coverage, you can purchase smaller and smaller policies. And that is another way to save money.

Here's a second thing to consider: When you go to purchase life insurance, you need to choose between a term policy and a cash-value policy. You might already know that there is an ongoing, raging debate about which is the better type of policy.

I have no particular axe to grind with the insurance industry, but I have to tell you that a cash-value insurance policy is very likely not the better deal for you. Yes, I've heard all the arguments, pro and con. And I've looked closely at maybe a couple of dozen policies over the years. But everywhere I look, you get a much better deal by getting a renewable, noncancellable term life insurance policy than you do by getting a cash-value policy. If you want to save some money in a tax-deferred savings account, which is what a cash-value policy offers, you'll almost certainly come out ahead by buying term insurance and then stashing what you save over the cash-value policy in your employer's 401(k) or a deductible Individual Retirement Account.

## Protect Your Assets

There's one final element to your financial safety net—asset protection. Basically, if you have significant assets—investments, a house, a car, and so forth—you want to protect them by buying property insurance: a homeowner's policy or renter's policy for your home and the stuff in your home, an automobile policy for your car and any damage you might do with your car. If you've accumulated a substantial amount of wealth, you need a personal liability insurance policy as well.

To learn more about this, talk to a good insurance agent. Find someone you can trust. Then ask him or her for advice.

**An Important Warning.** *Never cancel one insurance policy until you have a new policy in force. You don't want to cancel one policy and then find, for some reason, that you've become uninsurable.*

*Cash-value insurance also goes by the names whole life insurance and universal life insurance.*

# In Conclusion

Personal financial planning isn't complicated. It's really all quite simple. Sit down with your family and build a budget that everyone can live with. Pick out a long-term goal or two (be reasonable), and start working toward the goal. Finally, make sure there's a financial safety net to catch you or your family in case something bad happens. Doing this is common sense. Anybody who tells you differently is probably trying to sell you something you don't need.

# Retirement Planning

I may obsess too much about retiring, but I think this chapter is the most important in this book. I feel this way because so many people—including most of my friends and much of my family—aren't preparing for retirement. Unfortunately, by not preparing for retirement, people unnecessarily complicate their lives and reduce the joy of living.

The irony is that almost everyone can prepare for retirement. If you have a job (it doesn't even have to be a very good job), you can start preparing for retirement. It's that simple. All it takes is a decision—a decision that you want to maintain your standard of living when you're too old or infirm to work or when you're tired of the rat race. So let me talk a little more about why it's important for you to plan for and prepare for retirement.

## The Good News and the Bad News about Social Security

If you've read much about social security, you probably know that the system, while under no immediate danger, has some fundamental long-term problems. There are several complex reasons for this. Adding to the confusion are the strong emotions that swirl about the subject of social security. We all know people who probably couldn't survive without social security benefits. (My grandmother is an example.) We all also know people who either through dumb luck or clever design get money they don't need and don't really deserve. (Sorry, Mom.)

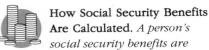 **How Social Security Benefits Are Calculated.** *A person's social security benefits are calculated using a very complicated formula that, among other things, adjusts for inflation. One curious aspect of the formula is that people with modest incomes have a much greater percentage of their income replaced by social security than do people with higher incomes. For example (and these are all rough numbers), if you made an average of $12,000 a year when you worked, you might receive an annual benefit of $5,000. But if you made an average of $60,000 a year when you worked, you might receive an annual benefit of $12,000.*

Whatever your feelings, there is little disagreement that sometime early in the next century, the social security system will not be able to function as it does now. The mathematics simply won't work. There won't be enough tax revenue coming into the system to pay for the benefits people get today. There won't be any trust fund left. And there won't be enough young employees in the nation's work-force to generate the taxes to pay for their parents' retirement.

So what's going to happen to social security? I don't know. No one does, really. My guess is that the whole system will become means-tested. If someone isn't able to survive without social security, they will get it, but if someone can survive without social security—perhaps because they own a home or receive private pension benefits—they probably won't get social security.

That's the bad news.

But there's a good news element to all this, too. And it's very simple: The coming changes in social security don't have to matter to you individually. You can prepare for your own retirement. You don't have to rely on social security. All you need to do is begin a regular retirement savings program using a tax-deferred savings plan such as a 401(k), 403(b), Individual Retirement Account, Keogh, or SEP/IRA.

## A Few Words about Employer Pension Plans

Before I get into the mechanics of how you go about saving money for retirement, I should say that there is one wildcard here—your employer's pension plan. I think you can probably rely on your employer's pension plan. And it just may be that your employer's pension plan will provide you with all the retirement income you need. But you need to be careful.

One factor that you need to worry about a little is whether your retirement income benefits depend on your continued employment. Let me explain.

One kind of retirement plan, called a *defined benefit plan,* pays you retirement income based on your salary in the final year or years you worked. With this type of plan, for example, you might receive a pension benefit of $32,000 if you work forty years for a big company and make $40,000 in your final year.

A defined benefit plan such as the one I just described can be a great deal for employees. In fact, if your employer has a plan like this and you can be sure of some day receiving the benefits, you probably don't need to save a dime for retirement. No kidding.

But there's a problem with defined benefit plans if instead of working for one employer for many years, you work for a number of different employers. This is true even if all the employer's have the same "2 percent for every year you work" benefit formula.

The problem is that the figure on which your retirement income is based—your final year's or years' salary—will be very low for all but your last employer or two. Inflation causes this, of course. And so does the fact that people tend to make less in their early working years.

To see how this works, suppose that you work someplace for forty years, that you're making $40,000 a year in your final years, and that you receive a retirement benefit equal to 2 percent of your final salary for every year you worked. In this case, for your first ten years of work you would get $8,000 of retirement income (10 x 2% x $40,000). This would be true even though you were probably making far less at that time.

Now consider the case of your neighbor. Let's say she had four different jobs over her working years. Let's say her first job, the one she worked during the first ten years of her career, paid less because it was a less demanding job. And, of course, thirty years of inflation have passed since she left that job. So maybe her salary at the ten-year marker was $7,000. In this case, for her first ten years of work she'll get a retirement benefit from that employer of $1,400 (10 x 2% x $40,000).

*A common defined benefit retirement calculation is that you receive 2 percent of your final salary for every year you work.*

Do you see the scary part of this? You, for your first ten years of work, accumulate $8,000 of retirement income, but your neighbor, for her first ten years of work, accumulates $1,400. Your neighbor's situation is even worse if she switched jobs more frequently—say, every couple of years or so. If that was the case, because of the way that pension benefit calculations work, it's possible for your neighbor to have *no* retirement benefits at all for her first ten years of work.

**Defined Contribution Plans.**
*Defined contribution plans are the other basic retirement income plan. With a defined contribution plan, your employer contributes money to your account. A defined contribution plan is a better deal for people who change employers, as long as they get to keep the money the employer contributes.*

What I've just described is, in a nutshell, the problem with defined benefit retirement programs. They can be wonderful deals for long-term employees, but for people who switch jobs frequently, they don't amount to such a good deal. Please note, too, that even if you have the best of intentions about staying someplace for your entire career, you can't really be sure you'll do this. Companies downsize. Industries decline. What you want to do with your life may change.

## Setting a Retirement Income Goal

The first step in planning for retirement is to set a retirement income goal. People throw around all sorts of rules of thumb about this figure. In my case, for example, I figure that I want to live pretty much the same way when I'm retired as I do right now. Of course, when I'm retired, I won't have to make my mortgage payment—my mortgage will have long since been paid by then. And I won't have to pay social security or Medicare taxes—you only pay social security and Medicare taxes on earned income, not on unearned income, which is what retirement income is. So if I take my current income and subtract my mortgage payment and my social security and Medicare taxes, I get a retirement income number that lets me live the same way I do now.

I should probably tell you that I don't really have work expenses. Or at least not very many. And the house I live in now is one that I'll probably still live in when I retire. If I had a bunch of work expenses, for example, or if I planned to move to a smaller house or apartment, I might need to adjust my retirement income figure for these amounts, too. For example, I'd want to subtract the work expenses that I currently pay but that I won't have to pay once I quit working. And if I lived in a big house but planned to move to a small condominium, for example, I might be able to reduce my retirement income even more for this change.

Your situation, of course, probably differs from mine. But the basic calculations you make for determining your retirement income are roughly the same as the calculation I make:

1 Look at your current income.

2 Adjust it for expenses you won't have once you're retired.

The caution I'll give, however, is that you don't want to be too optimistic about reducing your expenses. It's pretty safe to assume that you won't have a mortgage payment when you retire at age 62 if, for example, your mortgage will be paid off by age 59. And while no one knows how the tax laws will change between now and the time you retire, I also think it's pretty safe to assume that your retirement income won't be subject to social security and Medicare taxes. But I'd be cautious about assuming you can, for example, tighten up your living expenses. Or get by with just one car if you and your spouse now drive two.

## Calculating Retirement Savings

Once you know how much retirement income you want, you need to determine from where you're going to get it. As I mentioned earlier, I think it's safest to assume that you will not get any retirement income from social security if you're still years and years away from retirement.

What this means, then, is that your retirement income will have to come from one of two sources: either employer retirement plans or your savings. Your employer can tell you what income you can expect from your retirement plan. Whatever is left over must come from your own savings.

**How Can I Find Out about My Social Security Benefits?**

*If you're very close to retirement—and I'd say this means you're planning on retiring in the next half dozen years or so—you probably can count on social security. What's more, you can telephone Social Security at 1-800-722-1213 and request the SS-4 form. A few days later, when you get this form, fill it out and send it in. The Social Security Administration will send you a statement that reports your earnings and estimates your benefits.*

**A Little Saving Goes a Long Way.** *Take the case of a 27-year-old gambler with a $10-per-week lottery ticket habit. If this person quits gambling and saves the lottery ticket money in an IRA, he or she can accumulate roughly $325,000 in retirement savings by the time of retirement. (This amount would produce $33,000 a year for twenty years.) If this person quits gambling and saves the lottery ticket money in a 401(k) plan with 50-percent employer matching, he or she can accumulate roughly $500,000 in retirement savings by the time of retirement. This amount would produce $55,000 a year for twenty years. That may not sound like that much money, but get this: the typical $1,000,000 lottery pays only $50,000-per-year for twenty years!*

 **A Depressing Fact.** *If a worker earning $30,000 a year didn't have to pay social security and could instead invest the amounts he and his employer pay for social security into an Individual Retirement Account, he would accumulate roughly $1,000,000 by retirement—an amount that would produce roughly $75,000 a year in retirement income. In comparison, this worker's annual social security benefit will probably be around $8,000 a year.*

Once you know what portion of your retirement income needs to come from your savings, you can use Money's Retirement Planner to calculate how much you need to save for retirement. To do this, follow these steps:

1 Click the Planning Wizards button when the Money Contents window is displayed. Money displays the Planning Wizards window.

2 Click the Retirement Planner button. Money displays the first Retirement Planner dialog box. It asks about your age and when you want to retire.

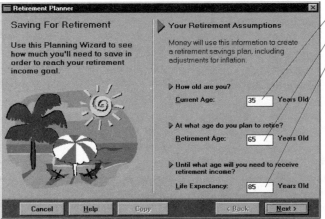

Enter your current age.

Enter your retirement age.

Enter your last year of retirement. Life expectancy in the United States is around 77 or 78, but Money says it is 85. Setting it at 85 is a good idea because you want to make sure that your money lasts longer than you do.

3 Click Next. Money displays the second Retirement Planner dialog box. It asks how much retirement income you want your savings to produce and whether you've already started saving.

**Don't Worry about Inflation.**
*Don't worry about inflation when you enter your retirement income goal. Money adjusts your input for the inflation that will occur between now and the time you retire. For example, if you say you want $25,000 of retirement income in twenty-five years, Money assumes that what you want is a retirement income figure equivalent to $25,000 in today's dollars. Assuming that inflation runs 3 percent annually over the next twenty-five years, Money inflates the $25,000 figure to roughly $61,000.*

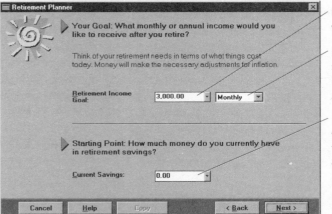

Enter the retirement income you want.

Indicate whether you've specified your retirement income as a monthly or an annual amount.

Enter any retirement savings you've already accumulated. You could enter amounts you've saved in Individual Retirement Accounts, 401(k)s, 403(b)s, RRSPs and so on.

4 Click Next. Money displays a dialog box that asks what rate of return you'll earn over the years you work and save and over the years you're retired.

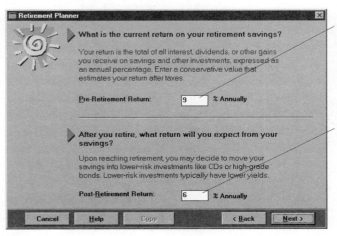

If you're not sure what you should enter here, leave the 9 in the box. Then read the next section in this chapter, "A Few Words on Rates of Return."

If you want to, replace the Post-Retirement Return with some other value.

**Average Annual Returns.**
*Common stocks have averaged about 10 percent over the last seventy or so years. Long-term bonds over the same period have averaged about 5 percent. Finally, small company stocks over the same seventy-year period have averaged between 12 and 13 percent. These are gross return numbers. Your return would be reduced by any investment expenses you pay.*

*Over the last sixty or seventy years, annual inflation has averaged 3.3 percent.*

**5** Click Next. Money displays a dialog box that asks what you expect the inflation rate to be over the years you work and save. (The dialog box also calculates the effect of **inflation** on your desired retirement income and the retirement savings you'll need to accumulate.) Money initially uses 3 percent as the expected annual inflation rate, which is probably a good guess. (If you want to enter a different inflation rate, however, enter it, and then click Calculate.)

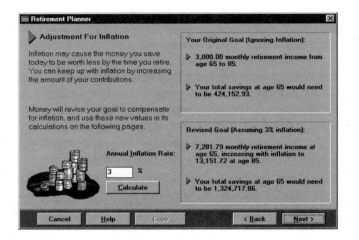

**6** Click Next. Money displays a dialog box that shows you how much you need to save to reach your retirement savings goal. Actually, there are two savings plans. One shows how much you need to save if you save the same amount every month. The other shows how much you should start saving if you adjust your savings amount each month for inflation.

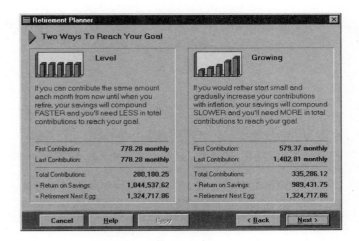

7 Click Next. Money displays a schedule that shows how your retirement savings grow over time.

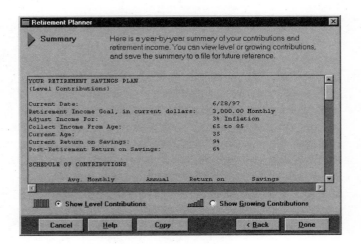

**Printing a Copy of the Retirement Summary.**

*To print a copy of the retirement savings summary, click Copy. Then start the WordPad application and choose its Edit Paste command. This pastes the retirement saving summary schedule into the WordPad document. To print the document, choose WordPad's File Print command.*

8 Use the Show Level Contributions and Show Growing Contributions option buttons to specify which savings plan you want to summarize. Under the level contributions plan, you accumulate retirement savings faster because you pay more during the early years of saving. Under the growing contributions plan, however, you'll find it easier to save initially because you'll be saving smaller amounts.

9 If you scroll down the summary, you'll first see columns that show your monthly contribution, interest income, and accumulated retirement savings. If you scroll down even farther, you'll see columns that show your monthly income, interest income, and diminishing retirement savings.

10 Click Done. Money returns you to the Planning Wizards window, but it saves all your retirement planning information.

# A Few Words on Rates of Return

The two trickiest inputs in retirement planning calculations are the pre-retirement return and the post-retirement return. Money suggests pre-retirement and post-retirement returns of 9 and 6 percent, respectively. But these may be wildly inappropriate depending on the way you choose to save your retirement money. It's possible to beat these numbers, but more likely you'll fall far short of the 9-percent pre-retirement return.

The problem isn't that Money's suggestions are bad. The problem is that it's easy to make investment decisions that preclude any chance of achieving these sorts of returns. For example, the seventy-year average return on an investment in the stock market is about 10 percent. You might think, then, that a 9-percent input for the pre-retirement return is reasonable. Perhaps even conservative. But there are at least two reasons why it probably isn't.

The first reason is that your retirement savings probably aren't 100 percent invested in **stocks.** You may have 50 percent of your retirement savings in stocks, for example, and another 50 percent in long-term **bonds,** which have averaged only 5 percent over the last seventy or so years. In this case, it might make more sense to say that you expect to earn about 7.5 percent, the average of the 10 percent in stocks and the 5 percent in bonds, for your pre-retirement return.

**A True Confession.** *I should tell you that I helped Microsoft pick the pre-retirement return and post-retirement return inputs. So it would be poor form of me to be too critical.*

**A Tip for Mutual Fund Investors.** *A mutual fund's quarterly report includes an income statement that shows the fund's expenses as a percentage. You can use this percentage to adjust the fund's expected gross return for expenses.*

The second reason why the 9-percent input for the pre-retirement return is a challenging target has to do with expenses you have to pay. Let's say that you're 100-percent invested in the stock market and the stock market returns 10 percent on your investments. You won't actually earn 10 percent. You have investment expenses to pay. If you're investing through **mutual funds,** for example, you indirectly pay annual expense ratios of between .25 percent (for index mutual funds) to more than 2 percent (for actively managed mutual funds). So, even if the stocks in your mutual fund earn 10 percent, paying 1 percent in expenses means that you earn 9 percent. If you invested in a balanced mutual fund that holds both stocks and bonds and has earned, say, 7.5 percent, paying 1 percent in expenses means you actually earn 6.5 percent. You see the dilemma.

The decision that some people come to is to put more and more of their money in stocks. And that's not a bad idea. (Almost all of my retirement money is in stocks, for example.) But it's not a risk-free strategy. On a daily, weekly, or even yearly basis, the stock markets bounce up and down like a yo-yo. Over the last century, the general direction has always been up if you look at twenty- or twenty-five-year periods of time. But there have been decades when the market hasn't gone up, when it's gone sideways, and even gone down.

Should you use a different pre-retirement return than the one Money suggests? The answer is "yes" if you're investing in something other than common stocks or if your investment expenses are high. If you're investing in, for example, stocks and bonds, you should use a weighted average of the estimated long-term returns on stocks and bonds. And you should be sure to adjust gross returns for your investment expenses.

By the way, I think using 6 percent as a post-retirement return input is pretty safe as long as you keep a significant percentage of your retirement savings in common stocks and you keep your investment expenses low. For example, if you keep 70 percent of your retirement savings in long-term bonds that earn 5 percent and keep 30 percent of your retirement savings in common stocks that you expect to earn 10 percent, the weighted average gross return of your investments equals 6.5 percent. If your investment expenses run an economical .5 percent (half a percent), your net return equals 6 percent.

**How Do I Calculate a Weighted Average Rate?** *To calculate a weighted average return, multiply the percent of your portfolio invested in a particular investment type by the expected gross return on the investment. Then add up all the percentages. For example, if 70 percent of your portfolio consists of bonds that earn 5 percent and 30 percent of your portfolio consists of common stocks that earn 10 percent, your weighted average gross return is calculated as (.7 x .05)+(.3 x .10), which equals .065, or 6.5 percent. To get the net return, you subtract the investment expenses percentage from the gross return: for example, .065 – .005, which equals .06, or 6 percent.*

# Ideas on Coming Up with the Money You Need to Save

If you use Money's Retirement Planner to plan for your retirement, the results can be pretty dismal. If you're like most people, you'll find that you need to save an impossibly large amount of money. But don't get discouraged. There are several ways to come up with the large chunks of money you need to save.

## Get the Government's Help

If you invest in tax-deductible, tax-deferred investments like Individual Retirement Accounts (IRAs), 401(k) plans, 403(b) plans, or, for Canadians, RRSPs, the government subsidizes your savings in two big ways. Let's say, for example, that your calculations reveal that you need to save $4,000 a year. Let's also say that this is an insurmountable sum for you.

The way the government helps you is by letting you use your contributions as a tax deduction. If you participate in a 401(K), 403(b), or SEP/IRA plan, for example, you can probably save about $1,200 in federal income taxes with a $4,000 contribution. If you use the tax savings to make part of your contribution, you only need to come up with $2,800 yourself because your tax savings provide the other $1,200 ($2,800 + $1,200 equals $4,000).

The government also helps you save for retirement in a second way: It doesn't tax your returns. And that lowers your investment expenses. For example, if your retirement savings earn a 10-percent gross return but you have to pay a 28-percent federal income tax, your net return is 7.2 percent. (You calculate this by multiplying the 10-percent gross return by the 28-percent federal income tax rate to get 2.8 percent—the portion of your return that you need to pay in income taxes—and then you subtract the 2.8 from the 10 percent.)

Federal income tax rates start at 15 percent and go to more than 40 percent. So, having to pay income taxes on the income that your retirement savings produce erodes the gross return.

The bottom line when it comes to retirement savings is that you almost have to use tax-deferred, tax-deductible investment options like Individual Retirement Accounts, 401(k) Plans, and 403(b) Plans.

## Get Your Employer's Help

Many employers offer 401(k) plans. In a 401(k) plan, an employee contributes a portion of his or her salary to a retirement savings account. In many cases, employers add to the savings. A 50-percent matching contribution is quite common. If you need to save, say, $6,000 a year, you would need to come out-of-pocket for only the first $4,000. Your employer would kick in the next $2,000.

If you read the preceding section, "Get the Government's Help," you know that you would also receive a tax deduction for your $4,000 contribution. This deduction would produce tax savings that could be used to fund another large chunk of retirement savings. In the preceding section, I guessed that for many readers, a $4,000 tax deduction would produce $1,200 in tax savings. So if you did need to save $6,000 a year, you might very possibly be able to get $2,000 from an employer and $1,200 from the federal government. In other words, more than half of your retirement savings money could very likely come from someplace other than your budget!

## Make Healthy Choices

In the previous chapter I pointed out that by quitting smoking a person could amass a tidy little nest egg. I like this example for a couple of reasons. One is that people with modest incomes can usually figure out how to pay for their cigarettes. Obviously, the fact that nicotine is addictive makes it easier for a smoker to make cigarettes a top spending priority. But the fact remains: People with modest incomes figure out how to buy a pack a day. That means that people who don't smoke or people who quit smoking should be able to save a dollar or two or three a day, too. In fact, anyone who starts early enough can accumulate a few hundred grand.

**Can You Deduct an IRA Contribution?** *To deduct $4,000 of IRA contributions, you need to be married, both you and your spouse must have earned at least $2,000 each, and neither of you can be covered by your employer's retirement plan. (If you or your spouse are covered, your deduction or some part of it might be deductible. You have to use a complicated formula to figure out how much of the contribution is deductible.)*

**The Highest Income Tax Rate.** *The highest federal income tax rate is 39.6 percent. But the real, or marginal, income tax rate of taxpayers who pay the 39.6-percent rate is higher than that because special rules limit these high-income taxpayer's itemized deductions and personal exemptions.*

But there's also a second reason that I like to use the quitting smoking example. It's an example of a healthy life-style decision that produces not only a better quality of life but also helps achieve financial success. I'm not suggesting you give up all your bad habits. And I'm certainly not going to tell you about all of my bad habits—nor about the ones that I should give up. (I did quit smoking thirteen years ago.) But I do want to alert you to the big financial benefits that healthy life-style choices deliver.

If you're a moderate drinker, quitting the drink will produce savings equivalent to those of quitting smoking. Becoming a vegetarian or even just eating less meat saves money and reduces your cholesterol. Eating fewer sweets means spending less on junk food, saving dental care costs, and looking better in a swimsuit. You don't need to give up all of your bad habits. But if you do give up or moderate even one or two of your bad habits, and you save what you were spending on them, the savings will add up very quickly.

## Make Your Big Decisions Carefully

Let me make one final observation about saving for retirement: The handful of big decisions you make largely determine how you spend your money. A home or car. Marriage. Children. It would be pretty bold of me to tell you what kind of house or apartment you should live in. Or what model car you should drive. And it would be inappropriate for me to make any suggestions concerning your marriage, your childbearing, or your childrearing. It does seem fair to point out, however, that the big decisions you make in these areas of your life largely set the course of your financial affairs. Accordingly, the big decisions largely determine how easy it is for you to save for retirement.

People who choose to live in larger homes won't ever be able to save as much as people who live in smaller ones. The same thing is true of people who choose to drive nicer cars. Getting married or getting divorced has a major impact on your financial life. And about the only thing more expensive than a couple of kids is three kids.

Of course, you may have strong philosophical or religious feelings about some of the big decision areas. But if in the big decision areas of your life you can consider the financial aspect of your choices, I encourage you to do so.

# In Conclusion

Most people need to prepare for retirement, yet the economists who study such things say most people aren't preparing. You get to choose what you want with your life, of course. But I really encourage you to figure out what you need to do to retire and then begin doing it. If you start now, you'll find the task much, much easier than it will be if you wait five or ten years. And if you choose to completely ignore your own future retirement, no good thing can come of it.

By the way, if what you've read here has convinced you that it's time to begin preparing for retirement or helped you start that preparation, I'd love to hear from you. You can write to me in care of the publisher. Or you can e-mail me at stphnlnlson@msn.com.

# Planning for College

**A**t the time I'm writing this (the summer of 1996), four years at a public university cost almost $30,000. Four years at a private university cost around $70,000, and four years at a select private university cost close to $100,000. In spite of the high costs, however, your kids can go to college. Make no mistake. If you read no further, at least go away with this thought. That said, however, you'll make things much easier by doing a little early planning and saving.

## Is College a Good Investment?

Despite the enormous cost of college, it's probably a good investment. U.S. Department of Commerce data show that if you're a male, a college education adds about a $1,000 a month to your salary. Go on to a professional school and the payoff gets even better: A man earns an extra $3,000 a month compared to a high school graduate. Please be sure you read this carefully. Those figures are per *month*. Over thirty or forty years, college can be a very, very good investment.

The education-vs.-earning correlation is just as strong for women, although the payoff is considerably less. College adds an average of $600 to the monthly wages of a woman and professional school adds roughly $1,700. I still think you can make a very strong argument for college as a good investment for both men and women. The census data includes a large group of men and women—not just recent college graduates. I personally suspect this means that gender dis-

**Return on a College Education.**
*If you work out the math with a financial calculator or a spreadsheet, college as a financial investment returns a yield of somewhere between 10 percent for a private university and as much as 30 percent for a public university. Given that the stock market has historically returned about 10 percent (a number that's pretty darn impressive), these returns aren't just good, they're astounding. Note, too, that these sorts of calculations view college purely as a financial investment and not one that also delivers other benefits, such as a more satisfying career, more job security, or—and let's be honest—a more interesting and more affluent spouse. .*

crimination from twenty and thirty years ago is still showing up in the salary data. (Of course, Perry Mason made more than this secretary, Della Street. But don't we all suspect that Paul Drake, Perry's private investigator, made more than Della, too?) What's more, there are presumably more part-time women workers and nonworking women than there are part-time men workers and nonworking men. The family stereotypes those *Leave It To Beaver* reruns depict aren't out of date—they're only less prevalent.

## What Will College Cost?

College costs vary widely by region. In addition, public universities cost much less than private universities. For this reason, the best tactic for estimating college costs is to look up the actual tuition of the colleges you think your child may one day attend.

## Do You Need to Save?

Do you even need to save for your kid's college expenses? You probably do. Unless you've already been through the college financial aid and admissions process, you probably think there is more "free money" than there really is.

It's only fair to point out, however, that in a couple of instances, parents may not need to save.

If you live on a low income, you should be able to get substantial financial aid money. For example, if you're raising a family of four on $15,000 a year and you have savings of a few thousand dollars or less, the federal government, some state governments, and a host of private sources will gladly lend a helping hand. (You'll probably get a few thousand in grant money and the rest in low-interest student loans.)

If your income allows you to easily pay an extra $1,000 to $2,000 a month to put a kid through college—or perhaps an extra $2,000 a month to put a couple of kids through college—you may not need to save, either. Of course, if you can afford to pay that much later, you can also afford to save that much now. So, why not save now?

Parents who are neither rich nor poor need to save substantial amounts before college or repay substantial loans after college. This is true, for example, even if you make a respectable but modest $25,000 or $30,000 a year.

# But What about All That Financial Aid?

You're right. Your child may be eligible for financial aid in the form of either outright grants (money someone gives the young student) or loans (money you or the student has to repay). It's possible. But let me tell you a little bit about how the process works and how eligibility is determined.

## Determining Eligibility

To determine whether a student is eligible for financial aid, you (the parent or guardian) fill out the Free Application for Federal Student Aid, or FAFSA. (You can pick one up at your local library or high school.) The information you provide on this statement determines the amount the government and colleges expect you to contribute to your child's educational expenses. That doesn't sound so bad, really. But here's a reality sandwich: The financial aid formulas expect you to live at the poverty line—$15,000 for a family of four, for example—and then contribute between 10 and 20 percent of the income you make in excess of the poverty line to your kid's college expenses. Your child is expected to earn and contribute about $1,000 per year and pay whatever savings he or she has toward the expense of college. Whatever amount is left over after deducting all these amounts determines the amount of financial aid the child is eligible for.

## Reviewing Financial Aid Programs

A number of different financial aid programs are available. Most, as I've already pointed out, are really loan programs. In general, there isn't any free money. Or at least not very much of it. Following is a summary of federal financial aid programs that are available at the time I'm writing this.

**Two Warnings about Financial Aid.** *Unless you're raising a family on an income close to the poverty level, almost all financial aid will come in the form of loans that you have to repay. Also, if your child is very young, it's foolish to rely on financial aid. Much of the financial aid that's available is federally funded—either directly or indirectly. With the budget deficit and the changing demographics of the population, it seems likely that less and less money will be available for student loans and grants.*

## Pell Grants

Pell grants are a great deal if you can get them because the federal government gives students up to $2,300 a year. Pell grants are available only to the neediest undergraduate students. When you fill out the Free Application for Federal Student Aid (FAFSA), you will be automatically considered for the Pell Grant.

## Direct and FFEL Program Loans for Students (Stafford Loans)

Stafford loans offer $2,625 the first year, $3,500 the second year, and $5,500 the third and fourth years. They offer $8,500 per year to graduate students. In the case of Direct Stafford Loans, the federal government loans you the money, and all you do is fill out the FAFSA. For Federal Family Education Loans (FFEL), you must find a bank to lend you the money. You must pay a loan fee equal to 4 percent of the value of the loan. Both direct loans and FFEL program loans come in subsidized and unsubsidized versions. If a student qualifies for a subsidized Stafford loan, Uncle Sam pays the interest while the student is in school. For the unsubsidized version, which is not based on financial need, the student pays the interest on the loan while in school but doesn't have to start repaying the principal until six months after he or she graduates. By the way, a student can't borrow more than about $23,000 for undergraduate studies nor more than about $65,500 in total for both undergraduate and graduate studies.

## PLUS Loans

Parent Loans for Undergraduate Students (PLUS) cover the annual cost of college, less any financial aid. As with Stafford loans, you borrow the money either from the federal government (Direct Plus Loans) or from a private lender (FFEL Program PLUS Loans). PLUS loans charge higher interest than Stafford loans and require a separate application. PLUS loans are not based on need. You must pay a 4 percent loan fee to secure the loan, and you must pay interest on the loan while the student is in school. You begin paying principal on the loan when the student graduates.

### FSEOG Grants

Federal Supplemental Educational Opportunity Grants, known as FSEOG grants, are campus-based, which means that the amount of aid depends on the availability of funds at the student's school. FSEOGs pay up to $4,000 per year. Like a Pell grant, Uncle Sam gives the student educational money outright. Unlike Pell grants, however, there's no guarantee that every eligible student will receive an FSEOG.

### Perkins Loans

Perkins loans, also campus-based, offer up to $2,500 each year for undergraduate study and $3,000 each year for graduate study. Students can possibly defer payments by joining the Peace Corps or the military, or by teaching in an inner-city school. Interest rates on Perkins loans are 5 percent, beginning after graduation. Perkins loans require no loan fee. Apply through the college's financial aid office.

### Federal College Work Study Programs

This is pretty simple. The student gets a job with an approved employer. Uncle Sam helps the employer with payroll.

The one thing I want to emphasize, however, is that this information probably applies only if your child is going to attend college in the very near future. If little Winston or Amelia is still in middle school or grade school (or in diapers), it probably makes most sense to save as much as you can. I'm rather a worrier. But I don't think it's all that pessimistic to assume that you *won't* be able to count on financial aid when your child or children attend college.

**Why the Retirement Planner?**
*It may seem weird to use the Retirement Planner to estimate a child's college costs and how much you need to save. On the other hand, it may help you to think about college, basically, as four years or so of retirement. And, in the years before your child temporarily retires, you and the child will need to accumulate enough savings to pay for those four years of retirement.*

# Saving Money for College

So how much should you save for college? As long as you have an idea about what kind of college your child will attend, you can use Money's Retirement Planner to come up with a pretty good guess. To do this, follow these steps:

1 Click the Planning Wizards button when the Money Contents window is displayed. Money displays the Planning Wizards window.

**2** Click the Retirement Planner button. Money displays the first Retirement Planner dialog box.

*If you are already considering specific colleges for your child, you should be sure to obtain the average time it takes for students attending that college to complete a four-year degree. Believe it or not, it's usually more than four years nowadays, since colleges are feeling the economic crunch and can't offer every quarter every class that a student needs to complete his or her major.*

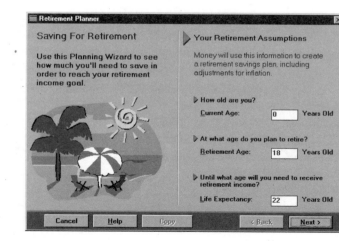

**3** Enter your child's current age into the Current Age text box.

**4** Enter your child's age at the time he or she will enter college in the Retirement Age text box. For example, if your child will start college at age 18, enter 18.

**5** Enter your child's age when he or she will complete college in the Life Expectancy text box. For example, if your child will finish college at age 22, enter 22.

**6** Click Next. Money displays the second Retirement Planner dialog box.

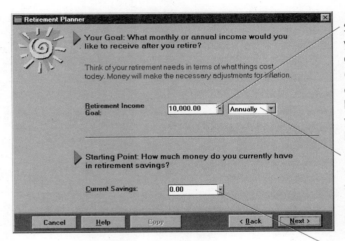

Specify how much money your child will need for college on an annual basis. (This figure shouldn't include college costs that will be paid by financial aid or through your child's summer earnings, however.)

Indicate whether you've specified the cost of sending your child to college (the retirement amount in the Planner) as a monthly or annual amount.

Enter any college savings you've already accumulated with your current savings.

**7** Click Next. Money displays a dialog box that asks what **rate of return** you expect to earn over the years you work and save and over the years your child goes to college.

*To earn 9 percent on your college savings, you'll probably need to invest a significant portion of the money in the stock market.*

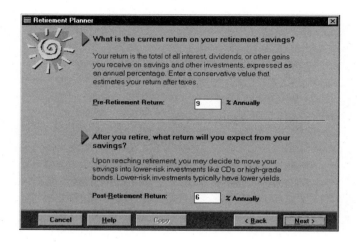

**8** If you want to, replace the Pre-Retirement Return rate with some other value. If you're not sure what you should enter here, leave the input set to 9. Then read "A Few Words on Rates of Return" in Chapter 13.

**9** If you want to, replace the Post-Retirement Return rate with some other value.

**10** Click Next. Money displays a dialog box that asks what **inflation** you expect over the years you work and save. Money initially uses 3 percent as the expected annual inflation, which is probably a good guess. If you want to enter a different inflation rate, however, enter it, and then click Calculate.

*Don't worry about inflation when you enter the annual college costs figure in the Retirement Income Goal text box. Money will adjust your input for the inflation that will occur between now and the time your child attends college.*

**What Is the Right Inflation Rate?** *If your child will attend college in a year or two, you may want to use a 7-percent inflation rate, the rate we've seen over the last few years for college costs. On the other hand, if your child is still quite young, you may want to use the roughly 3.3-percent historical inflation rate.*

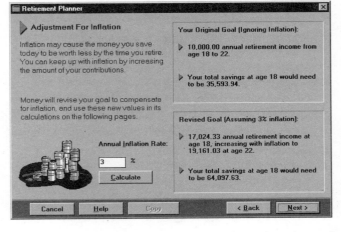

11 Click Next. Money displays a dialog box that shows how much you need to save to reach your college savings goal. Actually, Money presents two savings plans. One plan shows how much you need to save if you save the same amount every month. The other plan shows how much you should start saving if you adjust your savings amount each month for inflation.

*To print a copy of the retirement savings summary shown on the next page (really your college savings plan summary), click Copy. Then start the WordPad application and choose Paste from its Edit menu. This pastes the college savings plan summary schedule into the WordPad document. To print the document, choose Print from WordPad's File menu.*

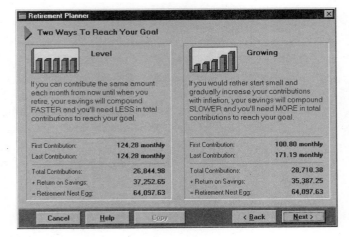

**Will College Costs Continue to Skyrocket?** *Over the past several years, college costs have increased by 7 percent annually, but I don't believe a 7-percent inflation rate is sustainable. With a 7-percent inflation rate in the cost of sending a child to college and a 3-percent general inflation rate, the real, inflation-ignored cost of a college education more than doubles between the time a child is born and the time a child enters college. In real terms, this means that a public university that costs $9,500 a year on the day a child is born will cost $19,000 a year in uninflated dollars by the time the child enters college. (These numbers assume there is no inflation over this eighteen-year period and parents will have received no cost-of-living adjustments.) Most people won't be able to afford to send their children to college if the real costs of a college education continue to skyrocket. For example, could a four-person family earning a healthy $70,000 a year afford $38,000 a year to send two children to college? There's no way they could. So, either this ridiculous 7-percent inflation rate will abate shortly or no one but the very rich will be able to afford to send their kids to college.*

**12** Click Next. Money displays a schedule that shows how your retirement savings grow over time (you'll use these savings for your child's college costs, of course).

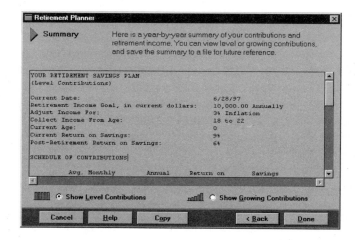

**13** Use the Show Level Contributions and Show Growing Contributions option buttons to specify which savings plan you want to summarize. Under the level contributions plan, you accumulate savings faster because you pay more in during the early years of saving. Under the growing contributions plan, however, you'll find it easier to save initially because you'll be saving smaller amounts.

**14** Click Done. Money returns you to the Planning Wizards window, but it saves all your planning information.

# Where Should You Save?

If you've just calculated how much money you should be (supposedly) saving for your child's or children's college expenses, you are probably in shock right now. Don't get discouraged, however. Or at least not yet. At the end of this chapter, I'll give you some ideas on how to reduce the costs of college. And I'll explain why your savings figure may be more than you really need.

Before we get to that stuff, however, let's assume that you're going to save at least something for your kid's college expenses. Once you make this decision, you need to decide in whose name the college savings should be put: the parent's or the child's. And you need to decide where to invest the savings—in **stocks, bonds,** bank accounts, and so forth.

## In Whose Name Should You Put the College Savings?

You have two choices about in whose name the college savings money should be put. You can hold the savings in your name, in which case you'll be taxed on the investment income the savings produce, or you can give the savings to your child, in which case your child will be taxed. In general, you pay less income tax by putting money in your child's name. If the child is 14 years old or less, the first $600 or so of investment income is tax-free and the next $600 is taxed at the lowest marginal income tax rate. If the child is 15 years old or more, the first $3,400 of income is tax-free (this might include both investment income and earned income if the child now has a job) and roughly the next $20,000 of income is taxed at the lowest marginal rate.

The one awkward thing about putting the money in a child's name is that the money really does become the child's. You can't borrow it temporarily—even if you have a good reason to. And when children reach the age of majority, either 18 or 21, they can spend the money on anything they want.

I once ran into a woman who illustrated perfectly the major downside of custodial accounts. Her great-grandmother had set up custodial accounts for all her great-grandchildren to help provide for their college educations. Unfortunately, the great-grandchild I met was a methamphetamine addict and an alcoholic when she reached the age of majority. You can guess what two things she

**About Those Income Tax Savings.** *Six-hundred dollars may not sound like all that much money. But you can actually accumulate a good-size chunk of money and still have most of your income tax-free. For example, if you invest a young child's college money in a stock **index fund,** the child can accumulate roughly $20,000 before the investment income is taxed. If you invest a young child's college money in bonds, the child can accumulate roughly $10,000 before the investment income is taxed.*

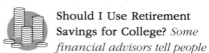 **Should I Use Retirement Savings for College?** *Some financial advisors tell people to save their kids' college money in a retirement plan, such as a 401(k), rather than in a custodial account. Saving money in a retirement account can work for two reasons. One is that a family's retirement savings aren't considered available money for college costs. Second, with retirement money, you get to borrow money from the government tax-free and then keep the interest you earn on the money. (This more than makes up for any penalty you pay if you start saving early—like when a child is still in preschool.) Saving college money in a retirement account won't work, however, if you're currently taking maximum advantage of retirement savings vehicles like 401(k)s, 403(b)s, Keoghs, and Individual Retirement Accounts to prepare for retirement. You, my friend, need to use these tools to fund your retirement—not your kids' college expenses.*

spent the money on. Fortunately, this story has a happy ending. The woman has been clean and sober for many years now and, last I heard, was working her way through college.

You probably don't need to worry about these kinds of extreme problems. But young adults are capable of piddling away at least some of the money that their parents intended for college tuition. Spring break in Ft. Lauderdale. Expensive stereos. Concert tickets.

The other tricky thing about deciding whether to put the savings in the child's or in the parent's name has to do with current financial aid regulations. These regulations assume that basically all of a child's savings are available for college but only a portion of his or her parent's savings are available.

In spite of the risks, I recommend using a custodial account to save money for college expenses if you're going to initiate a long-term, substantial college savings program. If you're not going to initiate a long-term, substantial savings program, I'd say go ahead and keep the money in your name.

## Where Should You Invest College Savings Money?

Once you decide in whose name the college savings should be put, you need to decide where to invest the savings. The challenge comes with the discouraging fact that college costs have been increasing at an annual rate of 7 percent, double the overall inflation rate of roughly 3.5 percent. This exorbitant inflation rate, in addition to provoking justice department investigations of a number of well-known private universities, has meant that parents either need to pursue the higher returns delivered by riskier stock investments or save much more money (and rely very little on compound interest.)

You've got three basic choices for funding a child's college expenses—or a goodly portion of them. Which you choose will depend on your feelings about investment risk. Read on.

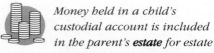

*Money held in a child's custodial account is included in the parent's **estate** for estate tax purposes if the parent dies. This isn't a factor if the parent's estate is less than $600,000. But if your estate exceeds $600,000, you ought to consider this not as a saving for college issue but as an estate-tax planning issue.*

*A bond matures when the bond's issuer, either the government or a corporation, redeems the bond by paying the bond-holders back.*

## What to Do If You're a Conservative Investor

Suppose you're a conservative investor, someone who routinely uses the words "stocks" and "gambling" in the same sentence. Someone who still has nightmares about the crash of 1987 or 1929.

If this sounds like you, stick with interest-bearing investments. You'll miss out on the chance to achieve the really impressive returns possible in the stock market, but your conservatism will pay off in one important way. You'll know with absolute certainty how much money you'll earn. All you have to do is buy high-quality U.S. government bonds and then hold the bonds to maturity. You should invest in individual bonds that mature about the middle of every summer so you can get a chunk of cash to pay the following year's tuition and room and board payments.

While planning for college years, you'll probably save several hundred dollars a month. So, you might want to accumulate a few months' savings and buy a U.S. Treasury bond two or three times a year. (These come in thousand-dollar denominations.) Or you can buy Series EE savings bonds every month. The only thing you must do—and this is crucial—is buy bonds that mature in a way that provides a huge pot of cash every summer for the following year's tuition and college expenses. Matching your child's expected tuition payment dates with the dates that the bonds mature is the secret.

The one thing you need to watch carefully if you follow the conservative investor approach is inflation. If inflation heats up, and particularly if education costs inflate wildly, you'll have to boost your savings. You can periodically recalculate how much you need to save by recalculating the amount that college tuition will cost.

## What to Do If You're an Aggressive Investor

As long as you start early—preferably while your child is still in diapers and definitely not long after your child starts grade school—I think it makes sense to invest college savings money in the stock market. Go for something that's well-diversified and inexpensive. (A no-load stock **index fund** based on the Standard & Poor's 500 is what I've got my kids' college money in.)

You probably need to save about half of what the ultraconservative bond investor does. If you figure on the stock market delivering its historical average of 10 percent and you subtract about .2 percent for expenses, you can figure on your college savings money earning about 9.8 percent. That's pretty good.

Then, at some point in the future, you'll want to begin moving money from the stock market into something very safe. Some financial writers advocate moving money from stocks to short-term bonds or certificates of deposit four to five years before you need it. This means moving a child's college freshman year money from the stock market to bonds at roughly the time the child is a high school freshman. Move more money into safer investments in each of the next three years to provide for the child's sophomore, junior, and senior years of college.

"Move money early" isn't a bad rule, although it seems quite conservative. I think it makes more sense to leave the money in the stock market as long as possible. I'll probably move money from my 4-year-old and 5-year-old daughters' stock market funds into bonds or certificates of deposit sometime during the year before they need it. As I said, though, I'm a pretty aggressive investor.

If the stock market does take a sharp dip during a daughter's senior year in high school, I could be in a bit of a pickle. I'll either have to withdraw a larger share of her college savings and hope later good years make up the difference, or I'll have to quickly figure out another way to make up the difference. Perhaps I'll have to borrow the money, for example. Or maybe my daughter will have to attend a less expensive school. In my case, however, these kinds of options don't scare me all that much. You need to think about these sorts of contingencies.

**Predictability for Profits.** *With the conservative approach, you eliminate the risk of losing your principal. But you have to save substantially more money because bonds, while more predictable, are less profitable. That's the tradeoff: predictability for profits.*

**How Can I Minimize My Investment Risk?** *One way to minimize stock market risk is by investing in the stock market for longer periods of time. By investing your first years of savings in the stock market and using this money for your child's last years of college costs, you further reduce the risk that comes with investing in the stock market.*

## The Middle Road

If you're not all that aggressive nor all that conservative, you might think about blending the conservative and aggressive approaches described here. The one thing I would do, however, is use the more aggressive approach for the first half of the years you save (and use this money to pay for the junior and senior years) and then use the conservative approach for the last half of the years you save (and use this money to pay for the freshman and sophomore years).

## A Couple of Ideas for People Who Don't Like Stocks and Bonds

Not excited about investing in stocks and bonds? I have one other idea for you. But I'd like your promise that you won't try this until you are sure your retirement savings are taken care of. (The thought of you not being prepared for retirement terrifies me much more than the thought of your kids going to college on a shoe-string budget.)

That said, here's my idea. Between now and the time your kids start college, stick money in your retirement account—especially that employer-sponsored 401(k) or 403(b) plan—and pay a little extra on your mortgage. The goal here is to have your mortgage paid off and your retirement fully funded by the time your kid starts college. (This may not be as tough as you think.) You won't have any savings for college, of course. But if, during your child's senior year, you stop saving a few thousand a year for retirement and stop making, say, a $1000-a-month house payment, you should be able to pay for tuition and room and board with the money you were using to save and pay off your mortgage.

If you do go with this approach, recognize that you're relying on your income to put your kids through college. And that means you want to make sure you either have a secure job or more than adequate rainy-day savings. You also want to make sure that you have appropriate life insurance and disability insurance coverage.

# What to Do If You Can't Possibly Afford College

Even if you can't afford a dime for your kid's college education, your kids can still figure out a way to go to college and even on to graduate and professional school. They will have to be a bit more flexible. They may need to be a bit more creative. But with some work and planning—and perhaps, more importantly, the desire—any kid can go to college. It's more important to offer emotional support and encouragement than cold, hard cash.

I should also mention that the calculation method I described earlier in this chapter probably overstates the amount you need to save for college. The calculations I described assume that you need to have all the money saved by the time your child starts college. (Remember, however, that you won't need to pay the sophomore, junior, and senior year expenses until the following years.) For this reason, don't worry if you can only save, say, 50 or 75 percent of what your calculations show as necessary. If you can just start saving money regularly—especially if you start early—you can make wonderful progress in your saving.

Let me also mention that I have several friends who successfully and solely paid their ways through both college and graduate and professional school. They all describe the experience as positive and a source of real pride. But enough said. Let's look at the down-and-dirty mechanics of saving serious money.

Basically, saving for college comes down to reducing either of the variables in the following formula:

`Annual College Costs x Years of College = Total College Costs`

If you start brainstorming, you can quickly come up with a lot of good ideas for reducing the costs of college. In the lists that follow, I describe the best ways I know of to reduce annual college costs as well as the number of years it takes to complete college.

Here are ways to reduce the cost of going to college:

- ➤ Attend a community college for the first two years rather than a public university. This saves $8,000 over the first two years.

- ➤ Attend an equivalent public university instead of a private university. This saves $28,000 over four years.

- ➤ Live at home rather than in student housing and attend a college as a commuter student. Your savings with this tactic are about $1,200 a year (the net of commuting costs).

- ➤ Get a part-time student job, such as a dormitory resident assistant. This saves $3,000 (usually paid as free room and board).

- ➤ Do a one-quarter work-for-credit study that pays a real salary. This saves $3,000 in earnings during the quarter.

Here are ways to reduce the amount of time spent in college:

- ➤ Take Advanced Placement (AP) classes in high school. (If your child's high school doesn't offer advanced placement classes, you can also arrange for College Level Examination Program, or CLEP, examinations.) Many high schools offer half a dozen AP classes and some offer twice that many.

- ➤ Take a transferable community college class during the summer breaks. You can shave off one quarter or even a semester this way.

- ➤ Take an extra class a year. Or take an extra class each quarter or semester if you can take the extra class for free.

I know that some of the tricks and techniques included in the two preceding lists aren't exactly appealing. But if someone has to choose between going to college on a shoe-string budget or not going at all, college on a shoe-string budget is the better choice, by far.

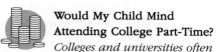

**Would My Child Mind Attending College Part-Time?**
*Colleges and universities often provide free or discounted tuition to full-time employees. Sure, it takes longer to get a degree by working full-time and attending college part-time, but this option is one you should consider if other, better options aren't workable.*

One final point about these cost-saving ideas: Before you broach the idea of an accelerated degree with your young scholar, I should mention something to you. I took an extra class a quarter to finish my Masters degree early and I still have occasional nightmares because of it. In my nightmare, it's the week before finals and I'm wandering the halls of graduate school. I still haven't had any time to study for the final. I haven't even started on the 100-page term paper. And, of course, I'm naked.

## In Conclusion

While college is a great investment for your kids, I don't think it makes sense for you to replace saving for retirement with saving for college. I can guess that if you're reading this, you're a pretty good parent. You're thinking about the things that you can do to make sure your son or daughter's life is better. And that's great. But make sure your future is secure before investing in your child's. Your kids should go to college if they want to and they have the right skills and attitude. But if they really want to go to college, they can do it on their own.

# Getting Started with Your Investments

**M**icrosoft Money provides wonderful tools for **investment** record-keeping. If you're an investor, you've probably already considered whether and how to use Money to make this part of your financial life—investment record-keeping—easier and less time-consuming.

This chapter helps you get started with investment record-keeping by discussing whether you even want to do it (it's a lot of work!), by explaining how to set up investment accounts, and by explaining how to describe your current investment **portfolio.** You need to complete these preliminary tasks before you can use Money for day-to-day financial record-keeping.

## Why You May Not Want to Do This

Before you jump right into the business of setting up the investment accounts you need and recording transactions that describe your current portfolio, let me suggest that you stop for a moment and consider whether you even need to keep investment records with Money. At first blush, that may seem like a kooky statement. You might think that Money users who invest should keep track of their investments with Money. But that's not quite true. You actually shouldn't keep investment records unless you have a good reason to. In general, there are only two good reasons for going to all that work.

> Your investments affect your income taxes. In this case, you need to track your investments with Money so that you know the taxable investment income that your investments produce and so you know about any capital gains or losses that occur (which will be taxable) when you sell an investment.

> You want to use Money's investment reports to assess the performance of your investments. By using Money's investment performance report, you can calculate the rate of return for the investments you're holding.

**What Is a Tax-Deferred Account?** *A tax-deferred account is one for which you don't have to pay income taxes on the investment income or capital gains it generates. For example, an Individual Retirement Account—even if the account is in a self-directed IRA brokerage account—is a tax-deferred account. So are 401(k), 403(b), Keogh, and SEP/IRA accounts.*

If you think about these reasons for a couple of minutes, you'll realize that many investors don't need to use Money. For example, if you're investing money in tax-deferred accounts (and this is a smart thing to do), you won't have any taxable investment income because you won't have any **capital gains** or **losses** from your investments. What's more, if you're sticking with **mutual funds,** you don't need Money's investment reports to monitor the performance of your investments. The mutual-fund management company does this for you.

Accordingly, many smart, sophisticated, and even very wealthy investors don't need Money to track their investments. Not only do you get better returns, but you substantially reduce the amount of time you spend record-keeping if you do all of your investing in tax-deferred mutual funds (as you probably should be doing with your retirement money, for example).

What's more, you don't need to track your investments with Money if you're investing in mutual funds or interest-bearing investments like certificates of deposit (CDs), money-market accounts, and U.S. savings bonds, or if you're holding the CDs or savings bonds until they mature and you're spending the investment income you earn. You don't need to track these investments because you can record the dividend or interest income you earn when you deposit it into your checking account. And you can also tell how well an investment is doing by looking at its interest rate or annual return.

Now that I've told you who *doesn't* need to use Money for investment record-keeping, let me tell you who *does*:

➤ Anyone who buys and sells investments that aren't part of a tax-deferred account should use Money to calculate capital gains and losses.

➤ Anyone who reinvests their dividends or interest to buy additional shares of a **stock** or mutual fund should use Money for the same reason.

➤ Investors who can't get annual investment return information somewhere else should use Money to calculate these figures on their own.

Many investors, then, need to use Money. And this is true even if their investment portfolios are not very large. If you've saved a few dollars for your kid's college expenses, for example, you should use Money. And if you've collected a few stocks and **bonds** over the years and occasionally add to your portfolio, you should use Money.

 **How Do I Track My Net Worth?** *If you don't need to keep investment records with Money but want to track your net worth, you may want to add an asset account to your Money files and use it to get a rough estimate of the total market value of your investments. The procedure for setting up asset accounts is described in Chapter 8.*

## Setting Up an Investment Account

To track your investments, set up at least one investment account. The general rule is to set up one investment account for each brokerage account statement you receive. For example, if you receive a statement from, say, The Vanguard Group, which might show two mutual funds, and you also receive a statement from Charles Schwab, which might show a cash-management account and a handful of stocks and bonds you've purchased as well as a mutual fund, you need to set up two investment accounts.

To add an investment account, follow these steps:

1 With the Money Contents window displayed, click the Account Manager button. Money displays the Account Manager window.

2 Click the New Account button. This tells Money to start the New Account Wizard.

**3** Optionally enter the name of the finance institution associated with the account.

**4** Click Next. When the Wizard asks what kind of account you want to set up, click Investment.

**5** Click Next. When the Wizard asks what name you want to use for your investment account, enter it.

 **What Records Do I Need to Save?** *If you invest in tax-deferred mutual funds, you should probably save your year-end statements in a desk drawer or a box someplace. By collecting and permanently saving year-end statements, you have a record of your annual contributions, investment profits, and year-end account balances.*

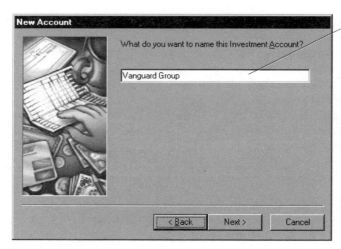

If you're setting up one investment account for each monthly statement, you may want to provide the name of the mutual-fund management company or stock brokerage company that sends the statement.

*If you enter the name of a new bank or financial institution in step 3 of Setting Up an Investment Account, Money will ask if you want information about the online services the bank offers before you exit the procedure.*

**6** Click Next. When the Wizard asks whether or not this account's investments are tax-deferred, click either the No, or the Yes, button. As mentioned earlier, there's little reason to track tax-deferred investments, so you'll probably mark the No, The Account Is Not Tax Deferred button.

*An associated cash account is a checking account or money-market account that you use either to collect the cash you receive from investments or to provide cash for investments.*

**7** Click Next. When the Wizard asks whether this account has an associated cash account, click either the Yes or No button. As this page of the New Account Wizard dialog box suggests, most brokerage accounts have an associated cash account.

**8** Click Next. When the Wizard asks for the cash account's balance, enter the ending balance from your last monthly statement.

**9** Click Finish.

Money returns you to the Account Manager window. It shows a new investment account, and, if you said that your new account has an associated cash account, it shows a new investment cash account, too. If you need to set up additional investment accounts, repeat steps 2 through 8.

*Chapter 17 describes how you work with associated cash accounts.*

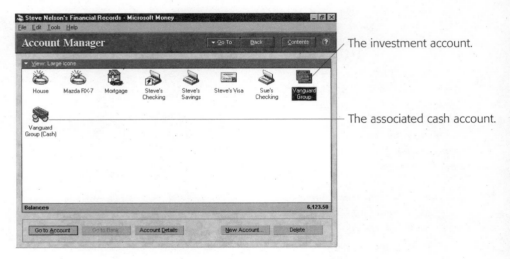

The investment account.

The associated cash account.

**Treat Lots As Separate Investments.** *For the purposes of calculating capital gains taxes, the federal income tax laws let you arbitrarily pick which **lot** you sell. (A lot is just a chunk of mutual-fund shares that you purchase at one time.) For example, say that you purchase two lots of Vanguard Index Trust 500, one at $10 a share and one at $30 a share, and you later sell the shares for $20 a share. If you say that you're selling the shares you purchased for $10, you show a $10 capital gain per share (because a $20 share price minus a $10 share cost equals a $10 capital gain). If you say that you're selling the shares you purchased for $30, you show a $10 capital loss per share (because a $20 share price minus a $30 share cost equals a capital loss of -$10). This record-keeping trick, known as "specific identification," often lets you control when you recognize capital gains. To use specific identification, set up each of your lots as separate investments. For example, instead of having one investment named "Index Trust," you might have two investments named "Index Trust-$10" and "Index Trust-$30." When you record the sale, you can choose whichever lot makes the most sense for your income taxes.*

When you finish working with the Account Manager, you can return to the Money Contents window by clicking the Back button. If you want to add details about the account, select the account you just created, click the Account Details button, and enter additional information about the investment account in the dialog box that Money displays.

# Describing Your Current Portfolio

Once you've set up your investment account, you're ready to describe the investments in your portfolio. To do this, display the Account Manager window, and then double-click your investment account. Money displays the investment account version of the Account Register window.

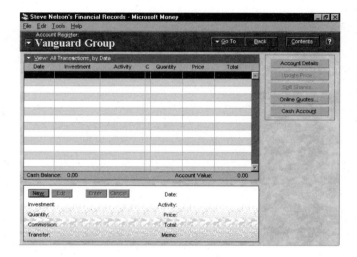

1 Click New.

2 Enter the date you first purchased the investment in the Date text box.

**An Idea for High Income Taxpayers.** *If you're a high income taxpayer, you may make more money by investing in tax-exempt bonds and money-market funds than you will by investing in taxable bonds and money-market funds—even though the taxable investments pay a higher interest rate. To determine whether a tax-exempt or a taxable investment makes more sense, you need to compare the tax-exempt investment's interest rate with the taxable investment's after-tax interest rates, which you calculate by multiplying the taxable investment's interest rate by the factor (1+ marginal tax rate). The marginal tax rate is the percentage you pay in income taxes on your last dollar of income.*

**3** Enter a name for the investment in the Investment text box.

**4** Press Enter or Tab. When you do, Money displays the Create New Investment dialog box. (Remember, we're not really dealing with new investments yet, but updating the new Money account to reflect the investments you currently hold in your portfolio.)

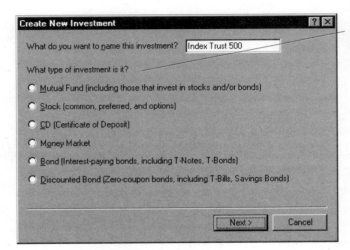

Click the option that most closely describes the investment you're adding.

**5** Click Next. Money displays another dialog box that asks for additional information about the investment. Use the boxes and buttons that Money provides to describe the investment in more detail. Here, you see the New Mutual Fund dialog box, which you use to describe a mutual fund investment. You complete a slightly different dialog box, however, for other types of investments

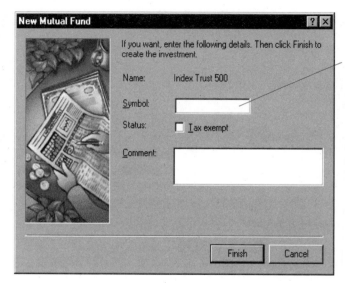

*Chapter 20 describes how you use Online Quotes.*

If you plan to use Money's Online Quotes feature, you need to enter the security symbol.

**6** Click Finish once you've described the investment. Money closes the dialog boxes, returns you to the Account Register window, and activates the Activity drop-down list box.

**7** Select the Buy entry from the Activity drop-down list box and press Enter. Money adds text boxes to the input area so you can describe the investment.

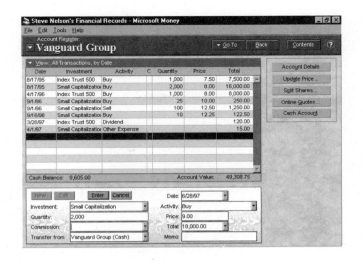

8 Use the Quantity text box to describe how many shares of the investment you own. (If you're describing the quantity of some other investment, such as bonds or precious metals, you can enter the number of bonds, number of ounces, or whatever measure is most appropriate.)

9 Use the Price text box to give the cost per unit you paid for the quantity you're describing.

*To calculate the average price of lots purchased at different prices, divide the total price you paid for all the lots by the total shares in all the lots.*

This can be a little tricky in the case of existing investments because you may have purchased different **lots**, or chunks of the investment, at different prices. So, it's actually a good idea to enter each investment lot separately. If you don't want to go to this much work, you can just enter all of the lots together as one big lot. In this case, use the average price you paid.

10 If necessary, use the Commission box to record the sales commission you paid to purchase the investment. Once you record this bit of data, Money calculates the total purchase price and displays this value in the Total box.

11 If necessary, edit the contents of the Total box. This shouldn't be necessary, but it is possible for a minor rounding error to cause a small error in the total.

12 Delete the account name shown in the Transfer From drop-down list box. Money initially shows the associated cash account, if you told it to create one. But you don't want to reduce the cash balance for this transaction if it's an old investment purchase. (Remember, we're building the investment account to reflect your current holdings, not new transactions.) In effect, the decrease in the cash account's balance already shows because you purchased the investment.

13 Click Enter. Money records the investment in the investment account.

14 Repeat steps 1 through 13 for each of the other investments you hold in your portfolio.

**Speeding Up Your Record-Keeping.** *If you describe additional purchases of an investment you've already described once, you can activate a drop-down list box when you move the selection cursor to the Investment box and select one of the investments that is named.*

# Updating the Prices in Your Portfolio

Once you've described all of the investments in your portfolio, you're ready to enter current price information. You'll want to do this so your investment records reflect current market values. Follow these steps:

1 Display the investment account in an Account Register window. You can do this by displaying the Account Manager window and double-clicking the investment account.

**An Interesting Fact about Professional Money Managers.** *Research into the performance of professional money managers reveals a curious fact: The vast majority of professional money managers don't even achieve the stock market average. During the 1980s, for example, the average annual return of Standard & Poor's 500 beat two-thirds of the professionals. Because of this fact, many sophisticated investors choose to invest in* **index funds,** *which deliver the stock market's average return. By choosing an index fund, these investors will probably do better with their investments than two out of every three professional money managers.*

**2** Click the Update Price button. Money displays the Update Price dialog box.

**3** Activate the Investment drop-down list box and select the investment whose current market price and value you want to update.

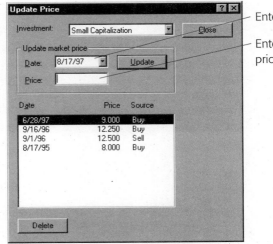

Enter the current date.

Enter the current market price.

**4** Click Update. Money adds the price to the list it shows on the Update Price dialog box.

**5** Repeat steps 2 through 4 for the other investments you're holding.

**6** Click Close when you're done.

# Viewing Your Portfolio

Once you've set up your investment accounts, described your investments, and updated their price, you can use the Investment Portfolio window to monitor your investments. To display the Investment Portfolio window, click the Investment Portfolio button, which appears on the Money Contents window.

This list box shows your investments. Activate the triangle menu at the top of the list box and choose a command to change the way your investments are summarized.

If you click an investment and then click the Investment Portfolio window's Go To Account button, Money displays the account register for the investment.

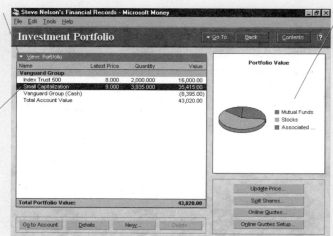

This chart shows the composition of your investment portfolio by investment type. By right-clicking the various parts of the chart, you can see a menu of commands for changing the appearance of the chart.

If you click the New button in the Investment Portfolio window, Money asks whether you want to create a new investment account or describe a new investment. Answer this question and Money either starts the New Account wizard (so you can create a new account) or displays the Create New Investment dialog box (so you can describe a new investment).

If you click an investment you've already set up and then click the Details button in the Investment Portfolio window, Money displays information about the investment in the window.

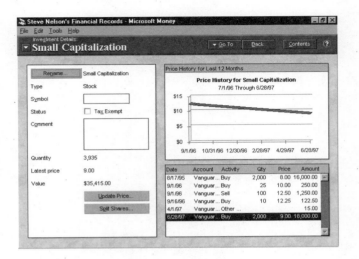

# In Conclusion

Once you've set up investment accounts, described your current portfolio, and provided current market prices for your investments, you're ready to begin using Money for day-to-day record-keeping. The next three chapters describe in detail how you can use Money to keep records of mutual funds (Chapter 16), stocks and bonds (Chapter 17), and real estate (Chapter 18). In Chapter 19, I explain how to handle special investments and show how good investment record-keeping can help with some common problems.

# 16

# Mutual Funds

Once you've set up your investment accounts and described your current **portfolio,** you're ready to begin using Money for day-to-day record-keeping. The simplest way to start doing this is to keep track of any **mutual funds** you own, so that's what I'll describe here. Even if you're not a mutual-fund fan, you should read this chapter. In the chapters that follow, I'll assume you know the information this chapter covers.

## Recording Mutual Fund Purchases

Whenever you purchase shares of a mutual fund, you need to describe the purchase in the mutual fund's account register. To do this, display the Account Manager window and then double-click the investment account. Money displays the investment account version of the Account Register window.

### What Are Mutual Funds?

*Mutual funds pool the money of a number of individuals and then invest the pooled money on behalf of those individuals. Different funds have different purposes, and, accordingly, they invest in different types of securities. For example, there are mutual funds that invest solely in low-grade bonds, high-grade bonds, stocks of domestic companies, stocks of foreign companies, and so forth. The advantages of mutual funds are many. You get the benefits of a professional money manager and you pay very low expenses. You can also diversify your investment portfolio and do so by starting with modest sums of money—often as little as $500.*

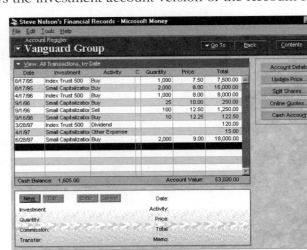

To describe the purchase of mutual-fund shares, follow these steps:

**1** Click New.

**2** Enter the purchase date in the Date box.

**3** Enter a name for the investment in the Investment combo box.

If you have purchased shares of this mutual fund before, you can select the name of the mutual fund from the Investment drop-down list box. If you haven't purchased shares of this mutual fund before, enter the name of the fund in the combo box and click enter. When Money displays the Create New Investment dialog box, mark the Type button that most closely describes the investment you're adding. Click Next. Money displays another dialog box that asks for additional information about the security. Use the boxes and buttons to describe the investment in more detail. Click Finish once you've described the investment. Money closes the dialog boxes, returns you to the Account Register window, and activates the Activity drop-down list box.

**4** Choose Buy from the Activity drop-down list, and Money adds more boxes to the input area so you can describe the investment.

*If you intend to use Money's Online Quotes feature, you need to enter the security symbol. See Chapter 20 for more information about Online Quotes.*

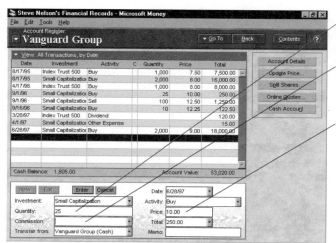

Indicate how many mutual-fund shares you're purchasing.

Record any sales commission you paid to purchase the shares.

Enter the price per share you're paying for the mutual fund.

**How Do I Pick a Mutual Fund?** *Don't rush out and buy last year's hottest fund. Chances are good that a fund that's done very well in the past won't do as well in the future. Statisticians call this effect "regression to the mean," but you don't need to be a scientist to understand the logic: Over time, fund returns tend to average out, so a fund that's done well in the past might do more poorly in the future. Instead, find a fund with a low expense ratio—and preferably select it yourself so you don't pay a commission. Make sure you're comfortable with the fund's investment objective, as described in the prospectus. Finally, unless you're going to be investing in a bunch of different funds, choose one that invests in a diversified portfolio of stocks or bonds.*

5 Verify the contents of the Total box. If necessary, edit the value in the Total box so it correctly reflects the total purchase amount. (This might be necessary if a minor rounding difference caused a small error in the total.)

6 Identify the bank account or associated cash account you are using to pay for the purchase. Select the account from the Transfer From drop-down list box. Money initially shows the associated cash account if you told it to create one. But you can select another account—for example, your regular checking account—if you're using money from somewhere else to make the purchase.

7 Click Enter. Money records the mutual-fund purchase.

## Recording Mutual Fund Sales

When you sell shares of a mutual fund, you describe the transaction by following a series of steps similar to the steps you follow to purchase shares. To do this, display the account in an Account Register window as described in the preceding section of the chapter, and then follow these steps:

1 Click New.

2 Enter the sale date in the Date box.

3 Identify the name of the mutual fund whose shares you're selling by using the Investment box. You can type the name into the combo box or you can select it from the drop-down list.

**4** Choose Sell from the Activity drop-down list, and Money adds text boxes to the input area so you can describe the sale of shares.

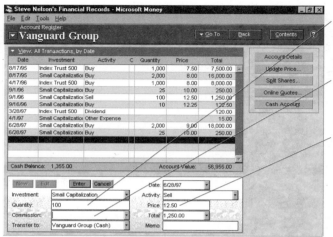

Describe how many mutual fund shares you're selling.

Record the commission you paid to sell the shares, if any.

Give the price per share you're receiving for the mutual fund shares.

### How Often Should I Update My Investment Records?

*Here's a record-keeping trick. For long-term investments such as retirement money or college savings for your kids, don't worry about updating your investment records at the end of every month or the end of every quarter. Instead, wait until the end of the year. Then use the year-end statement to record a year's worth of distributions and reinvestment. You'll probably have only a handful of transactions to record, anyway. And by batching them together, you'll save time. What's more, if the investment money you're tracking is a long-term investment, it doesn't really matter if you're several months behind in your record-keeping.*

**5** Verify the contents of the Total box. If necessary, edit the value so it correctly reflects the total purchase amount. (This might be necessary if a minor rounding difference caused a small error in the total.)

**Trading in Tax-Deferred Accounts.** *The more you buy and sell mutual fund shares, the more record-keeping you have. However, as I noted at the start of Chapter 12, you actually don't need to keep records for the mutual-fund investments you have in tax-deferred accounts. For that reason, if you're someone who frequently buys and sells mutual funds—attempting to trade, in other words—consider doing your trading in a tax-deferred investment vehicle such as your Individual Retirement Account or your Keogh account. Then you can save yourself time by* not *keeping records of this tax-deferred account. Keep in mind, however, that academic research does not support the notion that individual investors can profit by trading. So probably a better option is simply to stop trading.*

**6** Identify the bank account or associated cash account in which you'll deposit the sale proceeds by selecting the account from the Transfer To drop-down list box. Money initially shows the associated cash account, but you can select another account in which to deposit the money from the sale.

**7** Click Enter. Money records the mutual fund sale.

# Recording Mutual Fund Dividends

Periodically, of course, you'll receive a mutual fund dividend distribution. To record this transaction, follow these steps:

**1** Display the account in the Account Register window, and then click New.

**2** Enter the dividend date in the Date text box.

**3** In the Investment combo box, identify the name of the mutual fund that is distributing the dividend.

**4** Select an appropriate entry from the Activity drop-down list: Interest for an **interest** distribution, Dividend for a dividend distribution, S-Term Cap Gains Dist for a short-term **capital gains** distribution, or L-Term Cap Gains Dist for a long-term capital gains distribution. (We'll cover some of the other dividend options that are listed in the next section.) Money adds text boxes to the input area so you can describe the dividend distribution.

**What Kind of Distribution Is It?** *The mutual-fund statement identifies whether the distribution is an interest distribution, a dividend, a short-term capital gains distribution, or a long-term capital gains distribution. You don't have to worry about making this determination.*

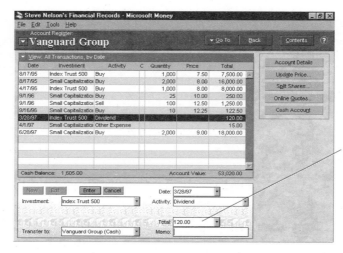

Specify the amount of the distribution here.

**5** Identify the bank account or associated cash account in which you'll deposit the distribution by selecting the account from the Transfer To drop-down list box.

**6** Click Enter. Money records the mutual-fund distribution.

# Reinvesting Mutual Fund Distributions

With a mutual fund, you usually have the option of reinvesting the distributions you receive when the mutual fund returns a profit. By reinvesting, you continue to accumulate more and more shares. Typically, reinvested distributions aren't subject to the same sales commissions that regular purchases are. To describe the reinvestment of a mutual fund distribution, follow these steps:

**1** In the Account Register window, click New.

**2** Enter the reinvestment date in the Date box.

**3** Enter the name for the investment in the Investment combo box.

**4** Choose an appropriate entry from the Activity drop-down list: Reinvest Interest for a reinvested interest distribution, Reinvest Dividend for a reinvested dividend distribution, Reinvest S-Term CG Dist for a reinvested short-term capital gains distribution, or Reinvest L-Term CG Dist for a reinvested long-term capital gains distribution. Money adds text boxes to the input area so you can describe the reinvestment.

![](What Kind of Distribution Am I Reinvesting?) **What Kind of Distribution Am I Reinvesting?** *The mutual fund statement identifies whether the distribution you're reinvesting is an interest distribution, a dividend, a short-term capital gains distribution, or a long-term capital gains distribution. You don't have to worry about making this determination.*

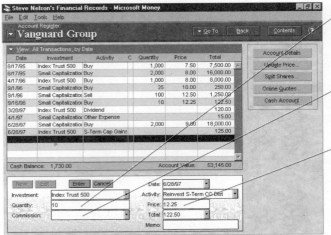

Describe how many mutual fund shares you're purchasing by reinvesting the distribution.

Record the commission you paid to purchase the investment, if necessary.

Give the price per share you're paying for the new mutual fund shares.

**5** Verify the contents of the Total box. If necessary, edit the value so it correctly reflects the total purchase amount. (This might be necessary if a minor rounding difference caused a small error in the total.)

**6** Click Enter. Money records the reinvested dividends.

# Recording Other Income and Other Expense Amounts

Money also lets you record other income and other expenses that are related to a mutual fund account. For example, if you have income that can't correctly be categorized as interest, dividends, or capital gains, you use the Other Income investment activity. If you have an investment expense such as an annual fee that you pay to maintain an account, use the Other Expense investment activity.

To record Other Income or Other Expense investment activity, follow these steps:

1 In the Account Register window, click New.

2 Enter the transaction date in the Date box.

3 Enter a name for the investment in the Investment combo box.

4 Choose either Other Income or Other Expense from the Activity drop-down list. Money adds text boxes to the input area so you can describe the investment.

 **What If I Pay an Account Maintenance Fee by Selling Shares?** *With mutual funds, sometimes you pay an account mainte- nance fee by selling shares and then using the sales proceeds as payment. To record this transaction with Money, you need to enter two transactions. The first records the sale of the shares and the second records the payment of the account maintenance fee. Even though you don't really ever move money into and out of one of your bank accounts, you need to record the transaction that way. The trick is to make sure that you use the same bank account for both transactions. That way, the transactions offset each other.*

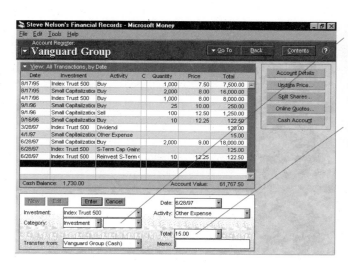

Categorize the income or expense amount. Do this the same way you record a category for a bank account transaction.

Enter the income or expense amount.

**5** Indicate into which account you'll deposit the income or from which account you'll pay the expense by using the Transfer To or Transfer From drop-down list box.

**6** Click Enter. Money records the income or expense amount.

## In Conclusion

Even if you're only an occasional investor who relies on mutual funds, investing can turn into a lot of work. You've got statements to read, records to keep, and decisions to make. Fortunately, Money helps you with the most tedious and time-consuming of these tasks: the record-keeping part. By using Money for your mutual fund record-keeping, you spend less time on this effort.

# Stocks and Bonds

**M**oney's record-keeping features work wonderfully well for **investments** you have in **stocks** and **bonds.** In fact, once you know how to set up an investment account and how to handle the simpler **mutual fund** investments, you'll find it very easy to track stocks and bonds.

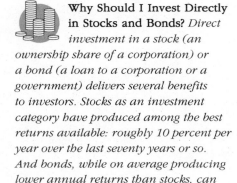

**Why Should I Invest Directly in Stocks and Bonds?** *Direct investment in a stock (an ownership share of a corporation) or a bond (a loan to a corporation or a government) delivers several benefits to investors. Stocks as an investment category have produced among the best returns available: roughly 10 percent per year over the last seventy years or so. And bonds, while on average producing lower annual returns than stocks, can produce consistent income year-in and year-out over the life of the bond. While you can invest in stocks and bonds indirectly by purchasing shares of a mutual fund, direct investment gives you more control over such things as which corporations you invest in or loan money to and when you realize **capital gains** and losses.*

## Recording Stock and Bond Purchases

Whenever you purchase more shares of a stock or additional bonds, you describe the purchase in the investment account's Account Register window. To do this, display the Account Manager window and then double-click the investment account. Money displays the investment account version of the Account Register window.

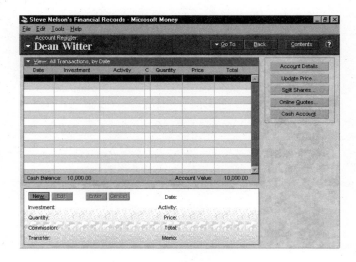

To describe the purchase of a stock or bond, follow these steps:

1 Click New.

2 Enter the purchase date in the Date text box.

3 Enter a name for the investment in the Investment box, and click Enter. Describe the type of investment you're making in the Create New Investment and New Stock or New Bond dialog boxes. If you have purchased shares of this stock or another bond in the same bond issue before, you can select the name of the stock or bond issue from the Investment drop-down list box.

4 Choose Buy from the Activity drop-down list and Money adds text boxes to the input area so you can describe the investment.

**What If I Haven't Yet Named the Investment?** *If you haven't purchased shares of this stock or another bond in the same bond issue before, enter the name of the stock or bond in the Investment combo box. Then, when Money displays the Create New Investment dialog box, mark the Type button that most closely describes the investment you're adding. Click Next. Money displays another dialog box that asks for additional information about the investment. Use the boxes and buttons to describe the stock or bond in more detail. Click Finish after you've described the investment. Money closes the dialog boxes, returns you to the Account Register window, and activates the Activity drop-down list box.*

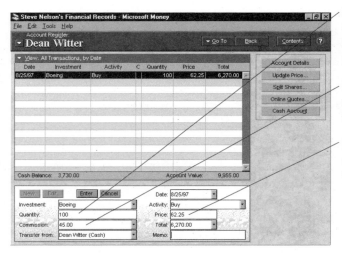

Indicate how many shares of stock or the number of individual bonds you're purchasing.

Record any sales commission you paid to purchase the stock or bond.

Enter the dollar price per share or the price per bond you're paying.

*If you intend to use Money's Online Quotes feature, you need to enter the security symbol for the stock or bond. (You can get this information from the local newspaper's stock page.) See Chapter 20 for information about Online Quotes.*

5 Verify the contents of the Total box. If necessary, edit the value in the total box so it correctly reflects the total purchase amount. (This might be necessary if a minor rounding difference caused a small error in the total.)

6 Identify the bank account or associated cash account you're using to pay for the shares or the bonds by selecting the account from the Transfer From drop-down list box. Money initially shows the associated cash account if you told it to create one. But you can select another account if you're using money from somewhere else.

7 Click Enter. Money records the stock or bond purchase.

## Recording Stock and Bond Sales

When you sell shares of a stock or individual bonds, you describe that transaction, too. To do this, display the account in an Account Register window as described in the preceding section of this chapter. Then, follow these steps:

1 Click New.

2 Enter the sale date in the Date text box.

3 Identify the name of the stock or bond you're selling by using the Investment combo box. You can type the name in the combo box or you can select it from the drop-down list box.

4 Choose Sell from the Activity drop-down list. Money adds text boxes to the input area so you can describe the investment.

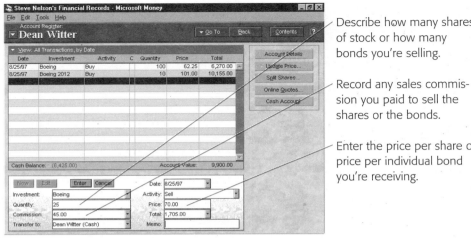

Describe how many shares of stock or how many bonds you're selling.

Record any sales commission you paid to sell the shares or the bonds.

Enter the price per share or price per individual bond you're receiving.

5 Verify the contents of the Total text box. If necessary, edit the value so it correctly reflects the total purchase amount.

6 Identify the bank account or associated cash account into which you'll deposit the sale proceeds by selecting the account from the Transfer To drop-down list box. Money initially shows the associated cash account, but you can select another account as the one into which you'll deposit the money from the sale.

7 Click Enter. Money records the stock or bond sale.

# Recording Dividends

Many stocks pay dividends, so you will probably have to record dividends periodically. To record dividends, follow these steps:

1 In the Account Register window, click New.

2 Enter the dividend date in the Date text box.

**How Money Handles Bond Prices.** *Money follows the standard convention of specifying bond prices as a percentage of the bond's **par value**. If the bond's par value is $1,000 and the dollar price is $950, for example, you specify the price as 95. You specify the par value, by the way, when you describe the bond investment—typically the first time you record a transaction for the bond. If you want to change the way Money handles bond prices, choose the Tools Options command, click the Investments tab, and unmark the Treat Bond Prices As A Percentage Of Par Value check box.*

**3** Identify the name of the stock distributing the dividend in the Investment combo box.

**4** Choose Dividend from the Activity drop-down list. Money adds text boxes to the input area so you can describe the dividend.

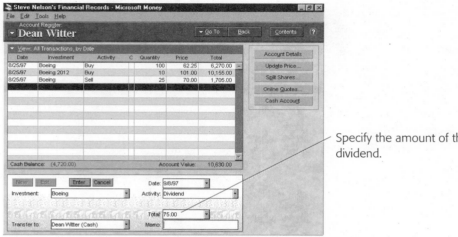

Specify the amount of the dividend.

**5** Identify the bank account or associated cash account in which you'll deposit the dividend by selecting the account from the Transfer To drop-down list box.

**6** Click Enter. Money records the dividend.

# Reinvesting Dividends

Some companies offer shareholders the opportunity to buy more shares with their dividends. These dividend reinvestment programs, often called DRIPs, let investors add to their holdings at a low cost because DRIPs typically don't require a brokerage commission.

**How Do I Calculate Annual Returns on My Investments?**

*Money provides two reports that calculate the annual return you earn on investments: the Performance by Investment Account and the Performance by Investment Type. To produce either report, use the Report And Chart Gallery window, which I describe in Chapter 4. A list of all the investment reports, including the two mentioned here, appear when you click the Investments button.*

To describe the reinvestment of dividends, follow these steps:

**1** Click New.

**2** Enter the reinvestment date in the Date text box.

**3** Enter a name for the investment in the Investment combo box.

**4** Choose Reinvest Dividend from the Activity drop-down list. Money adds text boxes to the input area so you can describe the dividends and the reinvestment.

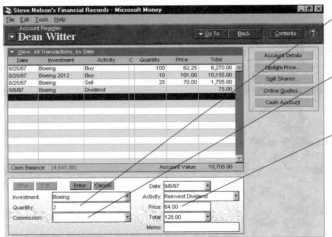

Describe how many new shares you're purchasing by reinvesting the dividend.

Record the sales commission you paid to purchase the investment.

Enter the price per share you're paying for the new shares.

**5** Verify the contents of the Total box. If necessary, edit the value in the total box so it correctly reflects the total purchase amount.

**6** Click Enter. Money records the reinvested dividends.

# Recording Stock Splits

Companies whose share prices are growing quickly sometimes *split* shares of their stock to reduce the price per share. For example, a company whose stock is selling at $100 per share might split its stock in two so that the shares sell for $50 each, not $100. If you, the investor, own a hundred of the old shares worth $100 each, or $10,000 in total, the company compensates you with additional shares so that you don't lose money. After the split, you would own two hundred shares worth $50 each or $10,000 in total. Stock splits don't really change the value of a company. They just make it easier for people to buy individual shares and even **lots** because the shares and the lots are less expensive.

To describe a stock split, display either the Investment Portfolio window or the investment account register. Then follow these steps:

**1** Click the Split Shares button. Money displays the Split Shares dialog box.

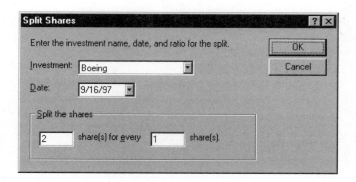

**2** Use the Investment combo box to identify the stock that's splitting.

**3** Enter the stock split date in the Date text box.

What Are Odd and Even Lots? *An even lot equals a hundred shares. The brokerage commission on even lots is less than the commission on odd lots, which are share sales or purchases of less than a hundred shares.*

**4** Use the Split The Shares text boxes to give the number of old shares and the number of new shares, or the old share to new share ratio. For example, if the stock split is a two-for-one split (meaning you get two new shares for each old share), enter 2 in the first Split The Shares text box and 1 in the second Split The Shares text box.

**5** Click OK. Money records the stock split.

# Recording Bond Interest

Bonds typically reward their holders by regularly paying interest. To record this interest income, you follow these steps:

**1** Click New.

**2** Enter the interest payment date in the Date text box.

**3** Identify the name of the bond paying the interest in the Investment combo box.

**4** Choose Interest from the Activity drop-down list. Money adds text boxes to the input area so you can describe the interest payment.

*Some bonds don't pay interest regularly, by the way. A zero-coupon bond, for example, doesn't pay interest over the course of the bond's life. Instead, it pays interest at the very end, when the bond is redeemed, or paid back. See Chapter 19 for information about how to treat zero-coupon bonds in Money.*

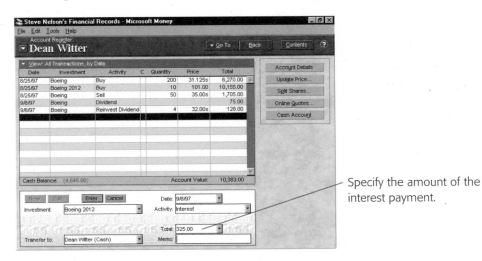

Specify the amount of the interest payment.

**5** Identify the bank account or associated cash account in which you'll deposit the interest payment by selecting the account from the Transfer To drop-down list box.

**6** Click Enter. Money records the interest.

**How Do I Look at All My Investments at Once?**
*Remember that the Investment Portfolio window, described in Chapter 15, gives you neat ways to view your investments. To display the Investment Portfolio window, click the Investment Portfolio button in the Money Contents window.*

# Recording Brokerage Account Fees and Miscellaneous Income

As I mentioned in Chapter 16 about mutual funds, Money lets you record "Other Income" and "Other Expense" investment activity, too. You use these two investment activities to record income and expense amounts that don't fit another category. For example, if income can't correctly be categorized as interest, dividends, or capital gains, use the Other Income investment activity. And for an investment expense such as an annual brokerage account fee that you pay, you use the Other Expense investment activity.

To record an Other Income or Other Expense investment activity, follow these steps:

**1** Click New.

**2** Enter the transaction date in the Date box.

**3** Enter a name for the investment in the Investment combo box if the income or expense amount is associated with a specific investment. (If the income or expense amount is related only to, say, the brokerage account in general, you leave the Investment combo box empty.)

**4** Choose either Other Income or Other Expense from the Activity drop-down list. Money adds text boxes to the input area so you can describe the investment.

**5** Use the Category boxes to categorize the income or expense amount. This works the same way as recording a category for a bank account transaction.

**6** Use the Total box to give the income or expense amount.

**7** Indicate into which account you'll deposit the income or from which account you'll pay the expense by using the Transfer From or Transfer To drop-down list boxes.

**8** Click Enter. Money records the income or expense amount.

# Working with Money's Associated Cash Accounts

When you set up an investment account, Money asks if the investment account has an associated cash account. This account stores the cash you use for additional investments and also the cash you receive when your investments produce profits or you sell an investment. If you tell Money that your investment account has an associated cash account, Money sets up this special cash account.

You work with an associated cash account the same way you work with any bank account. To display a list of transactions for the account, display the Money Contents window, click the Account Register command button, and then use the Account Register triangle menu to select the associated cash account.

*Money names the associated cash account by tacking the parenthetical phrase "(Cash)" on the end of the account name. For example, if the investment account is named "The Vanguard Group," the associated cash account is named "The Vanguard Group (Cash)."*

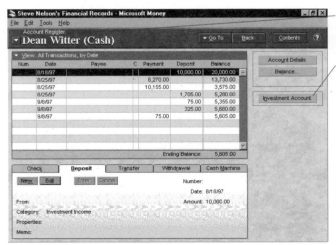

Click here to activate a triangle menu that lists all the accounts.

Click here to return to the investment account.

*Chapter 2 describes how to record checks, deposits, transfers, withdrawals, and automated teller machine (ATM) transactions for bank accounts. Chapter 5 describes how to reconcile a bank account. The same techniques and tricks described in Chapters 2 and 5 apply to associated cash accounts.*

To record checks, deposits, account transfers, withdrawals, and automated teller machine (ATM) transactions, you click one of the tabs at the bottom of the window, click New, and fill in the boxes that Money provides. To reconcile an associated cash account, you click the Balance button.

## In Conclusion

With the information covered in this chapter, you can handle most of your stock and bond record-keeping. If you have unanswered questions about how to handle a special investment or need to solve a problem you've encountered with an investment account, refer to Chapter 19.

# Real Estate

**M**any investors prize real estate because it is a hedge against **inflation** and because many types of real estate **investments** deliver solid cash returns. Real estate investments present unusual record-keeping challenges, however. Recording the income and expenses of passive real estate investments (such as limited partnership units or shares and real estate investment trusts or REITs) is more complicated than, say, recording the income and expenses that pertain to **stocks** or **bonds.** (Don't worry if you don't understand this lingo yet—I'll go into more detail in a minute.) Active real estate investments, such as rental income properties, require you to set up business bookkeeping systems. In spite of these challenges, however, Money provides real estate investors with a wonderful set of tools and possibilities.

### How Can I Get Started Investing in Real Estate?

*Probably the best way to start investing in real estate is to own your own home. On average, home ownership investment has delivered returns roughly equal to those from the stock market. Note, however, that it's difficult to make money on any real estate investment— including the purchase of a home— unless you hold the investment for a lengthy period of time. Typically, you need several years of appreciation just to pay for the selling costs.*

## Passive Real Estate Investments

Passive real estate investments include limited partnership units and shares in real estate investment trusts. At first glance, these investments resemble stocks, but they actually work quite differently because not all of the cash you receive comes in the form of interest or dividends. Typically, a substantial portion of the distributions from a passive real estate investment represents a return of capital. In spite of their complexity, however, you can use Money to keep accurate financial records of passive real estate investments.

**Why Might I Want to Invest in Real Estate?** *The allure of real estate investments often stems from financial leverage. Financial leverage simply means you borrow money to buy an investment. As long as your investment delivers an annual return in excess of the annual interest rate you're paying on the borrowed money, you come out ahead. For example, if you invest $10,000 in the stock market and earn a 10-percent return, your profit equals $1,000. In comparison, if you take your $10,000, borrow another $90,000 at 8 percent, and then invest the $100,000 total in a rental property that delivers a 10-percent return, your profit equals $2,800. (In effect, you earn 10 percent, or $1,000, on your $10,000, and you earn 2 percent, or $1,800, on the $90,000.) Financial leverage has its downside, however. Just as it magnifies your profits, it magnifies your losses. What's more, relatively small changes in the value of a real estate investment can wipe out the value of your investment. For example, if you put $10,000 down on a $100,000 rental property and the rental property later decreases in value by 10 percent, your investment may be worthless.*

# Recording Passive Real Estate Investment Purchases

Whenever you purchase partnership units or shares in a real estate investment trust, you need to describe the purchase in the investment account's Account Register window. To do this, display the Account Manager window and double-click the investment account. Money displays the investment account version of the Account Register window.

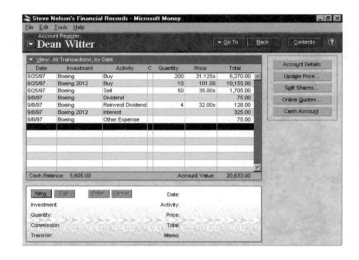

To describe the purchase of units or shares in a passive real estate investment, follow these steps:

**1** Click New.

**2** Enter the purchase date in the Date text box.

**3** Enter a name for the investment in the Investment combo box. If you have purchased units or shares of this real estate partnership or investment trust before, you can select the name from the Investment drop-down list box.

**What Are Passive and Active Real Estate Investments?** *In a passive real estate investment, you don't actively manage the investment. For example, you don't pick a property manager, collect rent, or arrange financing. If you purchased shares of a real estate investment trust (REIT) or invested in a real estate project as a limited partner, your investment is probably passive. With an active real estate investment, you actually manage or monitor the real estate investment yourself. For example, you might do the accounting, collect rents, and fix the leaky roof. If you purchased a rental house, your investment is probably an active one.*

*You need an investment account to track the passive real estate investments you make. Chapter 15 describes how to set up an investment account.*

*If you're describing a publicly traded real estate investment and you intend to use Money's Online Quotes feature, enter the security symbol. Refer to Chapter 20 for information about Online Quotes.*

**4** Choose Buy from the Activity drop-down list. Money adds text boxes to the input area so you can describe the investment.

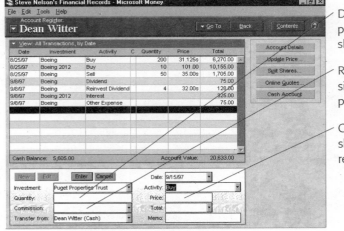

Describe how many partnership units or trust shares you're purchasing.

Record the sales commission, if any, you paid to purchase the investment.

Give the price per unit or share you're paying for the real estate investment.

**5** Verify the contents of the Total text box. If necessary, edit the value in the total box so it correctly reflects the total purchase amount.

**6** Identify the bank account you're using to purchase the investment or associated cash account by selecting the account from the Transfer From drop-down list box. Money initially shows the associated cash account, if you told it to create one. But you can select another cash account if you're using money from somewhere else.

**7** Click Enter. Money records the real estate investment purchase.

**What If I Haven't Yet Named the Investment?** *If you haven't purchased units or shares before, enter the investment name in the Investment combo box. When Money displays the Create New Investment dialog box, click the Type that most closely describes the new investment you're adding. You'll probably choose either Stock or Bond because these are the investment types that most closely match real estate investments. Click Next. Money displays another dialog box that asks for additional information about the investment. Use the boxes and buttons to describe the real estate investment in more detail. Click Finish once you've described the investment. Money closes the dialog boxes, returns you to the Account Register window, and activates the Activity drop-down list box.*

# Recording Real Estate Investment Sales

When you sell units or shares of a real estate investment, of course, you describe that transaction, too. To do this, display the account in an Account Register window as described in the preceding section of this chapter. Then follow these steps:

1 Click New.

2 Enter the sale date in the Date text box.

3 Identify the name of the real estate investment you're selling by using the Investment combo box. You can type the name in the combo box or select it from the Investment drop-down list box.

4 Choose Sell from the Activity drop-down list. Money adds text boxes to the input area so you can describe the investment.

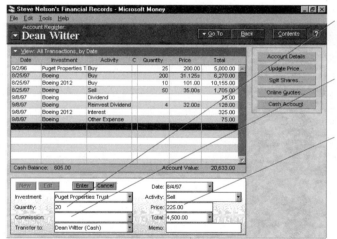

Describe how many partnership units or trust shares you're selling.

Record any sales commission you paid to sell the units or shares.

Give the price per share or per unit you're receiving.

*To describe a purchase, you need to enter at least three of the following four inputs: Quantity, Price, Commission, and Total. If you leave one of these inputs blank, Money uses the other three inputs to calculate the fourth.*

5 Verify the contents of the Total text box. If necessary, edit the value in the total box so it correctly reflects the total purchase amount.

6 Identify the bank account or associated cash account in which you'll deposit the sale proceeds by selecting the account from the Transfer To drop-down list box. Money initially shows the associated cash account, but you can select another account as the one in which you'll deposit the money from the sale.

7 Click Enter. Money records the real estate investment sale.

## Recording Real Estate Investment Distributions

At the end of the quarter or at the end of the year, you usually receive a real estate investment fund dividend distribution. To record this transaction, follow these steps:

1 Click New.

2 Enter the distribution date in the Date text box.

3 Identify the name of the real estate investment fund making the distribution in the Investment combo box.

4 Choose an appropriate Activity from the drop-down list: Interest for an **interest** distribution, Dividend for a dividend distribution, S-Term Cap Gains Dist for a short-term **capital gains** distribution, L-Term Cap Gains Dist for a long-term capital gains distribution, or Other Income. Money adds text boxes to the input area so you can describe the distribution.

**What Type of Distribution Is It?** *The quarterly or year-end distribution statement you receive identifies whether the distribution is an interest distribution, a dividend distribution, a short-term capital gains distribution, a long-term capital gains distribution, or some other distribution. You don't have to worry about making this determination.*

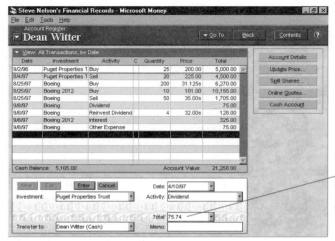

Specify the amount of the distribution.

**5** Identify the bank account or associated cash account in which you'll deposit the distribution by selecting the account from the Transfer To drop-down list box.

**6** Click Enter. Money records the distribution.

# Return of Capital Transactions

Sometimes a distribution isn't a share of the real estate investment's profits but a *return of capital*—a return of a portion of the price you originally paid. To record this type of transaction, called a return of capital transaction, follow these steps:

**1** Click New.

**2** Enter the return of capital date in the Date text box.

**3** Identify the name of the real estate investment returning capital in the Investment combo box.

**4** Choose Return of Capital from the Activity drop-down list. Money adds text boxes to the input area so you can describe the return of capital transaction.

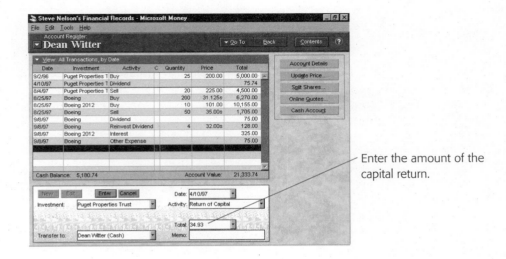

Enter the amount of the capital return.

**5** Identify the bank account or associated cash account in which you'll deposit the return of capital by selecting the account from the Transfer To drop-down list box.

**6** Click Enter. Money records the transaction.

# Active Real Estate Investments

If you're an active real estate investor—meaning you actively buy, manage, and sell real estate investments yourself—you can also use Money to simplify and expedite your record-keeping.

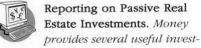

**Reporting on Passive Real Estate Investments.** *Money provides several useful investment reports, which you produce by using the Reports and Charts Gallery. These reports provide information about the market values, investment income and expenses, and annual returns of your passive real estate investments. Refer to Chapter 4 for information about how to print reports.*

In essence, you'll use Money in three ways:

➤ To track the adjusted cost basis of your properties

➤ To track the mortgages associated with any of your real estate properties

➤ To track the income and expenses that individual properties produce

## Setting Up Your Property Accounts

To track the adjusted cost basis of real estate investments, you set up asset accounts for each individual property you own.

To set up an asset account, follow these steps:

**How Do I Choose A Mortgage for an Investment Property?** *Chapter 7 describes how you can use Money's Mortgage Planner Wizard to choose a home mortgage and make refinancing decisions. You can also use the Mortgage Planner for choosing mortgages on an investment property and for making refinancing decisions about an investment property.*

1 With the Money Contents window displayed, click the Account Manager button. Money displays the Account Manager window.

2 Click the New Account button. This tells Money to start the New Account Wizard. Leave the Bank or Financial Institution box blank.

3 Click Next. When the Wizard asks what kind of account you want to set up, click Asset.

4 Click Next. When the Wizard asks what name you want to use for your asset account, enter it.

5 Click Next. When the Wizard asks for the account's opening balance, enter the original purchase price of the property.

6 Click Finish. If you need to set up additional accounts, repeat steps 2 through 5.

When you finish working with the Account Manager, return to the Money Contents window by clicking the Back button. Or, if you want to be more descriptive about the accounts you've set up, select an account, click the Account Details button, and use the dialog box that Money displays to enter more information about the account.

# Setting Up Your Property Classifications

If you own more than one piece of property, you'll also want to create classifications to track each property's income and expenses. To create property classifications, you need to complete two sets of steps: First you turn on the classification feature, and then you create a classification for each property you own.

To turn on the classification feature, follow these steps:

**1** Display the Money Contents window.

**2** Click the Payees and Categories command button. Money displays the Payees and Categories window.

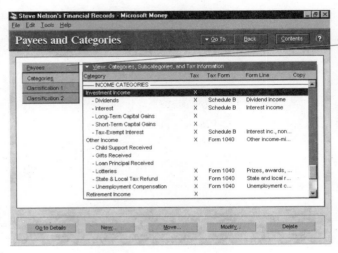

*You can also create and use subclassifications to track a particular property's income and expense in even greater detail. The process for creating a subclassification mirrors that for creating a classification.*

Use these buttons to select what you want to see in this window: income and expense categories, payees, or classifications.

**3** Click the Classification 1 button. Money displays the Add Classification dialog box.

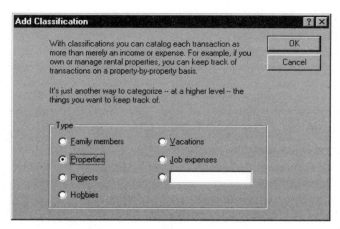

**4** Click the Properties option button, and then click OK. Money redisplays the Payees and Categories window, only this time it shows an empty property classifications list.

To create each of the classifications you need for your record-keeping, follow these steps:

**1** Display the Money Contents window.

**2** Click the Payees And Categories button.

**3** Click the Properties button.

**4** Click the New button. Money displays the New Properties or Sub-Properties dialog box.

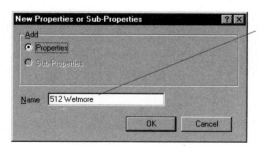

You may want to use a property's street address as its classification name.

**5** Enter the name of the real estate investment in the Name text box.

**6** Click OK.

**7** Repeat steps 3, 4, and 5 for each of your other real estate investments.

## Tracking the Adjusted Cost of a Property

Once you set up an asset account, you can use it to track improvements you make to the property (because improvements increase the property's adjusted cost) and your annual **depreciation** (because depreciation decreases the property's adjusted cost). The adjusted cost basis of a property is important. When you someday sell the property, you calculate the capital gain or loss by subtracting the adjusted cost from the net sales price.

To record capital improvements to a property, record a check in the usual way. When you get to the Category boxes, however, specify the transaction as a transfer to the property's asset account. Money updates the bank account for the check and adds a transaction to the property's asset register.

**Capital Improvement vs. Repairs and Maintenance.**
*When you spend money fixing up a real estate property in some way, you need to determine whether the expenditure is a capital improvement or a repairs and maintenance expense. You add capital improvement expenditures to the property's asset account, thereby increasing the adjusted cost. You use repairs and maintenance expenditures only to calculate the current year's profit or loss. Because you usually want to reduce your taxable income, it typically makes more sense to call an expenditure a repairs and maintenance expense than it does to call it a capital improvement. You can't make this determination willy-nilly, however. The IRS has very specific ideas about what does and what doesn't constitute a capital improvement. The general rule, however, is that if an expenditure adds to a property's useful life or its functionality, it's a capital improvement. For more information in this area of the tax law, consult a tax advisor.*

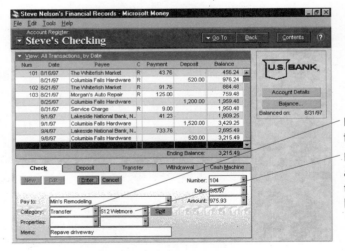

Enter Transfer in the first Category box.

Enter the property asset account name in the second Category box.

The next figure shows an account register for a real estate property, 512 Wetmore. Notice that the figure shows several capital improvements.

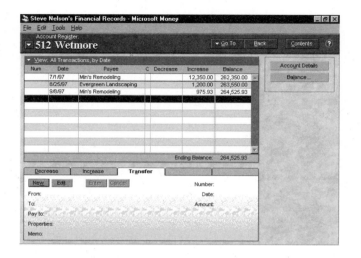

## Recording Depreciation on a Property's Asset Account

Depreciation is a little tricky, although record-keeping is not the tricky part. What is tricky is knowing how much depreciation to use in any given year's profit calculation. The tax laws treat different types of property differently when it comes to depreciation. What's more, how you depreciate a real estate property depends on the tax laws in effect in the year you placed the property into service. For these reasons, I'm not going to describe how you calculate depreciation here—only how you record depreciation you've already calculated.

Once you know how much depreciation you're supposed to charge in a year, however, it's easy to record the depreciation expense in the register. For example, suppose you have a $250,000 rental property and your tax advisor tells

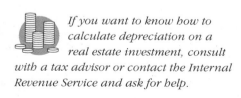

*If you want to know how to calculate depreciation on a real estate investment, consult with a tax advisor or contact the Internal Revenue Service and ask for help.*

you that you can depreciate it by $10,000 every year. In this case, you record $10,000 of depreciation expense for each year directly in the property's account register.

*You can enter each year's depreciation expense in the assets account register. By using transaction dates that correspond to the correct year, the depreciation expense gets counted correctly.*

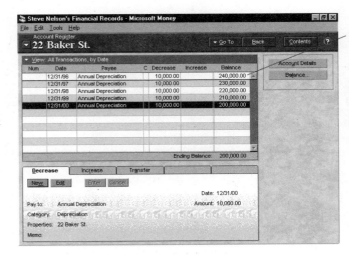

The account balance column shows the property's adjusted basis—its original cost less depreciation charged to date—for each of the years you hold the property.

1 Click the Decrease tab.

2 Enter the date for the asset depreciation transaction. If you're entering a series of annual depreciation transactions, use a different year for each so that each depreciation transaction gets counted in a different year's profit or loss calculation.

3 Optionally, enter a description of the asset depreciation in the Pay To text box. You might enter "Annual Depreciation on Carlton Heights," for example.

4 Enter the amount of the annual depreciation charge.

**5** Enter a new category, Depreciation, in the Category box. Money displays a dialog box that asks you to name and describe the category. Complete the dialog box and press Enter.

**6** Classify the real estate investments in the first Properties text box.

**7** Click Enter. Money records the depreciation and recalculates the asset's account balance.

## Tracking a Property's Mortgage

You track the mortgage associated with a real estate investment property in the same way you track the mortgage on a home. In Chapter 7, I describe in detail how to set up Loan accounts and how to use Money's powerful Loan Calculator and Mortgage Planner to analyze different loans. Refer back to that chapter if you have questions about how to track a mortgage.

*Refer to Chapter 21 for information about how to use the Internet to get real-estate investment advice, news, and information.*

## Keeping Records of a Property's Income and Expenses

To keep records of a property's income and expenses, you do two very simple things. You first create a list of categories specifically for tracking your real estate investments. Next, you use these real estate income and expense categories to record transactions related to your real estate investments. Neither of these tasks is difficult, but because it's important to start off right, let me talk about these two tasks in a bit more detail.

### Building a Real Estate Investment Categories List

While you can use any list of income or expense categories that you want, the following list shows the income and expense categories that you may want to use as a starting point. You need to use the income and expense categories shown here when you report your real estate profits or losses to the federal government:

*The categories in this list are based on the federal income tax form, Schedule E, which you use to report real estate profits and losses.*

**Income Categories**

Rents received

**Expense Categories**

Advertising

Auto and travel

Cleaning and maintenance

Commissions

Insurance

Legal and other professional fees

Management fees

Mortgage interest paid to banks

Other interest

Repairs

Supplies

Taxes

Utilities

Other

To add real estate income and expense categories to your categories list, display the Money Contents window and then follow these steps:

**1** Click the Payees And Categories button. Money displays the Payees And Categories window.

**2** Click the Categories button.

**3** Click the New button. Money displays the New Category Or Subcategory dialog box.

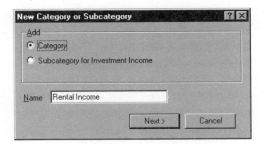

**4** Click the Category button.

**5** Enter a name for the new real estate category in the Name text box.

**6** Click Next. Money displays the second page of the New Category Or Subcategory dialog box. This one asks if the new category is an income or expense category.

**7** Indicate whether the new category is an income or an expense category by clicking the appropriate button.

**8** Click Next. Money displays the third page of the New Category Or Subcategory dialog box. This one asks if the next category is a tax-related category.

**9** Answer the question about the tax-related category by clicking Yes.

**10** Click Finish.

**11** Repeat steps 4 through 10 to add each of the income and expense categories you need.

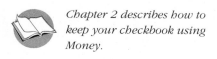

*Chapter 2 describes how to keep your checkbook using Money.*

## Recording Real Estate Income and Expense Transactions

Once you've created a list of income and expense categories, keep your checkbook as usual—except when you record an income or expense related to a real estate property, use the appropriate real estate income or expense category and describe the real estate investment by using the Properties boxes, as shown on the next page.

## Recording Real Estate Income and Expense Transactions

**1** Click the Checks tab to record an expense. Click the Deposit tab to record income.

**2** Enter the check number.

**3** Enter the check date.

**4** Enter the name of the person or business you're paying.

**5** Enter the amount of the check.

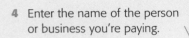

**6** Activate the Category drop-down list box and choose a real estate expense category that describes how the money is being spent or a real estate income category that describes where the money is coming from.

**7** Activate the Properties drop-down list and select the real estate property's classification.

**8** Click Enter. Money records the check or deposit and recalculates the account balance.

# Reporting on Your Active Real Estate Investments

Once you collect income and expense data for active real estate investments by using the techniques described in the preceding section, it is easy to get a report that summarizes income and expense data by property. To produce such a report, follow these steps:

**1** Display the Money Contents window.

**2** Click the Report And Chart Gallery button. Money displays the Report And Chart Gallery.

**3** Click the Spending Habits button.

**4** Double-click the Income Vs. Spending report. Money produces the report.

**5** Click the Customize button. Money displays the Customize Report dialog box.

**6** Activate the Columns drop-down list box and select the Properties entry.

**7** Click View. Money updates the Income Vs. Spending report, only this time it uses different columns to show income and spending by real estate investment.

**Where Do I Get Schedule E Data?** *To report on the profits and losses of active real estate investments, you use the Schedule E form. You can use an Income Vs. Spending report to get most of the data you need to complete this form.*

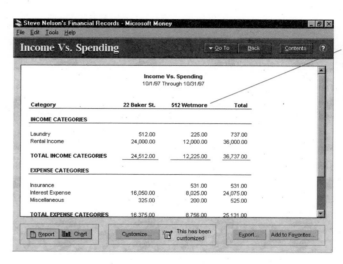

Each property's income and expense information appears in a separate column.

## In Conclusion

Real estate investments have made many people rich. But for real estate investments to produce good, solid profits, you need to monitor their income and expenses carefully. Fortunately, Money provides a powerful set of tools for this very purpose. And they really aren't difficult to use!

# 19

# Special Investments and Common Problems

In the previous three chapters, I describe the record-keeping techniques that people use for the most common **investments.** Unfortunately, you may encounter record-keeping complexities if you've chosen to put your money into specialized investments. In this chapter, I describe how you can handle specialized investments and how to solve common problems with investment record-keeping.

*In this chapter I assume you have set up an investment account and that you know how to perform basic investment record-keeping. If you don't have this knowledge, see Chapters 15 and 16.*

## Stock Dividends

A *stock dividend* is a dividend that's paid in **stock.** As a practical matter, however, a stock dividend works exactly like a stock split. For example, if a stock pays a dividend equal to one-twentieth of a share, you get 21 new shares for every 20 old ones. Another way of saying this is that the stock has a 21:20 split.

To record a stock dividend, treat it like a stock split. I describe how to do this in "Recording Stock Splits" in Chapter 17.

## Liquidating Dividends

Sometimes a dividend isn't a share of the corporate profit, which is usually the case, but a return of capital. A *return of capital* is a return of a portion of the price you originally paid. To record this sort of transaction, follow the steps on the next page.

## Recording a Liquidating Dividend

**1** In the Account Register window, click New.

**2** Enter the return of capital date in the Date text box.

**3** Identify the name of the stock or bond returning capital in the Investment combo box.

**4** Choose Return Of Capital from the Activity drop-down list.

**5** Enter the return of capital amount in the Total text box.

**6** Identify the bank account or associated cash account in which you'll deposit the return of capital by selecting the account from the Transfer To drop-down list box.

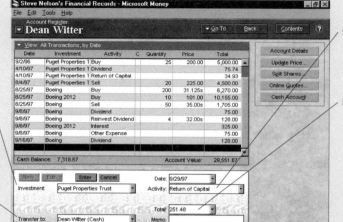

**7** Click Enter. Money records the transaction.

**How Will I Know a Dividend Is a Return of Capital?** *The statement you receive with the payment will identify the dividend as a return of capital.*

# Handling Short Sales

A *short sale* occurs when you sell stock before you purchase it—instead of the other way around. This sounds complicated, but here's how it works. You think that stock in the XYZ Corporation is going to drop from its current price of $50 a share, so you borrow shares from your broker and sell them for $50. If the stock does drop, to say $40 a share, you buy shares and replace the shares you borrowed. In effect, you bought shares for $40 and sold them for $50, so you made $10 per share in profit.

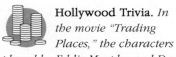

**Hollywood Trivia.** *In the movie "Trading Places," the characters played by Eddie Murphy and Dan Ackroyd made a fortune by selling short, or "shorting." In the movie, however, the protagonists weren't shorting stock. They were shorting an agricultural commodity, concentrated orange juice.*

**How Can Options Reduce My Investment Risks?** *As long as you write call options on stocks you want to own and put options on stocks you already own, you actually reduce your investment risks. For example, suppose you own shares of ABC Corporation that are worth $10 a share. If the stock goes down in value, you still get the $1 per share option price—and that subsidizes a portion of your investment loss. And if the option is exercised— say because the stock goes up in value dramatically, you in effect sold $10 stock for $11. (If the stock stays about where it is and the option expires without being exercised, you're still $1 ahead.)*

Money doesn't provide a way to handle short sales. If it's any consolation, the rumor mill says that Microsoft will add this feature to the next release of the product.

## Buying on Margin

Your broker, as you may know, will happily lend you money to purchase more stocks and **bonds.** This practice is called "buying on margin." Money lets you record margin purchases quite easily. If you purchase stocks or bonds and your purchase requires more money than you have in your associated cash account, Money shows the associated cash account's balance as a negative number.

To record *margin interest*—the interest costs that your broker charges you on the borrowed money—you record an Other Expense transaction. When you record this transaction, make sure that you categorize your margin interest by using an investment interest expense category. Your investment interest expense may be tax deductible.

## Derivatives

*Derivatives* are investments that get their value from other investments. The most common types of derivatives are call and put options. A *call* is an option to buy a share of stock. A *put* is an option to sell a share of stock. While these investments have received a lot of publicity—much of it bad—they have an important place in many people's investing, particularly as a way to hedge against price fluctuations in the stocks investors already own.

*Chapter 17 describes how to record stock and bond purchases and sales as well as Other Income transactions. Refer there for more information.*

## Selling Puts and Calls

Fortunately, the record-keeping for call and put options is straightforward. If you sell a put or call and the option is exercised, you record the option as a regular buy or sell transaction. If you sell a put or call and the option isn't exercised (in other words, if it expires without being used), you record the option as "Other Income."

## Buying Puts and Calls

If you invest in puts and calls (in other words, if you purchase them), the record-keeping works differently: You record the option as a new investment purchase. If the option expires without being exercised, you record the expiration as a sale with the sales price equal to zero. Of course, you don't actually sell the option for nothing. It simply becomes worthless upon expiration. But you need a way to show that the option value now equals zero, and a sale is the easiest and most accurate way to do so.

If you sell the option before it expires because it has value, you record the sale in the same way that you record the sale of any investment.

## Exercising Puts and Calls

While individual investors don't usually exercise puts and calls, it's still possible to do so. To deal with this situation, you record two separate transactions.

To record the exercise of a put option (an option to sell a stock), you first record the sale of the option with the sales price equal to zero. (This works the same way as recording an option's expiration.) Then you record a regular sale transaction for the stock with the sales price equal to the option price.

If you're recording the exercise of a call option (an option to purchase a stock), you first record the sale of the option with the sales price equal to zero. (Again, this works the same way as recording an option's expiration.) Then you record a regular purchase transaction with the purchase price equal to the option price.

**Exercising Your Options.** *For purposes of calculating the capital gain or loss on stock acquired by exercising a call option, the call option price must be included as part of the stock purchase price. For purposes of calculating the capital gain or loss on stock you sell when the option holder exercises a put option, the put option price must be included as part of the stock sales price.*

# Employee Stock Options

If you've been granted employee stock options in a publicly traded company, you can track the value of those options in an investment account. To do this, set up an investment called something like "XYZ Corporation Options." Then, enter the share price as the difference between the option exercise price and the market price. For example, if the price to exercise an option is $50 per share and the market price is $70 a share, your option value per share equals $20.

*As a practical matter, it makes most sense to track the value of only the options that you can exercise—in other words, options in which your right to exercise has vested.*

If you have more than one option grant, your record-keeping may be easier if you include the option exercise price as part of the investment name. For example, if you have two grants of options from XYZ Corporation, one at $50 a share and one at $65 a share, you would set up two investments: "XYZ Option $50/share" and "XYZ Option $65/share."

If the option exercise price exceeds the market price, the option value is zero. But don't remove the option from the investment account until it's expired. Share prices, as you know, bounce up and down. An option that is worth nothing today may be worth quite a lot next month or next year.

# Accrued Interest on Bonds

Unless you buy or sell a bond on the interest payment day, some of what you pay when you buy the bond and some of what you receive when you sell it represents accrued interest. Accrued interest is simply the interest the bond has earned since the last interest payment date. Unfortunately, accrued interest increases both the work and the complexity of bond record-keeping.

## Accrued Interest on Bonds You Purchase

*Chapter 17 describes how to record the purchase of bonds. An earlier section in this chapter, "Liquidating Dividends," describes how to handle return of capital transactions.*

To record the purchase of a bond with accrued interest, you record two transactions. For example, let's say you just purchased, for $1,020, a $1,000 bond with $20 of accrued interest. First, record the purchase of the actual bond without the accrued interest: $1,000. Then, record a return of capital transaction with a negative return of capital amount equal to the accrued interest (in this case, –$20). At this point, Money shows your bond's value as equal to $1,020.

When you get your next interest payment—let's say it's $60—you record two transactions: a return of capital transaction equal to $20 and an interest income transaction equal to $40. In this way, you don't count as income the $20 of accrued interest you actually paid when you purchased the bond. And you record as interest income only the $40 you actually earned.

## Accrued Interest on Bonds You Own

*Chapter 17 describes how to record bond interest income. An earlier section in this chapter, "Liquidating Dividends," describes how to handle return of capital transactions.*

Some bonds accrue interest but don't pay the interest. (The bond issuer typically reports this accrued but unpaid interest on form 1099-OID at the end of the year.) You need to record the interest income, however, because it's taxable. To do this, you record two transactions. First, you record the accrued bond interest as regular interest income. When you record this transaction, transfer the bond interest income to your associated cash account—even though there really won't be a deposit because the interest will only accrue. Then, record a negative return of capital transaction equal to the accrued interest. When you record this second transaction, transfer the bond interest income from your associated cash account. In this way, Money records the interest income and adjusts the bond value for the accrued interest.

## Bond Premiums

If you pay more for a bond than the redemption price, the extra amount you pay is called a **premium.** You might ask, why would you and other investors pay more for a bond than the borrower will pay to redeem it? Because the borrower agrees to pay a higher rate of interest than the current rate. For example, imagine that a borrower issues $1,000 bonds that pay 6.6-percent interest, or $66. Subsequent to the issue of the bonds, investors like you decide that 6 percent is the going bond interest rate; a bond that pays $66 is therefore worth more than $1,000 because $66 is 6 percent of $1,100, not $1,000.

**What Is the "Effective Interest Rate"?** *The effective interest rate is simply the total yield, from purchase to maturity—a figure you'll learn when you purchase the bond. The effective interest rate is also called the "yield to maturity."*

**What the IRS Says about Bond Premiums.** *The IRS doesn't require you to amortize bond premiums. You can simply charge the bond premium as an expense in the year you sell the bond. This approach simplifies your record-keeping, but it also costs more money. In the meantime, you pay income taxes on the premium. Eventually, because you are entitled to deduct the bond premium as an expense in the year that you sell, you'll get back your overpayment—but that might be ten or twenty years away. People typically want to accelerate their income tax deductions, not delay them.*

Bond premiums present an accounting problem. In effect, the $100 is an expense, or loss. Why? Although you might pay $1,100 for the bond described in the preceding paragraph, you only receive $1,000 when you redeem it.

For record-keeping purposes, you should spread the expense of the $100 bond premium over the years until the borrower redeems the bond. This is called **amortization.** To amortize the bond premium, multiply the effective interest rate the bond earns by its purchase price, and then subtract this amount from the actual interest the bond pays during the year. The difference is the bond premium expense that you will record the first year.

In the years that follow, you make only one minor modification in this bond-premium allocation formula. Instead of multiplying the effective interest rate the bond earns by the bond purchase price, you multiply the effective interest rate by the bond purchase price minus the bond premium amounts that you've already allocated.

Suppose, for example, that you purchase a $1,050 bond that pays an effective interest rate, or yield to maturity, of 6 percent. Further suppose that the bond pays $66 in interest annually. Given these facts, the bond premium charged as expense the first year would be calculated like this:

$66 – (6% × $1,050) = $3

During the second year, the bond premium that is charged as an expense would be calculated as follows:

$66 – [6% × ($1,050 – $3)] = $3.18

During the third year, the bond premium charged as an expense would be calculated like so:

$66 – [6% × ($1,050 – $3 – $3.18)] = $3.56

*Chapter 17 describes how to record investment expenses using the Other Expense activity.*

To record the allocations of bond premiums as expenses, you record two transactions as shown below:

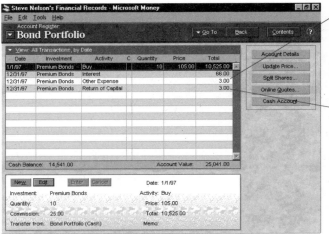

Record the bond premium allocation as an Other Expense for the bond, and specify the Transfer From account as the associated cash account.

Record a return of capital transaction equal to the bond premium allocation, and specify the Transfer To account as the associated cash account.

## Handling Bond Discounts

Bond discounts arise when buyers pay less for a bond than its redemption price. The difference between the purchase price and the redemption price is called the **discount.** Whereas a premium indicates that the borrower is paying more than investors require, a discount indicates that the borrower is paying less than investors require.

Accounting for bond discounts works much like accounting for bond premiums. Suppose, for example, that a borrower issues a $1,000 bond that pays 6 percent interest, or $60, and that subsequent to the issue, investors decide that 6.66 percent should be the going rate. In this case, a bond that pays $60 is worth less than $1,000, because $60 is 6.66 percent of $900, not $1,000.

The $100 difference is income because, although you might pay $900 for the bond described in the preceding paragraph, you'll receive $1,000 when you

**What the IRS Says about Bond Discounts.** *You are required to allocate bond discounts as income unless the effect of doing so is very, very small. Currently, for example, the basic rule is that if the difference between the effective interest rate and the stated interest rate is less than 0.25 percent, or one-quarter of one percent, you don't have to allocate the difference. The stated interest rate is shown on the face of the bond. The 0.25-percent rule may be out of date by the time you read this, however, so you may want to consult a tax advisor for up-to-date information.*

redeem it. You should treat the $100 bond discount you receive as income and spread it over the years between the purchase and the redemption.

To make this discount allocation, you multiply the effective interest rate the bond earns by the bond purchase price and then subtract from this figure the actual interest the bond paid for the year. The difference is the bond discount income you record for the year. The effective interest rate is simply the yield to maturity—a figure you'll obtain when you purchase the bond.

In following years, you modify this bond-discount allocation formula by multiplying the effective interest rate by the bond purchase price plus the bond discount amounts already allocated.

Here's an example of how to deal with a bond discount. Suppose that you purchase a $950 bond that pays an effective interest rate of 6.5 percent. This bond annually pays $60 in interest. Given these facts, the bond discount allocated as income the first year would be calculated like so:

(6.5% × $950) – $60 = $1.75

During the second year, the bond discount allocated as income would be calculated as:

[6.5% × ($950 + $1.75)] – $60 = $1.86

During the third year, the bond discount allocated as income would be calculated like this:

[6.5% × ($950 + $1.75 + $1.86)] – $60 = $1.98

To record the allocations of bond discounts as income, you treat the bond discount as accrued interest—which, in fact, is what it is. To do this, you first record the accrued bond interest (the bond discount allocation) as regular interest income. When you record this transaction, transfer the bond interest income to your associated cash account, even though there really won't be a deposit. (The interest will only accrue.) Then, record a negative return of capital transaction equal to the accrued interest. When you record this second transaction, transfer the bond interest income out of your associated cash account. In this way, Money records the interest income and adjusts the bond value for the accrued interest.

## Certificates of Deposit

How you keep records of certificates of deposit (CDs) depends on how you invest in them. If you buy CDs and hold them until maturity, you can treat them like regular bank accounts. (In this case, however, they won't show up in your Investment Portfolio or in any of Money's investment reports.)

If you buy and sell negotiable CDs, you can treat them just like bonds. In this case, the CDs show up in your Investment Portfolio as well as in Money's investment reports.

## Zero-Coupon Bonds

Some bonds, including U.S. Savings bonds, don't pay interest until the bond matures. Over the years that you hold these bonds, they only accrue interest. To keep a good record of these bonds, record the accrued interest annually. You do this as described in "Accrued Interest on Bonds You Own" earlier in this chapter.

## Precious Metals and Commodities

You can treat commodities like you do shares of stock. In other words, you can describe the investment by weight per unit (such as by ounces or bushels or gallons) and then record a price per unit. You can treat commodities futures like stock market put and call options, since they are really options to buy and sell.

## In Conclusion

As this chapter shows, if you get fancy in your investing, you dramatically increase the time it takes to manage your portfolio. When you think about your investments, therefore, you need to focus not only on risks and opportunities for profit but also on the amount of work, including the record-keeping, that they require.

Let me say one final thing before this chapter closes. As a general rule, you don't suffer in your investing by picking simpler investments. I suggest keeping it as simple as you can.

# Online Quotes

**W**ith Microsoft Money's Online Quotes service, you can download the latest prices of a **stock** or major **mutual fund** and, in so doing, automatically update your investment **portfolio.** The service costs $2.95 per month for six sessions. Additional downloads cost $.50 each.

If you track a lot of stocks (or are interested in tracking a lot of stocks), you can do it quickly with the Online Quotes service. Stock prices are updated every fifteen minutes. If the previous day's closing prices aren't good enough for you, the Online Quotes service represents a big advantage over tracking stock prices with the newspaper.

## How It Works

Like all of Money's online services, there's nothing mysterious or magical about the Online Quotes service. When you enter an investment in Money—whether you own it or not—the Online Quotes service can tell automatically that you're tracking it and download its latest price. But there's one important detail: You must enter the official, market-approved symbol for the investment in the Investment Details area. Otherwise, Money has no way of knowing what to update. The service tracks all stocks that trade on the NYSE, AMEX, and NASDAQ indexes, as well as most major mutual funds.

This service isn't for everyone. If you own just a couple of stocks and check their prices once every few weeks or so, you probably don't need it. You can update the prices manually from the local newspaper. On the other hand, if you track a lot of investments and you'd like to update them every week or so, the Online Quotes service can be a great time-saver.

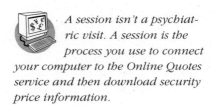

*A session isn't a psychiatric visit. A session is the process you use to connect your computer to the Online Quotes service and then download security price information.*

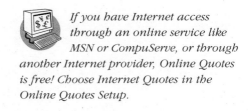

*If you have Internet access through an online service like MSN or CompuServe, or through another Internet provider, Online Quotes is free! Choose Internet Quotes in the Online Quotes Setup.*

## Setting Up Your Account
## to Use the Service

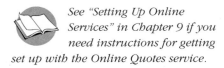

*See "Setting Up Online Services" in Chapter 9 if you need instructions for getting set up with the Online Quotes service.*

The first thing you need to do is set up Money to use the Online Quotes service. If you're already set up with the Online Bill Payment or Online Banking service, getting set up for Online Quotes should be very simple. Go to the Investment Portfolio and click the Online Quotes Setup button. From here, things are pretty self-explanatory. Read all the text in each dialog box and click the Next button when you're ready to move on.

## Entering Market Symbols
## for Stocks and Mutual Funds

Before you can start getting quotes electronically, you need to identify each stock or mutual fund you want to track and enter the market-approved symbol for each. If you don't know the official, market-approved symbol for a stock or mutual fund, call your stockbroker or check your local paper and see if it is listed there. In stock tables, it's often listed under the heading "Ticker."

If you want to check the market symbols you've already added or to enter new market symbols, follow these steps:

1 With the Money Contents window displayed, click the Investment Portfolio button.

2 Click the investment and then click the Details button.

3 Type the symbol in—you guessed it—the Symbol field.

Once you've displayed the Investment Details window, it's easy to switch between different investments. To do so, click the triangle menu next to the investment name.

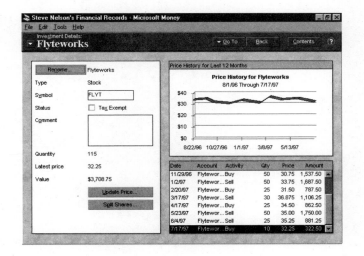

**How Do I Change the Portfolio Window's View?**

*You can use the Investment Portfolio window's View triangle menu to choose what you want the window to display: your entire portfolio, individual investments, or only a specified investment account. To display all the investments you're tracking (even those you don't actually own), click to display the View triangle menu and then choose Investments.*

# Electronically Downloading Market Prices

Once you've set up the Online Quotes service, identified all the investments, and entered the market symbol for each stock or mutual fund you want to track, you're ready to download prices. Follow these steps:

1 With the Money Contents window displayed, click the Investment Portfolio button. Money displays the Investment Portfolio window.

**2** Click the Online Quotes button. Money displays the Online Services dialog box. In the Online Services dialog box, all the investments for which you've entered market-approved symbols are listed. There should also be a check mark in the box next to each investment. If for some reason you don't want to update one of the investments listed here, click it to remove the check mark.

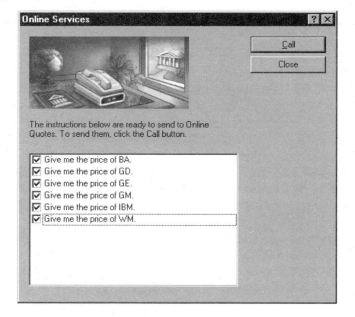

**A Slight Delay.** *The price information that Online Quotes retrieves is out-of-date by as much as fifteen minutes.*

**3** When you're ready, click the Call button. Money displays the Call Online Services dialog box. If this is the first time you've connected to the online services, Money also displays the Change PIN dialog box on top of the Call Online Services dialog box. It asks you to enter and change your Personal Identification Number (PIN). Once you enter this information, click OK to close the Change PIN dialog box.

**4** Optionally, click the Dialing Properties button to customize how Windows 95 handles your calls.

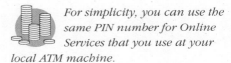

*For simplicity, you can use the same PIN number for Online Services that you use at your local ATM machine.*

*Call your local phone company to find out which code you need to disable call waiting.*

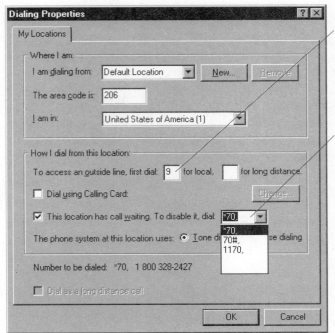

If you have to dial a special number in order to access an outside line (which you might have to do if you're dialing from an office), enter the number or numbers here.

If you have call waiting, you should check the box and then choose a disable code from the drop-down list. If you don't do this, your connection could be disrupted if someone calls while you're connected to the online services. Click OK.

**5** Now you're ready to receive the transactions. Click the Connect button.

**6** When Money displays the Call Summary dialog box, you can see the updated price of all your investments.

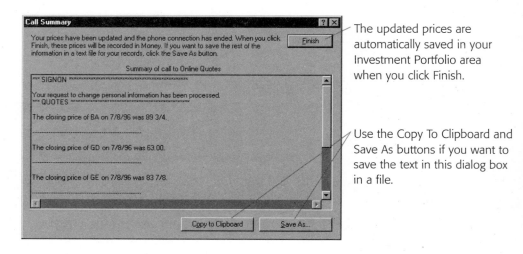

The updated prices are automatically saved in your Investment Portfolio area when you click Finish.

Use the Copy To Clipboard and Save As buttons if you want to save the text in this dialog box in a file.

**7** When you're ready, click the Finish button. The prices in your Investment Portfolio are automatically updated.

## In Conclusion

One of the neat things about the Online Quotes service is being able to tell instantly what your portfolio is worth. After you click the Finish button, all you have to do is look at the Total Portfolio Value figure at the bottom of your list of investments. But be careful. This can be addictive to the point of wanting to update your prices every day (or every hour) to see how the paper value of your portfolio is changing.

# Researching Investments Online

**T**he other chapters in this book talk about how to use Money for personal financial or business management tasks. This chapter takes a different course. It talks in general terms about ways to use your computer for online investment research. You don't need Money to do this. You do need your computer, a modem, and access to either the Internet or an online service.

*Because the Internet and the popular online services change rapidly, this chapter doesn't provide step-by-step descriptions of how to accomplish specific tasks. Rather, it describes how to find investing and personal financial information on the Internet. It also discusses the investment research tasks you can do with the online services.*

## On the Internet

The Internet is the richest source of investment and other personal financial information. Unfortunately, it's also the most disorganized. There isn't a single place to go to get all the information you want. You can get investment information from newsgroups, from mailing list messages, and on World Wide Web sites.

I'm not going to describe how to use all these features here. Doing so would require me to write an entire book. In fact, I have written an entire book on the Internet, *Field Guide to the Internet* (Microsoft Press, 1995). For purposes of this discussion, therefore, I assume you already have access to the Internet and that you know how to work with newsgroups, mailing lists, and World Wide Web sites. In this section, I'll tell you specifically where to locate investing and personal finance information.

## A Review of Available Newsgroups

An Internet *newsgroup* is really just an electronic bulletin board. Some people post messages on the bulletin board, and other people read them. A handful of newsgroups post messages on personal financial topics. As long as you have a newsgroup reader and access to the Internet, or subscribe to an online service that provides access to newsgroups, you can read the posted messages and even post your own.

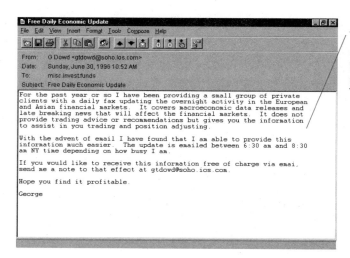

This is an article posted to the misc.invest.funds newsgroup. Notice that the article is really just a long e-mail message.

At the time I am writing this chapter, the following newsgroups are available and active enough to warrant at least a quick review:

| Newsgroup name | What it covers |
| --- | --- |
| misc.invest | All types of investment discussion |
| misc.invest.canada | Investments in Canada or of special interest to Canadians |
| misc.invest.funds | Mutual fund investing |
| misc.invest.real-estate | Real estate investing |
| misc.invest.stocks | Common stock investments |
| misc.invest.technical | Technical analysis (charting) of securities |

## A Review of Available Mailing Lists

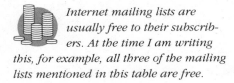

*Internet mailing lists are usually free to their subscribers. At the time I am writing this, for example, all three of the mailing lists mentioned in this table are free.*

Internet *mailing lists* are simply lists of electronic mail addresses. When someone mails a message to the mailing list, everyone whose name is on the list gets the message. This might seem like much ado about nothing, but because mailing lists cater to the interests of their members, mailing lists are powerful communication tools. Several Internet mailing lists provide useful investment information:

| Mailing list name | What it covers and how to subscribe |
|---|---|
| Investment-Talk | Discusses financial markets with emphasis on stock, bond, and fund markets. Send an e-mail message to *majordomo@mission-a.com*. Enter your message text as *subscribe investment-talk your e-mail address*, where *your e-mail address* is just that. To subscribe to Investment-Talk, I would enter the message text as follows: *subscribe investment-talk steven@cyberspace.com*. |
| persfin-digest | Answers general personal finance questions. Send an e-mail message to *majordomo@shore.net*. Enter your message text as follows: *subscribe persfin-digest*. |
| TNMA (The New Media Analyst) | Monitors publications for articles of interest to investors in high-tech stock and companies. Send an e-mail message to *tnma@idirect.com*. On the subject line of your message enter *SUBSCRIBE TNMA*. |

## Reviewing World Wide Web Sites

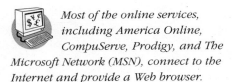

*Most of the online services, including America Online, CompuServe, Prodigy, and The Microsoft Network (MSN), connect to the Internet and provide a Web browser.*

The *World Wide Web* is a collection of multimedia documents connected by hypertext links. To view a Web site, you need an Internet connection and a Web browser. You jump from one document, or Web page, to another by clicking on hypertext links.

The Internet provides hundreds of popular World Wide Web sites related to personal finance and investing, but the two sites that I recommend that you view first are those of the Global Network Navigator and the *Wall Street Journal:*

*http://www.gnn.com/*
*http://update.wsj.com/*

To view a Web page, you provide the Web page's uniform resource locator (often referred to as a URL)—those things I italicized above this paragraph.

Here's where you specify the uniform resource locator, or URL.

You have to subscribe to the *Wall Street Journal*'s Money & Investing Web page. However, Dow Jones does offer a trial subscription to the service for free.

Let me quickly mention one other really useful Web site. The *http://www.yahoo.com/* Web site is an index of other Web pages. You can use this site to build a list of investment-related Web pages by entering the word "investing" in the Search text box.

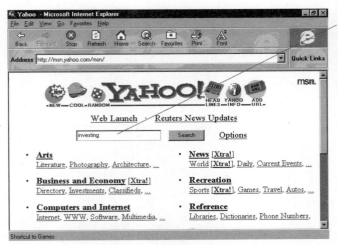

Enter the search word *investing* here. Then click Search. The Yahoo Web site then builds a list of Web pages that cover investing in some way.

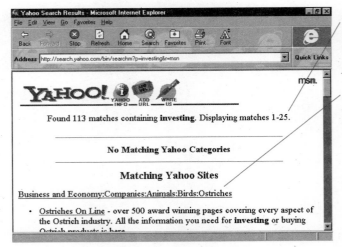

This is the list of the Web pages that Yahoo built the day I asked for investment information.

To view one of the referenced Web pages, click its name.

# On the Outernet

A while back, someone coined the term *Outernet* to describe the online services that aren't really part of the Internet but that are loosely connected to the Internet. Outernet services include America Online, CompuServe, Prodigy, and The Microsoft Network (MSN). In a general sense, these online services work the same basic way. Each provides up-to-the-minute news and delayed stock prices, special online columns and newsletters that cover personal financial topics, and personal financial chat rooms and bulletin boards where you can ask questions about investing. Most of the services also let you connect to online brokerage services such as the PC Financial Network.

Compared to the Internet, these Outernet services provide a unique advantage. Usually, you can simply click a button and the service displays a list of the personal financial or investing features it provides. I won't spend time describing the personal finance or investing features that the different Outernet services offer because whatever I might tell you would probably be out of date by the time you read it. The Outernet services add new features all the time.

Take the time to explore the offerings of these services, however, especially if you already have an account. The Outernet supplies investors with volumes of useful information.

# In Conclusion

For serious investors and for anyone who's a computer hobbyist, online investment research is both fun and fast. The Internet and the Outernet provide a staggering amount of financial information. The trick, however, is to first do a little exploring to find the handful of information resources that provide the information or perspective you want.

# Income Taxes
# and Money

I f you itemize your deductions and have business expenses, using Money for your record-keeping can save you hundreds of dollars a year in taxes. The reason? You can keep an exhaustive list of your deductions, and more deductions means paying less in income taxes.

Fortunately, using Money for tax-deduction record-keeping doesn't require you to do anything special. You need to use categories that mesh nicely with the tax deductions you intend to take. And you need to move the tax-deduction information you've collected with Money to your tax returns—either by hand or by exporting the Money data to a tax-preparation package like TurboTax.

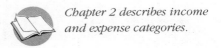

*Chapter 2 describes income and expense categories.*

## Building the Perfect Categories List

If you know how to use income and expense categories (and I presume you do if you're reading this), you don't need to do anything special to track your taxable income and tax deductions with Money. When you tag a check or deposit as falling into a particular category, you capture the taxable income or tax-deduction data you need. If you write a check to a local charity, for example, and you categorize it as a charitable donation, you've done everything you need to do in order to track the deduction.

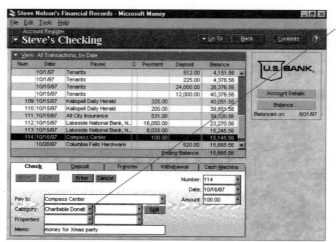

Categorizing this check as a charitable donation makes it easy to include this tax deduction on your return later on.

At the end of the year, as I'll explain later, you simply print a Tax Transactions report. You use the report's Charitable Donations total for your charitable-giving tax deduction. Money, as you might guess, provides all of the common taxable income and tax-deductible expense categories. You shouldn't need to add any new categories to Money's list of categories.

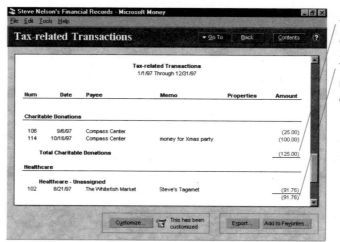

This number is your charitable-giving deduction.

This number is your medical and dental expenses deduction.

If you need to add a category for tax-accounting purposes, however, it's easy to do so. Just follow these steps:

**1** Display the Money Contents window.

**2** Click the Payees And Categories button. Money displays the Payees And Categories window.

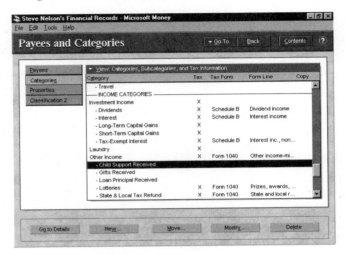

**Prevent Mixups.** *If you collect tax income and deduction information for more than one taxpayer, you'll want to use different Money files for each taxpayer. For example, if you're married but you and your spouse file separate returns, you should segregate your tax income and tax deduction data by using different Money files. To create a new file, use the New command on the File menu.*

**3** Click the Categories button.

**4** Click the New button. Money displays the New Category Or Subcategory dialog box.

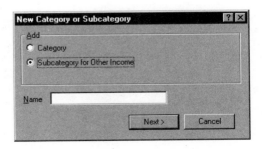

5 Click the Category option.

6 Enter a name for the new tax-deduction category in the Name text box.

7 Click Next. Money displays the second screen of the New Category Or Subcategory dialog box. This one asks if the new category is an income or expense category.

8 Indicate whether the new category is an income or an expense category by clicking the appropriate button.

9 Click Next. Money displays the third page of the New Category Or Subcategory dialog box. This one asks if the new category is a tax-related category. Click Yes.

10 Click Finish.

11 Repeat steps 4 through 10 to add all the income and expense categories you need.

 **A Tax Record-Keeping Shortcut.** *Don't spend time keeping records of taxable income or tax-deduction information that someone else—your employer or the mortgage company—keeps for you. You have to use their numbers anyway when you complete your return—you can't use your numbers. I keep records of things like charitable donations and personal property taxes, but I don't worry about my other deductions: mortgage interest, real estate property taxes, and so on. For that, I rely on someone else's handiwork.*

## Summarizing Your Income and Deduction Data at Tax Time

At the end of the year, you should produce a tax transactions report. It identifies each transaction you recorded under a taxable income category or tax-deduction expense category. You use the totals from the report to complete your tax return.

To produce the tax transactions report, follow these steps:

1 Click the Report And Chart Gallery button on the Money Contents window. Or, if you're working in another window, click the Go To triangle menu and then choose the Report And Chart Gallery command. Money displays the Report And Chart Gallery window.

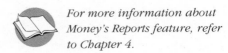

*For more information about Money's Reports feature, refer to Chapter 4.*

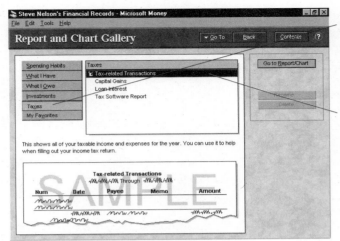

Click the Taxes button to see reports and charts that summarize taxable income and tax-deduction information.

Select the Tax-Related Transactions report by double-clicking it.

**2** Click the Go To Report/Chart button to have Money produce the report or chart. Money produces the report and displays it in its own window.

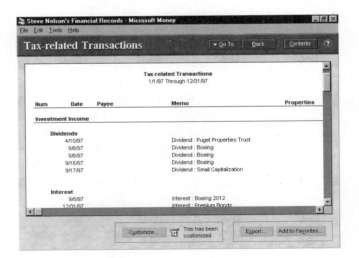

*Be sure to save the copy of the Tax-related Transactions report with your tax return. If you later have a question about some number that appears on your return, you can refer to the report.*

3 Choose Print from the File menu. Money displays the Print Report dialog box.

4 Click OK, and Money (with Windows 95's help) will produce the report.

## Should You Export Data to a Tax-Preparation Package?

A couple of years ago, personal finance programs like Money and Quicken started including features that make it possible to export data directly to tax-preparation programs like TurboTax and TaxCut. The people who review personal finance and tax software in computer magazines all thought this was a great idea—a real winner. But I want to discourage you from doing this. No, exporting data is not mechanically difficult. It's actually very easy. But that's sort of a problem. By automating the process—and letting Money and, say, TurboTax handle the entire process on their own without your supervision—you run the risk of not getting the numbers right.

The problem basically boils down to this: Money exports the data in its account registers for a particular calendar year. If you're exporting 1996's taxable income and tax-deduction data, for example, Money just grabs information from 1996. And that sounds right, but it usually isn't. Some of the checks and deposits you made at the very beginning of 1996 were probably for the tax year 1995. And some of the checks and deposits you made at the very beginning of 1997 should really be counted in 1996, not 1997. Unfortunately, Money isn't smart enough to correct these errors. (Neither is any other checkbook program, by the way.) You need to correct them yourself. The only practical way of doing this is by reviewing the checks and deposits that appear on the tax transactions report and then making adjustments where necessary.

If you're still thinking that you want to export the Money data to a tax-preparation program, let me say one more thing. Exporting doesn't actually save much time because you don't export very many numbers. Most of the numbers you use for preparing a return (including wages, interest income, dividend income, mortgage and home equity loan interest, and real estate taxes) come from the informational returns that other people send you: W-2s, 1099s, 1098s, and so forth. This information isn't stored in Money.

# The Five Best Tax-Saving Gambits

Occasionally, a new acquaintance pulls me aside, tells me he or she is paying "way too much" in taxes, and asks me for the secret to saving on taxes. Whenever someone asks me this, I tell them that there isn't a magic formula or super-secret loophole. Then I describe the following tax-saving and tax-delaying ideas.

## Take Every Deduction You're Entitled To

This maybe sounds silly, but I continually run into people who don't take all the deductions they're entitled to. Some of them think they increase their risk of being audited by taking too many deductions. Others think maybe they're being a little unpatriotic by taking too many deductions. But not taking every deduction you're entitled to is a big mistake. The U.S. Congress writes the tax laws with the assumption that taxpayers will take every deduction to which they're entitled. The entire system is built on this assumption. Therefore, you should take every deduction you're entitled to. And you should arrange your affairs in a way that produces the maximum dollar amount of deductions.

If you routinely give away clothing your kids have outgrown to the local thrift shop, for example, be sure to collect a receipt, assign a fair value, and then take the amount as a charitable donation deduction. If you're spending money on night school so you can acquire new skills and do a better job, take the amount as an employee business expense deduction.

# Bunch Your Deductions

Perhaps the best way to save money on income taxes without giving up anything in return is to bunch your deductions so you take the standard deduction in some years and itemize deductions in other years. This effectively increases your deductions. Let me explain. Let's say you're married and that you routinely have about $8,000 a year in itemized deductions:

| Itemized deduction | Amount |
| --- | --- |
| Mortgage interest | $6,000 |
| Real estate taxes | $1,000 |
| Charitable donations | $1,000 |
| Total | $8,000 |

Furthermore, just to make the math simple, let's also assume that you can take a $7,000 standard deduction. In any given year, of course, it makes sense to take the $8,000 a year in itemized deductions because that reduces your taxable income the most and, therefore, reduces your income tax bill. But if you pay some deductions early and some deductions late, you can actually increase the total deductions you're taking over time. Why? Because (and this is the trick) in the years when your itemized deductions fall below the standard deduction amount, you can take the standard deduction. Let me show you how this works over a four-year time frame.

Let's say that your plan is to use the standard $7,000 deduction in years 1 and 3 and itemized deductions in years 2 and 4. In this case, you want to pay as many of your deductions as you can in years 2 and 4. For example, you could delay your final mortgage payment in years 1 and 3 and pay it in the following year. You could also pay the next year's first mortgage payment in years 2 and 4. This would increase the mortgage interest deduction in years 2 and 4 by about

**Why People Itemize.** *By law, you can deduct a preset amount, called the* standard deduction, *from your income for purposes of calculating taxable income. Alternatively, you can deduct what you spend on mortgage and home equity loan interest, real estate taxes, personal property taxes, state and local income taxes, charitable donations, a few other miscellaneous items, and sometimes a portion of what you spend on medical and dental expenses. This is called your* itemized deductions *total. If your itemized deductions total exceeds the standard deduction amount, you save taxes.*

$1,000, while reducing the year 1 and year 3 mortgage interest deductions. It might be possible—you'd have to check the cost of late fees and penalties—to bunch your real estate taxes in years 2 and 4. In other words, in year 2, you'd pay the real estate taxes for both year 1 and year 2. And you might be able to do the same with your charitable donations. The table below shows what your itemized deductions would really be in years 1, 2, 3, and 4 if you did this juggling.

| Itemized deduction | Year 1 | Year 2 | Year 3 | Year 4 |
|---|---|---|---|---|
| Mortgage interest | $5,500 | $ 6,500 | $5,000 | $ 7,000 |
| Real estate taxes | 0 | $ 3,000 | 0 | $ 3,000 |
| Charitable donations | 0 | $ 2,000 | 0 | $ 2,000 |
| Total | $5,500 | $11,500 | $5,000 | $12,000 |

You can probably guess what I'm going to say next. Because you get to choose whether to itemize or whether to use the standard deduction, you itemize in years 2 and 4, but you take the standard deduction in years 1 and 3. Over the four years, by bunching your deductions, you get to take $37,500 of deductions, calculated as follows:

| Deduction in | Amount |
|---|---|
| Year 1 | $ 7,000 |
| Year 2 | $11,500 |
| Year 3 | $ 7,000 |
| Year 4 | $12,000 |
| Total | $ 37,500 |

**Deducting Home Mortgage Interest.** *Home mortgage interest isn't automatically deductible. You can't deduct interest on a mortgage and home equity loans if the total debt exceeds the fair market value of the home, for example. In other words, you can't deduct the interest on a $200,000 mortgage if the home is worth $100,000. In addition, your mortgages can't exceed $1 million, and your home equity loans can't exceed $100,000.*

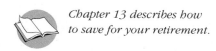

*Chapter 13 describes how to save for your retirement.*

Do you see what happens? If you itemize in each of the four years, you'll have $32,000 of deductions (four years times $8,000 a year). If you simply take the standard deduction, you'll have $28,000 of deductions (four years times $7,000). But by bunching your deductions and then flip-flopping between the standard deduction and itemized deductions, you can deduct $37,500—an extra $5,000 of deductions (as compared to the $32,000 itemized deductions) and an extra $10,000 (as compared to the $28,000 of standard deductions).

If this bunching business seems like too much work, I'll tell you that I agree. I don't do it. It just isn't worth it for me. It requires a lot of fiddling around. You may incur substantial tax savings, but you may also pay more in interest as well as late fees and penalties. But I describe bunching here because bunching deductions truly can save in taxes.

## Exploit Retirement Savings Options

I beat this drum earlier in Chapter 13 while discussing saving for retirement. But tax-deferred investment options like 401(k)s, 403(b)s, IRAs, SEP/IRAs, and Keoghs are such good deals that I have to mention them again. If you're saving for retirement (and you should be), these tax-deferred investment options are absolutely the best way to go.

## Don't Use Nondeductible Consumer Credit

Another very powerful tax-savings gambit is to convert nondeductible consumer credit interest on items such as car loans, credit cards, personal lines of credit, and so forth to deductible mortgage or home equity loan interest. To do this, you need to be a homeowner, of course. But assuming you are, you could take out, say, a $25,000 second mortgage home equity loan and use the proceeds to pay off your car loan, all your credit cards, that old student loan you're still paying on, and any other debts you have as well.

If you swap $25,000 of consumer credit that charges 10-percent interest with a $25,000 home equity loan that charges 10 percent, for example, you still pay $2,500 a year of interest, but you can use the $2,500 of home equity loan interest as a deduction. If your marginal, or highest, income tax rate is 28 percent, you save about $700 a year. If the home equity loan's interest rate happens to be lower than the average interest rate you're paying on all the consumer credit you replace—and it probably is—you save even more money.

Despite the substantial savings available, I caution you regarding this particular gambit, especially if you're someone who spends uncontrollably or likes to use a credit card. Sure, if you do one of these home equity loan things and use the proceeds to pay off your consumer credit debt, it may save on taxes. But you'll be in really sad shape if you go out and start charging up your credit cards again. And more than a few people complete a transaction like the one described in the preceding paragraphs and then find themselves with both a $25,000 home equity loan and a bunch of new credit card debts.

Let me mention one other problem: You could end up stretching out the repayment of your debt. Swapping a deductible home equity loan for a nondeductible car loan sounds like a good idea. And it really may save on taxes. But you might not get ahead if your car loan has three years of payments left and your new home equity loan lets you make payments over the next ten years.

*Consumer credit interest isn't deductible as an itemized deduction, but most mortgage interest is.*

*To make sure that you truly save money by swapping nondeductible consumer credit for deductible home mortgages and home equity loans, make sure you pay off the new debt as fast as you would have paid off the old debt.*

## Use Specific Identification for Your Investments

One final trick applies to investors who buy and sell stocks and bonds outside of tax-deferred accounts like self-directed IRAs, SEP/IRAs, and Keoghs. As described in Chapter 15, you can control when you recognize capital gains and losses by employing a technique known as specific identification. Because I describe this technique in Chapter 15, I'll refer you there rather than repeat myself.

# In Conclusion

I first started using a personal finance program similar to Money as a way to simplify my tax-deduction record-keeping. (This was many years before the Money program appeared.) In looking back over the years that I've been doing this, I can honestly say that tax-deduction record-keeping has been the biggest benefit of using a personal finance program. If you're anything like me, you'll save hours and hours of tax-preparation time and maybe even quite a bit of money by using the Money application.

# Part 3

# Managing a Small Business with Money

# Running Your Business from a Checkbook

**H**ere's a curious statistic concerning small business accounting programs: The ratio of users to purchasers is often very small. It's quite common, for example, for only 5 or 10 percent of the people who purchase a full-featured small business accounting program to actually use it. People sometimes cite this statistic as proof that small business accounting software isn't very good. But that's not true. Small business accounting software is some of the best software available. The problem with small business accounting software—and the reason for its low user-to-purchaser ratio—is that you need to know accounting to use these programs.

If you own or operate a small business, you still need to keep accurate and informative financial records. You probably know that already. What you may not know is that although Microsoft Money is chiefly a personal finance program, it is also perfectly suited for keeping financial records for many small businesses. Before you start using Money for small business accounting, however, you need to think about whether Money will work for you. You also need to understand the basic mechanics of using Money in a small business setting. This chapter covers these topics.

## Understanding the Big Picture

To successfully use Money as a business accounting program, you need to understand what a business accounting system does and whether Money can work for your business. So let's start here.

Unless you've been trained as an accountant, you may be a little vague about what an accounting system is supposed to do. You know it's supposed to keep the books and help with your finances, but you may not have a solid grasp of what this means. Fortunately, accounting systems aren't very complicated. No matter what the size of a business, accounting systems do four basic tasks:

> Print business forms

> Tally business income and expenses

> Keep records of assets, liabilities, and, in special cases, owner equity

> Simplify financial and accounting calculations

As long as you understand these tasks in a general way, you should be able to decide whether Money will work as well as a true small business accounting system. To help you make this decision, let me talk just a bit more about these four tasks and how they relate to using Money in a small business. Before you start using Money as your business's accounting system, you'll want to be sure you can use it successfully.

**Will Money Work for My One-Person Business?**
*Money works wonderfully well for most one-person service businesses in which there aren't a lot of business forms to produce or liabilities to track, and the only asset that requires precise record-keeping is cash.*

*Chapter 3 describes how to print checks.*

## Printing Business Forms

Printing business forms is the easiest-to-understand of the tasks that an accounting system does. If you need checks in your business, for example, your accounting system should be able to print them for you.

Okay, I know what you're thinking. If you're in business, you have checks to print. So Money can help you with that. But you have at least a few other business forms to print, too. Invoices, to take one example. "How," you're wondering to yourself, "can Money help with that?" Good question.

While printing business forms is a good thing, you don't need and don't want your accounting system to print each and every business form. You want it to print business forms that you use frequently. For example, if you write several dozen checks a month by hand, you want your accounting system to do that for you. But if you only have, say, two or three invoices to print each month, you won't save time by having your accounting system print out an invoice or two or three. You'll find it easiest to just use a word-processor or spreadsheet to produce neat, professional-looking invoices.

**What Forms Do Accounting Programs Produce?** *Small business accounting programs like QuickBooks for Windows and Peachtree Accounting for Windows print checks, invoices, customer statements, and purchase orders.*

**Cash-Basis vs. Accrual-Basis Accounting.** *Cash-basis accounting counts any checking account deposit as income and any checking account withdrawal as an expense. Cash-basis accounting is commonly employed in small businesses because it's easy to use. But it's usually less accurate than the alternative, accrual-basis accounting, in the way that it measures profits. Accrual-basis accounting counts income when you bill customers and counts expense when you charge or incur bills. The problem with accrual-basis accounting, however, is that to use it, you need to understand double-entry bookkeeping.*

The bottom line is this: If the only business forms you produce in great volume are checks, you'll be fine with Money. But if you need a good way to produce a bunch of other business forms, you shouldn't use Money unless you have other tools you can use to easily and efficiently produce these other business forms.

## Tallying Business Income and Expenses

Perhaps the most important task for a small business accounting system is tallying business income and expense. By tracking your business's sales and expenses, you learn whether you're making a profit. And you must make at least a modest profit to stay in business.

Fortunately, Money's checkbook makes it easy to tally income and expenses. (I talk a bit more about this later in this chapter in "Keeping Your Books with Money.") You can do that by using what's called cash-basis accounting.

## Keeping Records of Assets, Liabilities, and Owners Equity

Accounting systems must also keep accurate, up-to-date records of a business's assets and liabilities. You probably want to know at all times how much cash you have in the bank, for example. If you're a retailer, you want to keep an up-to-date inventory.

Money's strength, as you might guess, lies in its ability to keep track of cash and investments. Not surprisingly, then, Money does an excellent job of tracking business bank accounts and business investments.

But many businesses have items to track in addition to cash and investments. If your business holds inventory, for example, your accounting system should help you track that. If your business owns a bunch of machinery or real estate or equipment, your accounting system should help you track that, too. Finally, if you have significant accounts payable or loans payable, your accounting system should help you track these items. In any of these cases, Money can't do as much as more complete accounting programs.

**What If I Do Business as a Corporation or Partnership?** *If you're operating your business as a partnership or a corporation, you need to keep track of your owners equity, too.* Owners equity *in a corporation includes the money initially raised through a stock offering, retained earnings, and your dividends. Owners equity in a partnership includes the partners' capital accounts, partnership profit shares, and the partner draws. Unfortunately, owners equity accounting is pretty complicated, and Money doesn't handle it well. You're really better off using a more powerful small business accounting program.*

**Preparing the Payroll with Money.** *It's easy to prepare a payroll with Money if you have only salaried employees. Chapter 25 describes how to do this.*

# Simplifying Financial and Accounting Calculations

There's one final task that an accounting system should help you with: It should simplify the financial or accounting calculations that you make on a regular basis. Perhaps the most common set of calculations that an accounting system should make are related to payroll. If you have employees, for example, your accounting system should help you with the task of calculating employees' gross wages, their federal income tax withholding, social security taxes, Medicare taxes, and so forth.

And there are other calculations that accounting systems should make. In a business that owns a lot of depreciable assets—rooms of machinery or a fleet of delivery trucks—the accounting system should calculate **depreciation.** In a business like a construction company that bids on jobs or projects, the accounting system should calculate bid amounts.

Unfortunately, Money can't make any of these common accounting calculations for you. Money can't calculate payroll amounts. It can't calculate depreciation. It can't calculate or help you calculate bid amounts.

I should point out that no small business accounting system can make every financial or accounting calculation. But if you're making a calculation over and over again, you need a good way to do it. And typically, the best way to handle these calculations is by having your accounting system make them.

# Keeping Your Books with Money

Once you've decided to keep your books—that is, your financial records—with Money, you'll find it very easy to get going. There are, however, a few items you need to take care of first.

## Preparing for Business Accounting

Before you can start keeping your books, you need to have set up the bank account on which you'll write business checks and in which you'll make business deposits. Once you've done that, you need to create categories to track your business income and expenses.

**What If I Want a More Powerful Accounting Program?** *The more you ask of your accounting system, the more it asks of you. If you want to keep detailed records of all your assets and liabilities and you also want to make complicated accounting calculations, you need to understand a lot more about finance and accounting. You also need a powerful accounting program—one that is very likely time-consuming to learn.*

The table that follows lists the standard business income and expense categories used by sole proprietors to report their profits to the Internal Revenue Service. You can use this category list for your business, or you can create your own. You need to fill out your Schedule C business tax return using these categories, however.

## Income categories
Gross receipts or sales
Returns and allowances
Other income

## Expense categories
Advertising
Bad debts
Car and truck expenses
Commissions and fees
Cost of goods sold
Depletion
Depreciation
Employee benefit programs
Insurance
Legal and professional services
Meals and entertainment
Mortgage interest
Office expense
Other interest
Pension and profit-sharing plans
Rent on vehicles, machinery, and equipment
Rent on other business property
Repairs and maintenance
Supplies
Taxes and licenses
Travel
Utilities
Wages
Other expenses

To add business income and expense categories to a categories list, follow these steps:

1 Display the Money Contents window.

2 Click the Payees And Categories button. Money displays the Payees And Categories window.

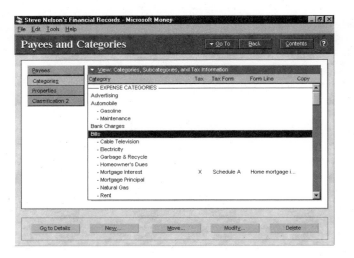

*If you're investing in loans—you're a small finance company, say—Money can calculate loan payments and amortize loans for you. Chapter 7 describes how to track loans and mortgages with Money.*

3 Click the Categories button.

4 Click the New button. Money displays the New Category Or Subcategory dialog box.

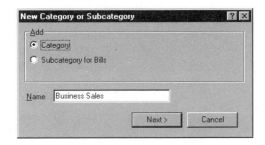

**Can I Use the Same Category List for Both My Business and Personal Record-Keeping?**

*If you're using the same category list to track personal expenses, you may want to start each category name with the word* Business *or the abbreviation* Bus *to identify it as a business category.*

**5** Click the Category button.

**6** Enter a name for the business income or expense category in the Name text box.

**7** Click Next. Money displays the second page of the New Category Or Subcategory dialog box. This one asks if the new category is an income or expense category.

**8** Indicate whether the new category is an income or an expense category by clicking the appropriate button.

**9** Click Next. Money displays the third page of the New Category Or Subcategory dialog box. This one asks if the next category is a tax-related category.

**10** Answer the question about the tax-related category by clicking Yes.

**11** Click Finish.

**12** Repeat steps 4 through 11 to add more business income and business expense categories, if you need them.

## Recording Business Income

Once you set up your accounts (if necessary) and create new categories (if any), you're ready to begin recording your business income and business expenses. To record business income, you enter a deposit in the Account Register window. To do this, you describe the date of the deposit, who paid you, and the amount of the deposit. Finally, you also categorize the deposit as falling into one of your income categories.

**Recording Business Income**

1 Click the Deposit tab.

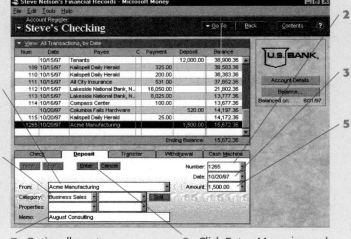

2 Enter the invoice number, if you want.

3 Enter the deposit date.

4 Enter the customer name.

5 Enter the amount of the deposit.

6 Activate the Category drop-down list box and select the category that describes the deposit's income category.

7 Optionally, enter a description of the deposit.

8 Click Enter. Money records the deposit and recalculates the account balance.

**Data-Entry Magic.** *Money provides several data-entry tricks you can use to speed the process of entering a deposit. You can press the + and - keys to adjust the deposit date. If you've recorded a deposit from this person or business before, you don't have to enter their name. You can activate the From drop-down list box and select the person or business from that list. And SuperSmartFill also fills out some (or, in a few cases, all) of the deposit text boxes for you.*

## Recording Business Expenses

To describe a business expense, you record a check using the Account Register window. In a nutshell, you click the Check tab and then describe the check by filling in the check number and date, the person or business you're paying, the amount, and the expense category.

**Recording Business Expenses**

1 Click the Check tab.

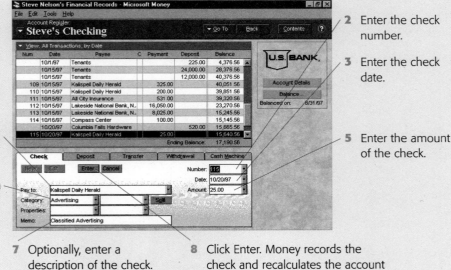

2 Enter the check number.

3 Enter the check date.

4 Enter the name of the person or business you're paying. Or activate the Pay To drop-down list box and select the name of the person or business you're paying.

5 Enter the amount of the check.

6 Activate the Category drop-down list box and select the category that describes the check's business expense category.

7 Optionally, enter a description of the check.

8 Click Enter. Money records the check and recalculates the account balance.

**Should I Use a Full-Featured Accounting Program?** *If you're unsure about whether it makes sense to move up to a powerful program and you've been using an awkward manual system (a shoebox, for example), I suggest trying Money first. A checkbook program like Money may be all you need.*

# If Money Doesn't Work for Your Business

If Money doesn't do all that you need from your accounting system—for example, if you need to print business forms Money can't print, or to use accrual-basis accounting, or to keep records of items Money can't track, or to make complex financial or accounting calculations—you can and should step up to one of the more powerful small business accounting systems. Three of these are QuickBooks for Windows, QuickBooks Pro for Windows, and Peachtree Accounting for Windows.

*Full-featured small business accounting programs such as QuickBooks and Peachtree Accounting do a lot more than checkbook programs like Money. The extra functionality is appealing, but it also means that the programs are more difficult to use.*

QuickBooks and QuickBooks Pro are easy-to-use, full-featured small business accounting programs tailored for a small business with few employees. Peachtree Accounting for Windows is a more powerful small business accounting program. It's probably better suited for larger businesses or those with a part-time or full-time bookkeeper or accountant.

## In Conclusion

Many small businesses can use a personal finance program such as Money to do their accounting. Personal finance programs such as Money aren't as powerful as full-blown small business accounting programs, but they are much easier to use.

# Billing and Collecting from Customers

In Chapter 23, I outlined how to use Money to keep the books for a small business. The gist of that chapter is that you can use Money to track business income and spending in the same manner that you use Money to track personal income and spending. While that's all good and true, Chapter 23 doesn't address another important topic: the ways that Money can help you keep the records for and track an important business asset—your accounts receivable.

## A Look at the Big Picture

Here's the big picture in a nutshell: Money isn't really set up to invoice customers and to track the amounts that you've billed to and collected from customers. But even so, you can use Money to do this. Accounts receivable accounting, as this area of record-keeping is called, really consists of three tasks:

➤ Producing the invoices that you use to bill customers

➤ Keeping track of the invoices you've produced and of the unpaid balances of those invoices

➤ Keeping track of the amounts that your customers pay

The trick to using Money for this stuff is to know that Money doesn't do the first task for you: It doesn't bill customers. It does everything else admirably, however. So you need to use another program—such as your word processor—to produce the invoices.

**A Word Processor for Invoices.** *One advantage of using a word processor to produce invoices is that you can create much nicer looking invoices. You have plenty of room to describe why you're billing a customer and to explain how you arrived at the invoice total. In fact, I suggest people think of their invoices as sales and marketing tools and, therefore, use their invoices to remind customers of any special benefits or services provided.*

This isn't difficult. Remember that all an invoice needs to do is describe why a customer or client owes you money and how they're supposed to pay. If your word processor can do this, and it probably can, you use Money to track the invoices you've produced (in other words, the amounts you've billed) and the amounts customers or clients have paid.

# Preparing for Accounts Receivable Accounting

To track accounts receivable with Money, you need to set up an accounts receivable account. To do this, follow these steps:

1 Display the Money Contents window. You can do this by starting Money or by clicking the Contents button at the top of most Money windows.

2 Click the Account Manager button. Money displays the Account Manager window.

3 Click the New Account button. Money starts the New Account Wizard. Click Next to bypass the first dialog box.

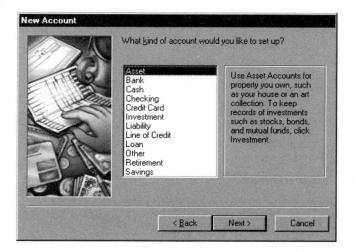

**4** In the second dialog box, click Asset to indicate that you want to set up an asset account.

**5** Click Next. Money asks what name you want to use for the new account. Name the new account by typing something in the What Do You Want To Name This Asset Account text box. You could type "Accounts Receivable."

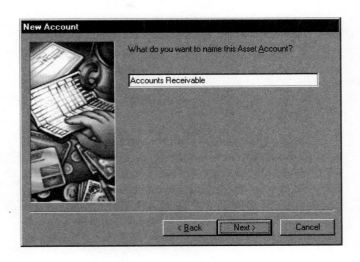

**6** Click Next. Money asks for the current account balance.

**7** Enter zero in the What's The Balance Of This Account text box.

**8** Click Finish. Money displays the Account Manager window.

# Tracking Accounts Receivable

You have a choice when it comes to tracking accounts receivable. You can track accounts receivable in a way that records your income whenever you deposit cash or in a way that records your income whenever you bill a customer. The first method really means you're using cash-basis accounting. The second method means you're using accrual-basis accounting for your business income.

# Using Cash-Basis Accounting

If you want to use cash-basis accounting, you simply use your accounts receivable account to list your unpaid invoices. In this way, you keep a record of the amounts that customers or clients owe you.

## Recording a New Customer Invoice

To record a new customer invoice, you describe the invoice date, the customer, and the invoice amount.

**Recording an Invoice If You're Using Cash-Basis Accounting**

**1** Click the Increase tab.

**2** Enter the invoice date.

**3** Enter the name of the customer.

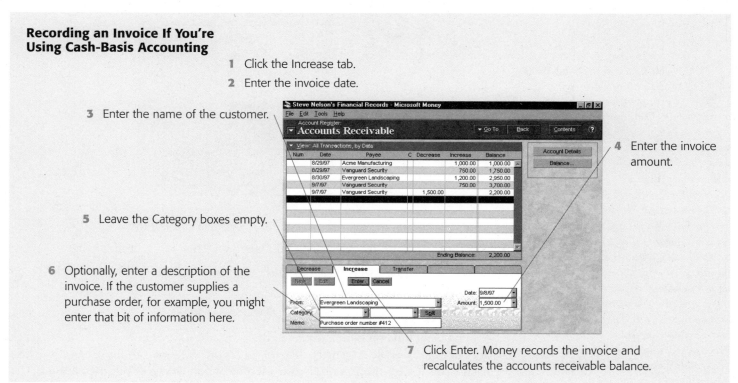

**4** Enter the invoice amount.

**5** Leave the Category boxes empty.

**6** Optionally, enter a description of the invoice. If the customer supplies a purchase order, for example, you might enter that bit of information here.

**7** Click Enter. Money records the invoice and recalculates the accounts receivable balance.

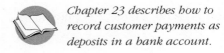

*Chapter 23 describes how to record customer payments as deposits in a bank account.*

## Recording a Customer Payment

To record a customer payment, you enter two transactions in the Money account registers. First you record the customer's check as a deposit in the bank account. Then you record the decrease in the accounts receivable balance. To record the decrease in the accounts receivable balance, display the accounts receivable account in the Account Register window and enter a transaction that decreases the account balance.

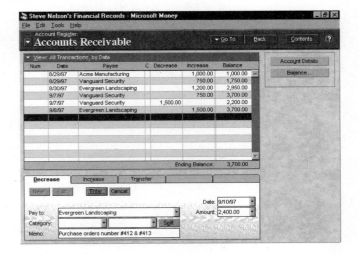

1 Click the Decrease tab.

2 Enter the payment date.

3 Select the customer's name from the Pay To drop-down list box.

4 Enter the amount of the check.

5 Leave the Category boxes empty.

6 Optionally, enter a description of the check, including the customer's check number, in the memo box.

7 Click Enter. Money records the customer payment.

8 Mark the invoices that the customer's check pays as reconciled. To do this, select the invoice transaction and then choose Mark As Reconciled from the Edit menu. Repeat this step for each invoice a customer's check pays.

9 Mark the customer's check as reconciled. Again, to do this you select the payment transaction and then choose Mark As Reconciled from the Edit menu.

# Using Accrual-Basis Accounting

Cash-basis accounting is easy to understand, but you record the same transaction twice: one time as a deposit in the bank account register and one time as a decrease in the accounts receivable register. You can reduce the work you do and, at the same time, more accurately measure your income by using accrual-basis accounting.

## Recording a New Customer Invoice

To record a new customer invoice, you describe the invoice date, the customer, and the invoice amount.

**Early Payment Discounts.**
*It's not unusual in some industries to offer customers a discount for paying invoices early. A common early payment discount scheme, for example, offers customers a 2-percent discount for paying in ten days instead of in thirty days. (This is usually referred to as "2-percent ten net thirty.") Be careful about offering customers early payment discounts, however. They amount to painfully expensive ways to borrow money. If you offer a 2-percent discount for paying twenty days early, for example, you're effectively paying 2-percent interest for twenty days. That 2-percent, twenty-day interest rate is equal to a 36-percent annual interest rate. (If you pay 2-percent interest every twenty days, you pay the 2 percent 18 times over the course of a 365-day year: 2% x 18 = 36%.)*

## Recording an Invoice If You're Using Accrual-Basis Accounting

**1** Click the Increase tab.

**2** Enter the invoice date.

**3** Enter the name of the customer.

**4** Enter the invoice amount.

**5** Use the Category box to specify the income category. By doing this, you count a customer invoice as income when you bill rather than when you collect.

**6** Optionally, enter a description of the invoice.

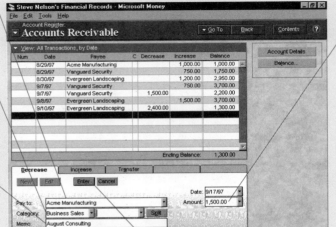

**7** Click Enter. Money records the invoice and recalculates the accounts receivable balance.

## Recording a Customer Payment

To record a customer payment, you record a deposit in the bank account. But instead of categorizing the deposit as business income, you transfer the money to the accounts receivable account.

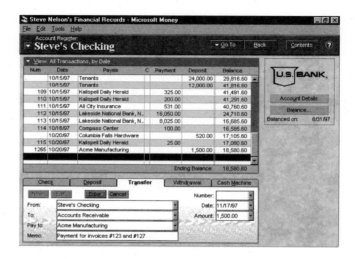

1 Click the Deposit tab.

2 Enter the customer's check number.

3 Enter the payment date.

4 Select the customer name from the From drop-down list box.

5 Enter the amount of the check.

6 Enter Transfer in the first Category box and the name of the accounts receivable account in the second Category box.

7 Optionally, enter a memo description of the check.

8 Click Enter. Money records the customer payment as a deposit in the bank account and as a reduction in the accounts receivable account balance.

9 Display the account register for the accounts receivable account. You can do this by activating the triangle menu at the top of the register area and choosing the accounts receivable account.

10 Mark the invoices that the customer's check pays as reconciled. To do this, select the invoice transaction and choose Mark As Reconciled from the Edit menu. Repeat this step for each invoice a customer's check pays.

11 Mark the transfer transaction as reconciled. To do this, select the transfer transaction and choose Mark As Reconciled from the Edit menu.

## Monitoring Accounts Receivable

On a regular basis, you need to review your accounts receivable. In particular, you want to watch out for delinquent customer invoices—invoices that should have been paid but haven't been paid. To do this, you can produce a report that summarizes the transactions in the accounts receivable account and sorts the information by customer name. Follow these steps to produce this report:

1 Display the Money Contents window.

2 Click the Report And Chart Gallery button. Money displays the Report And Chart Gallery.

3 Click the Spending Habits button.

4 Double-click the Account Transactions report. Money produces the report.

**Accounts Receivable Paperwork.** *You should keep permanent copies of customer invoices. Store any unpaid customer invoices in an "open invoices" file. Move paid customer invoices to a "paid invoices" file.*

**5** Click the Customize button. Money displays the Customize Report dialog box.

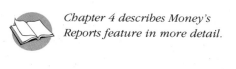

*Chapter 4 describes Money's Reports feature in more detail.*

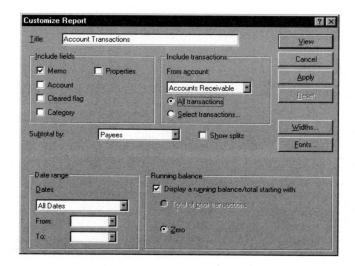

**6** Activate the From Account drop-down list box and select the Accounts Receivable account.

**7** Activate the Subtotal By drop-down list box and select Payees.

**8** Use the Include Fields check boxes to specify which pieces of register information you want to appear on the report. If you aren't using the Category boxes when you enter transactions (you would not be using them if you're using cash-basis accounting), you can unmark the Category check box. If you are using the Memo box to store information such as invoice numbers or check numbers, you can mark the Memo check box.

**9** Click the Select Transactions option button. (You'll find it at the bottom of the Include Transactions area.) When you do, Money displays the Select Transactions dialog box.

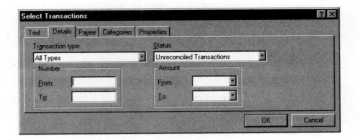

10 Click the Details tab of the Select Transactions dialog box.

11 Activate the Status drop-down list box and select the Unreconciled Transactions entry.

12 Click OK to return to the Customize Report dialog box.

13 Click View. Money updates the Account Transactions report. This time, it summarizes the invoices and payments by customer.

**Credit and Collections.** *When you spot a customer with an overdue invoice, you want to contact the customer to find out if there's some problem. Perhaps the customer didn't receive your invoice or has lost it. Or perhaps the customer didn't receive the product or service you thought you provided. In cases in which the customer can't make a payment because of cash-flow problems, you can discuss any payment options you're willing to offer. As a general rule—and perhaps this is obvious—you should begin collection efforts early. The older an unpaid invoice becomes, the more difficult it is to collect.*

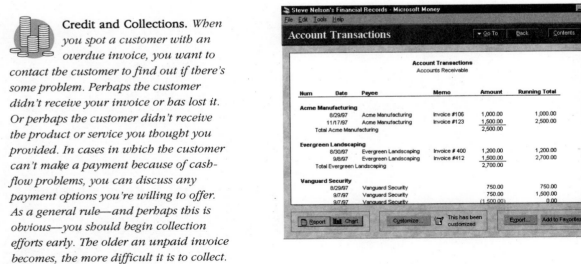

## In Conclusion

Money isn't perfectly suited to accounts receivable accounting. But as long as you don't have high volumes of customer invoices and payments to monitor, you can use Money to track your accounts receivable. If you do have high volumes of customer invoices and payments to monitor, however, your best bet is probably to step up to one of the full-featured small business accounting programs.

# Payroll

**M**oney doesn't provide a payroll feature as such, but it can dramatically reduce the work of preparing a payroll. You can use Money, for example, to record and print employee payroll checks. And the powerful reporting capabilities that Money provides make it easy to produce end-of-quarter and end-of-year reports that you can use to prepare payroll tax returns and forms.

This chapter describes what you need to do when you become an employer, how to set up the payroll accounts and categories you need for payroll processing, and how to prepare payroll checks and tax returns.

*While this chapter explains how a business uses Money to prepare its employee payroll, the information provided in this chapter also applies to household employees such as nannies and other child-care providers.*

## Becoming an Employer

Hiring the first employee is one of the major turning points in a business. Suddenly, the business owner has a regular payroll to meet, and another family depends on the continued success of the business. It's more than a little scary.

In addition to the financial burden and responsibility of having an employee, the amount of administrative work dramatically increases. As you'll soon learn if you don't already know, the accounting and bookkeeping burden of adding a single employee is staggering. You now have to prepare payroll checks, make regular payroll tax deposits, and file end-of-the-quarter and end-of-the-year payroll tax returns. And that's just the federal payroll tax work. You also have state and perhaps local payroll taxes and tax returns to deal with, too.

**Employee vs. Independent Contractor.** *When you look at the hassle of having employees, you may conclude that you should hire freelancers, or independent contractors, instead. That's not a bad tactic, but it's more difficult to do than you might imagine. The IRS says that in order for someone to be called an "independent contractor," he or she really should look and act like a small business. For example, independent contractors should do work for multiple customers, perhaps have independent contractors or employees of their own, probably provide their own work location and equipment, work with little supervision, and get paid by the job. If someone you would like to hire as an independent contractor works only for you and only at your location, doesn't really have any work expenses, relies on you for supervision and instruction, and gets paid by the hour, the IRS will probably say that your independent contractor is really an employee.*

Fortunately, both the federal and state government are usually very helpful in assisting small businesses to correctly process payroll.

# Federal Payroll Tax and Reporting Requirements

To meet the federal payroll tax and reporting requirements, your first step is to get an employer tax identification number. This number is equivalent to your personal social security number—it identifies you as an employer and is used by the government to track transactions relating specifically to your responsibilities as an employer. To get an employer tax identification number, contact the Internal Revenue Service and ask for an SS-4 form. This form, which is very simple to fill out, tells the IRS you want to hire an employee.

Once you fill out the SS-4 form, you can either mail it in or call the IRS and give them the information on the SS-4 form over the phone. The IRS will give you an employer identification number immediately. (You still have to fax or mail in the SS-4 because it has your signature on it.)

Once you request an employer tax identification number, the IRS knows you're an employer and sends you the federal tax deposit coupons you use to remit the money withheld from employees' paychecks. And, at the end of the quarter and the end of the year, the IRS sends you the payroll tax returns you need to complete: the end-of-quarter 941 return to report the wages you've paid for the quarter and the end-of-year 940 return to report any federal unemployment tax you owe.

The IRS also sends you a copy of the *Employer's Tax Guide*. This booklet, which is sometimes called a "Circular E," tells you how much federal income tax, social security tax, and Medicare tax you're supposed to withhold from an employee's paycheck. You need this booklet to prepare payroll checks. Watch for it and don't lose it.

*If you are reporting the wages paid over the quarter to a household employee such as a nanny, you use the 942 form instead of the 941 form.*

# State and Local Payroll Tax and Reporting Requirements

Your state also has payroll tax and reporting requirements that you need to meet. States, for example, require employers to pay unemployment insurance and disability insurance, also known as "workman's compensation." Most states have a state income tax that you, as an employer, need to withhold from employee checks and then remit to the state. You may also have local county or city payroll tax reporting requirements.

I can't give you precise instructions for meeting state and local payroll tax reporting requirements because they vary from state to state. Contact the state or local employment tax office and tell them you are hiring an employee or several employees. The office will put you on its list of employers. Typically, as soon as this happens, you get instructions on what you're supposed to do. And you periodically get payroll tax returns you're supposed to fill out and return. (End-of-quarter payroll tax returns are common, for example.)

# Other Employee Reporting Requirements

Let me mention one other item related to all this. In addition to the payroll tax and reporting requirements described in the preceding paragraphs, employers are also required to perform other tasks. The Immigration and Naturalization Service, for example, requires employers to verify that their employees are U.S. citizens, Permanent Residents, or have a work visa. Some states have special reporting requirements, for example, to help track down parents who aren't making court-ordered child support payments. And there are often other special reporting requirements as well.

I can't tell you which of these other requirements will apply in your situation. But you should be aware that as a new employer, you are often required to do additional work.

**How Do I Handle State and Local Payroll Taxes?**

*You may also need liability accounts to track other substantial state and local payroll taxes. But don't go overboard. As a general rule, track a payroll liability only if you need to keep track of what you owe so that you have enough money to pay the liability. Therefore, for payroll taxes that are very nominal—say, less than $100 a year per employee—you can simplify your record-keeping by not setting up a liability account. At the end of the year or quarter, or whenever you're supposed to pay the amount you owe, you can figure out what the liability is and pay it.*

*If you have questions about how the Account Manager window works, refer to Chapter 1. It describes the Account Manager in detail.*

# Setting Up the Payroll Accounts You Need

Once you're prepared to meet the federal, state, and local payroll tax and reporting requirements, you should set up payroll liability accounts to track the amounts you withhold from employee payroll checks and the expenses you incur because of a payroll check, but that you postpone paying. Specifically, you need liability accounts to track social security taxes, to keep track of Medicare taxes, and to monitor employees' federal income tax withholdings.

To set up these accounts, follow these steps:

**1** With the Money Contents window displayed, click the Account Manager button. Money displays the Account Manager window.

**2** Click the New Account button. This tells Money to start the New Account Wizard. Leave the Bank Or Financial Institution box blank.

**3** Click Next. When the Wizard asks what kind of account you want to set up, click the Liability account type.

**4** Click Next. When the Wizard asks what name you want to give your liability account, enter it. For example, you may use the account name "Social Security" to track the social security taxes you owe, "Medicare" to track the Medicare taxes you owe, or "Federal Income" to track the federal income taxes you withhold and owe. (Of course, if you need all of these, you will need to create a separate account for each.)

**5** Click Next. When the Wizard asks for the account's opening balance, enter what you currently owe for the tax. (If you haven't yet paid anyone, you don't owe anything, so enter zero.)

**6** Click Finish. If you need to set up additional accounts, repeat steps 2 through 6.

# Setting Up the Payroll Categories You Need

*You can also set up payroll expense subcategories for any of the other federal or state payroll taxes you pay. You can do this when you first set up the account or when you first write a check to pay a payroll tax expense.*

Once you've set up the payroll liability accounts you need, you need to set up several new payroll expense categories. Specifically, you need to set up a new Payroll expense category as well as Payroll expense subcategories for Gross wages, Employer's social security, and Employer's Medicare tax.

To set up the Payroll expense category, follow these steps:

1 Display the Money Contents window.

2 Click the Payees And Categories button. Money displays the Payees And Categories window.

3 Click the Categories button.

4 Click the New button. Money displays the New Category Or Subcategory dialog box.

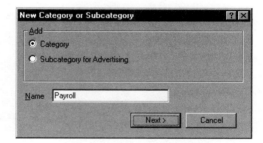

5 Click the Category option button.

6 Enter the new category name as Payroll in the Name text box.

7 Click Next. Money displays the second page of the New Category Or Subcategory dialog box. This one asks if the new category is an income or expense category.

**8** Click the Expense option button.

**9** Click Next. Money displays the third page of the New Category Or Sub-category dialog box. This one asks if the new category is a tax-related category.

**10** Answer the question about the tax-related category by clicking Yes.

**11** Click Finish.

To set up the Gross pay, Employer's Social Security, and Employer's Medicare expense subcategories, follow these steps:

**1** Display the Money Contents window.

**2** Click the Payees And Categories button. Money displays the Payees And Categories window.

**3** Click the Categories button.

**4** Click the Payroll expense category in the list box that Money displays in the Payees And Categories window.

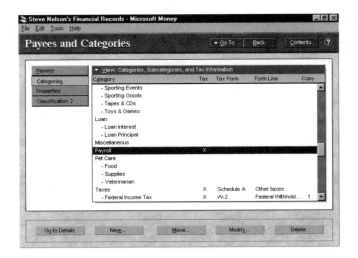

**5** Click the New button. Money displays the New Category Or Subcategory dialog box.

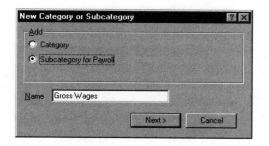

**6** Click the Subcategory For Payroll button.

**7** Enter the new category name as Gross Wages in the Name text box.

**8** Click Next. Money displays a third page in the New Category Or Subcategory dialog box. This one asks if the new category is a tax-related category.

**9** Answer the question about the tax-related category by clicking Yes.

**10** Click Finish.

**11** Repeat steps 4 through 10 to add the other payroll subcategories you need.

*An employee's W-4 form tells you which income tax filing status he or she uses to file a federal tax return. It also tells you how many personal exemptions he or she will claim on the federal tax return. With this information and the employee's salary, you use the tables provided in the Circular E* Employer's Tax Guide *to look up what taxes the employee owes.*

# Preparing Payroll Checks

Once you've set up the payroll accounts and payroll categories you need, preparing a payroll check is a snap. To illustrate how this works, suppose you have an employee whom you pay $600 twice a month. Further suppose that based on the employee's W-4 form and the current Circular E *Employer's Tax Guide*, you're supposed to withhold $70 per pay period for federal income taxes, that the employee's social security withholdings amount to $37.20 per pay period, that his or her Medicare taxes come to $8.70 per period, and that you must match the employee's social security and Medicare taxes. Given this information, you would enter the employee's semimonthly payroll information in the Split Transaction dialog box as follows.

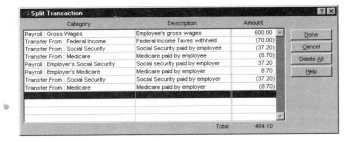

To record the employee's check, follow these steps:

1 Display the Account Register for the bank account on which you'll write the check.

2 Click the Check tab.

3 Click New, and then enter the payroll check number in the Number text box.

4 Enter the payroll check date in the Date text box.

5 Enter the employee name in the Pay To text box.

6 Click the Split command so Money displays the Split Transaction dialog box.

**7** Describe the gross wages amount on the first line of the Split Transaction dialog box. Do this by specifying the Category as Payroll and the Subcategory as Gross Wages, and by entering the amount as the total wages.

**8** Describe the federal income taxes you withhold on the second line of the Split Transaction box. Do this by specifying the Category as Transfer and the Subcategory as Federal Income, and by entering the amount as the federal income taxes withheld.

**9** Describe the social security taxes paid by the employee through withholding on the third line of the Split Transaction dialog box. Do this by specifying the Category as Transfer and the Subcategory as Social Security, and by entering the amount as the Social Security taxes withheld.

**10** Describe the Medicare taxes paid by the employee through withholding on the fourth line of the Split Transaction dialog box. Do this by specifying the Category as Transfer and the Subcategory as Medicare, and by entering the amount as the Medicare taxes withheld.

**11** Describe the employer's matching social security taxes on the fifth and sixth lines of the Split Transaction dialog box. Use the fifth line to record the expense by specifying the Category as Payroll, the Subcategory as Employer's Social Security, and the amount as the employer's matching social security. Use the sixth line to record the amount of money owed the federal government for social security tax by specifying the Category as Transfer, the Subcategory as Social Security, and the amount as the employer's matching Social Security.

**12** Describe the employer's matching Medicare taxes on the seventh and eighth lines of the Split Transaction dialog box. Use the seventh line to record the expense by specifying the Category as Payroll, the Subcategory as Employer's Medicare, and the amount as the employer's matching Medicare. Use the eighth line to record the amount of money owed the federal government for this Medicare tax by specifying the Category as Transfer, the Subcategory as Medicare, and the amount as the employer's matching Social Security.

 **What If I Employ People in More Than One State?** *If you employ people in more than one state, you must meet the payroll tax and reporting requirements of each state. For example, if you own a business that has employees who work in both Washington and California, you need to meet the Washington state payroll tax and reporting requirements for the employees who work in Washington and the California payroll tax and reporting requirements for the employees who work in California.*

**13** Click Done to close the Split Transaction dialog box.

**14** Click Enter to record the payroll check.

In our example, the net amount of the payroll check is $484.10, which is the sum of all the expenses categorized as well as the funds transferred in the Split Transaction dialog box. If you've performed the arithmetic correctly, the payroll check amount should also equal the gross pay amount minus the employee's social security and Medicare withholdings and the federal income tax withheld.

## Making Tax Deposits

On a periodic basis, you must pay the federal government the amounts you owe, based on the money withheld from the employee's gross pay for social security, Medicare, and income taxes, and your matching share of social security and Medicare contributions. (The IRS will tell you how often you're supposed to remit federal income taxes.)

Suppose that you use the payroll tax liability accounts shown earlier in the Split Transaction dialog box and that the transaction shown is the only one that affects payroll tax liability. When you write the check to pay the tax deposit, you split the transaction between the three accounts shown: $74.40 to the social security taxes payable account, $17.40 to the Medicare taxes payable account, and $70 to the income taxes withheld account. After you record the check, each of the four payroll tax liability accounts will have an ending balance of zero.

## Filing Quarterly and Annual Tax Returns

Employers need to complete a 941 or 942 payroll tax return quarterly. It requires employers to report the total wages paid, calculate and report social security and Medicare taxes, and report the federal income tax withheld. You calculate social security and Medicare payments by multiplying the percentage due by the total gross pay. To figure out how much federal income tax was withheld, look at the liability account for federal income taxes withheld. Chapter 4 describes how to print reports.

There is one potential problem with the approach described here. Employees pay social security taxes only on wages below a ceiling amount. (Medicare taxes equal 1.45 percent of a person's total wages—there is no ceiling.) For example, in 1995, employees paid social security taxes of 6.2 percent only on wages up to $60,600. But this ceiling amount increases every year, based on inflation. If you have employees who make more than the ceiling amounts, you won't be able to print out a report that summarizes the total Gross Wages expense category because social security and Medicare taxes won't be owed on the entire amount.

To get around this problem, print an Account Balances report that provides the account balances for the social security and Medicare tax liability accounts. Assuming you've figured these amounts correctly, you can then calculate wages subject to social security based on the social security taxes owed. For example, if you owe $6,200 of social security taxes, you know that half of the $6,200 is social security taxes employees paid on their wages because employers must match employee deductions for social security and Medicare. If the social security tax percentage is 6.2 percent, the total wages subject to social security is $3,100 divided by 6.2 percent, or $50,000.

Employers also file the annual 940 federal unemployment tax return. In a nutshell, to file the 940 federal unemployment tax return, you just add up what you've paid your employees and multiply this sum by a percentage. The only tricks to the calculation are that you don't need to pay a federal unemployment tax on amounts an employee makes in excess of $7,000. And the tax percentage depends on the way your state unemployment taxes work. Nevertheless, the 940 return is easy to fill out. Just carefully follow the instructions that come with the return.

## Preparing W-2 and W-3 Forms

The other payroll task you must complete is the annual preparation of W-2 forms and the W-3 form. You complete a W-2 for each employee to summarize the gross pay earned over the year, the social security and Medicare taxes withheld, and the federal income taxes withheld. You also complete a W3 form, which summarizes the W2s.

Although you can't use Microsoft Money to print these forms, you can use it to calculate the needed information. Simply print a report that summarizes your payroll transactions by employee, or payee, and that gives subtotals for the expense categories and transfer accounts used to split the transactions. To do this, follow these steps:

1 Display the Money Contents window.

2 Click the Report And Chart Gallery button. Money displays the Report And Chart Gallery.

3 Click the Spending Habits button.

4 Double-click the Who Is Getting My Money report button. Money produces the report. (If Money displays a chart, click the Report button.)

5 Click the Customize button. Money displays the Customize Report dialog box.

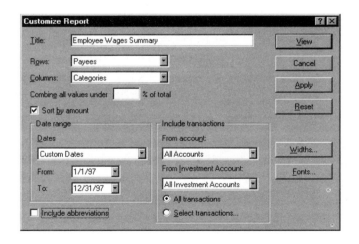

**6** Change the report's title by clicking the Title text box and typing **Employee Wages Summary**.

**7** Activate the Rows drop-down list box and select Subcategories.

**8** Activate the Columns drop-down list box and select Payees.

**9** Use the Date Range options to tell Money for which year you want to prepare the W-2s and W-3.

**10** Click the Select Transactions option button at the bottom of the Include Transactions area. Money displays the Select Transactions dialog box.

**11** Click the Categories tab.

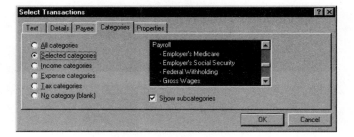

**12** Click the selected Categories option button.

**13** Use the list box on the right to select the Payroll expense category and subcategories. To select a category, click it. (The option button will change to Selected Categories.) To unselect a category you don't want to appear on the statement, click it again.

**14** Click OK to close the Select Transactions dialog and return to the Customize Report dialog box.

**15** Click View. Money produces the Employee Wages Summary.

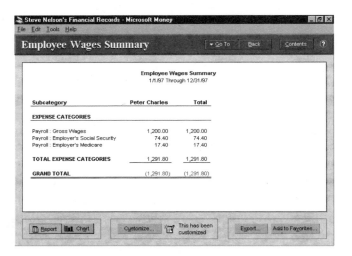

**16** Print the report by choosing Print from the File menu. Once you've got the printed report, you can use its information to complete your employee's W-2 forms and the W-3 form.

## In Conclusion

The techniques described in this chapter work just fine for small businesses with an employee or two and for households and businesses with only salaried employees. However, if you pay several employees by the hour, you'll find the process of calculating the gross wages and payroll deductions time-consuming. If this does become the case, you need to consider other options. For example, you may want to step up to a full-featured small business accounting program that has a payroll feature. (I recommend QuickBooks Pro for Windows from Intuit.) Or, you may want to consider having an outside payroll service bureau, such as ADP, do your payroll processing for you.

# Measuring Profits, Cash Flow, and Net Worth

**T**he three chapters that precede this one describe how to use Money to collect financial information about your business and how to use Money to handle common accounting transactions, including customer invoices and employee payroll checks. This chapter takes a step back from the details and talks about how to use the financial information you're collecting to measure your profits, cash flow, and net worth.

## Measuring Profits

There are many reasons for owning or operating a small business. Autonomy, for one. And superior financial rewards. Or just plain fun. But for a business to survive, the business must produce profits. Accordingly, on a regular basis, you need to calculate whether or not you're making a profit.

As long as you've been collecting information about your income and expenses by using the techniques described in Chapters 23, 24, and 25, it is easy to produce a profit and loss statement. To do so, follow these steps:

**1** Display the Money Contents window.

**2** Click the Report And Chart Gallery button. Money displays the Report And Chart Gallery.

**3** Click the Spending Habits button.

**4** Double-click the Income Vs. Spending report. Money produces the report.

**5** Click the Customize button. Money displays the Customize Report dialog box.

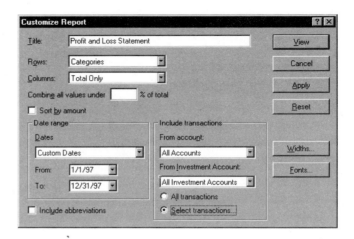

**6** Change the report's title by clicking the Title text box and typing **Profit and Loss Statement**.

*As a general rule, you want to measure profits on both a monthly and an annual basis.*

**7** Use the Date Range options to tell Money for which time period you want to measure profits. The Dates drop-down list box provides a bunch of common profit reporting periods.

**8** Click the Select Transactions option button. Money displays the Select Transaction dialog box.

**9** Click the Categories tab.

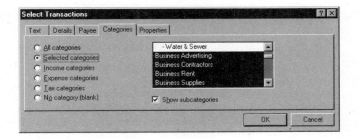

**10** Click the Selected Categories option button.

**11** Use the list box on the right to select the business income and expense categories that you want to appear on your profit and loss statement. To select a category, click it. To deselect a category that you don't want to appear on the statement, click it again.

**12** Click OK to close the Select Transaction dialog box and return to the Customize Report dialog box.

**13** Click View. Money produces the Profit And Loss Statement.

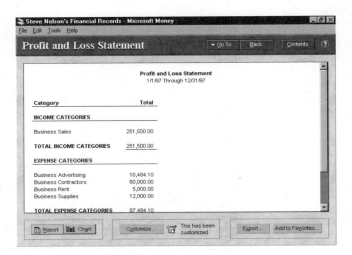

**Getting Information on Your Competitors' Profits.** *You can get information on your competitors' profits if you know where to look. Both Robert Morris & Associates and Standard & Poor's publish financial statistics on a variety of businesses. The data is arranged both by size of business and by standard industry classification, or SIC, codes. If you're running a $100,000-a-year insurance agency, for example, you can look up what other $100,000-a-year insurance agencies make and spend.*

*As a general rule, you want to measure cash flow on a monthly basis and on an annual basis.*

**14** Print the profit and loss statement by choosing Print from the File menu. To view your profit and loss statement in a bar chart, click the Chart button at the bottom of the Profit And Loss Statement window.

# Measuring Cash Flow

Over the long haul, a business can't survive without profits, but cash flow is more important in the short run. To make it through the next month or quarter, for example, you need to have enough cash to pay all your bills and to make any needed investments in new machinery or equipment. To produce a monthly cash-flow statement, follow these steps:

**1** Display the Money Contents window.

**2** Click the Report And Chart Gallery button. Money displays the Report And Chart Gallery.

**3** Click the Spending Habits button.

**4** Double-click the Monthly Cash Flow report. Money produces the report.

**5** Click the Customize button. Money displays the Customize Report dialog box.

**6** Use the Date Range options to tell Money for which time period you want to measure cash flow. The Dates drop-down list box provides a number of common profit reporting periods.

**7** Make sure the Include Transfers To Or From Asset Or Liability Accounts option button is selected.

**8** Click the Select Transactions option button. Money displays the Select Transactions dialog box.

**9** Click the Categories tab.

**10** Click the Selected Categories option button.

**11** Use the list box on the right to select the business income and expense categories that you want to appear on your cash-flow statement. To select a category, click it. To deselect a category you don't want to appear on the statement, click it again.

**12** Click OK to close the Select Transaction dialog box and return to the Customize Report dialog box.

**13** Click View. Money produces the Cash Flow Statement.

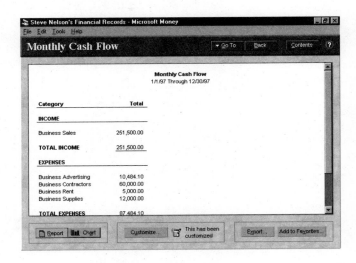

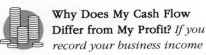

**Why Does My Cash Flow Differ from My Profit?** *If you record your business income when you deposit customer payments and you record your business expenses when you write checks, you use cash-basis accounting. In this case, your profit and loss statement will closely resemble your cash-flow statement. The only differences will result from account transfers to and from your bank accounts. These transfers appear on cash-flow statements because they involve cash moving in or out of a bank account. But they don't appear on profit and loss statements.*

**14** Print the cash-flow statement by choosing Print from the File menu and then clicking OK. To view a cash flow statement in a bar chart, click the Chart button at the bottom of the Cash Flow Statement window.

# Measuring Your Net Worth

The other financial statement that you want to produce and review regularly is a balance sheet. With a balance sheet, you tally your assets and liabilities and calculate the difference between these two amounts to get your business's net worth.

A balance sheet provides several pieces of useful information. It lets you assess the liquidity of your business, helps you calculate return on investment figures, and provides the information you need to determine how fast you can grow your business.

To produce a balance sheet, follow these steps:

1 Display the Money Contents window.

2 Click the Report And Chart Gallery button. Money displays the Report And Chart Gallery.

3 Click the What I Have button.

4 Double-click the Account Balances report. Money produces the report.

5 Click the Customize button. Money displays the Customize Report dialog box.

 **How Fast Can I Grow My Business?** *In general, you can grow your business only as fast as you can grow your net worth. For example, if you want to grow your business by 25 percent annually, you need to grow your net worth by 25 percent annually. Because a small business usually increases its net worth only by reinvesting profits, however, these reinvested profits limit your growth. For example, if reinvested profits as a percentage of net worth equal 20 percent, you can only grow your business by 20 percent.*

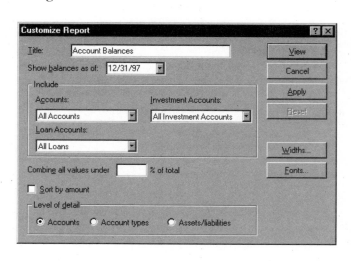

**6** If the report title is not already highlighted, highlight the Title text box, and then type **Balance Sheet**. (If the title is already highlighted, just type **Balance Sheet**.)

**7** Use the Show Balances As Of text box to specify the date for which you want the account balance calculated.

**8** Activate the Accounts drop-down list and click the Multiple Accounts option. Money displays the Select Accounts dialog box.

*The usual convention is to show account balances for the end of the month and the end of the year.*

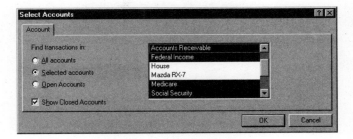

**9** Click the Selected Accounts option button.

**10** Use the list box on the right to select the business accounts that you want to appear on your balance sheet. To select an account, click it. To deselect an account you don't want to appear on the statement, click it again.

**11** Click OK to close the Select Account dialog box and return to the Customize Report dialog box.

**12** Click View. Money produces the balance sheet.

**What's on a Balance Sheet?** *A general rule of thumb is that the sum of your cash, accounts receivable, and any investments should be at least equal to your short-term debts. Your short-term debts include liabilities you have to pay in the coming year: any amounts you now owe employees or creditors, business credit-card balances, and the loan principal payments you'll make over the next year. You should be able to get all of this information from your balance sheet.*

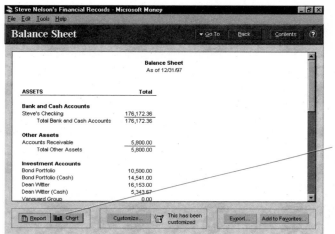

You can also view your balance sheet in a bar chart by clicking the Chart button at the bottom of the Balance Sheet window.

**13** Print the balance sheet by choosing Print from the File menu.

## In Conclusion

I don't think you can run a business purely by the numbers, although many financial types do. Too many business problems and opportunities defy quantification. You usually can't, for example, whip up a quick profit and loss statement to determine whether you'll make more money by providing better customer service. What's more, despite what they teach in many business schools, it's easy for the costs of a sophisticated accounting system to exceed its benefits. This "no net benefit" situation applies particularly to small businesses.

Nevertheless, you really will be more successful if you regularly measure your profits, cash flow, and net worth. I don't have any empirical data to back up this statement, only anecdotal data. But my experience is that entrepreneurs and managers who regularly review profit and loss statements, cash-flow statements, and balance sheets make better decisions, operate healthier businesses, and enjoy larger profits.

# Glossary

## A

**amortization** Refers to two financial calculations. On the subject of loans, amortization refers to periodic payments of principal that pay off the loan balance over time. On the subject of bonds, amortization refers to the way a bond premium or discount adjusts the bond's interest rate. See also *discount, premium*.

**appreciation** The increase in the value of an asset, such as real estate or an investment. For example, if a real estate investment increases in value by $10,000, you can say the investment appreciated by $10,000.

**asset** An item you own, for example a car, real estate, or investments such as stocks and bonds. See also *liability*.

## B

**balloon payment** An extra—and usually very large—loan payment made in addition to the last regular loan payment.

**bond** A bond is an investment instrument you can purchase that is really a loan to a corporation or a government agency. Over the term of the loan, the corporation or government agency pays interest. At the end of the loan term, the corporation or government agency redeems the bond by paying back the loan. See also *stock*.

## C

**capital gain** The profit an investor makes by selling an investment for more than he or she bought it for.

**capital loss** The loss an investor suffers by selling an investment for less than he or she bought it for.

# D

**depreciation** Refers to two financial calculations. Depreciation is a tax accounting and income measurement technique whereby the cost of an expensive, long-lived asset such as a building or car is allocated as an expense and is used in profit calculations over the asset's life. Depreciation also refers to a decrease in an asset's value. See also *appreciation*.

**discount** The amount by which a bond's price falls short of its par value. Bond discounts effectively increase the bond's interest rate. See also *bond, par value, premium*.

**discount points** A type of fee that mortgage lenders might charge a borrower so the borrower can obtain a loan. In effect, discount points amount to prepaid interest. See also *loan service fee*.

# E

**estate** The assets an individual owns, both real property and money.

**expense** The amounts an individual spends or the costs a business incurs to produce a profit. See also *income*.

# I

**income** The salary or wages an employee earns or the revenue a business produces. See also *expense*.

**index fund** A mutual fund that doesn't attempt to pick and choose individual stocks or bonds but instead buys a group of investments that closely match a market average. For example, a Standard & Poor's 500 index fund buys all of the 500 stocks in the Standard & Poor's 500 index. Index funds don't seek to beat the market averages; rather, they attempt to replicate a stock market or bond market average (something that most actively managed mutual funds can't do consistently).

**inflation** An increase in the price of some item with no corresponding increase in its quality or value. For example, if a loaf of bread cost $.40 a year ago but $.50 today, its price has inflated.

**investment** An asset purchased with the expectation that it will either produce regular income or steadily increase in value.

# L

**liability** An amount owed, such as a car loan, a mortgage, or back taxes.

**loan service fee**  A fee that lenders often charge borrowers for setting up a loan. A loan service fee is in addition to the interest charges the loan carries.

**lot**  Individual shares of stock or individual bonds that are purchased together, in a group, at the same time. Tracking investments by lot can save in capital gains taxes.

# M

**mutual fund**  A fund in which money from many investors is pooled and invested—usually in stocks and bonds. For this service, the mutual fund management company charges investors a fee that ranges from .2 percent to more than 2 percent of the fund's total assets.

# P

**par value**  Both stocks and bonds typically have par values. Stock par values aren't really of concern to investors, but bond par values are. A bond's interest payments are calculated by multiplying the bond's stated interest rate by its par value. Bond par values are also called face values. For example, if a bond's par value equals $1,000 and the bond's annual interest rate equals 7 percent, then the bond annually pays $70.00 in interest. Note, however, that you might pay more or less than $1,000 for the bond. See also *bond*.

**portfolio**  The collection of investments an investor owns.

**premium**  The amount by which a bond's price exceeds its par value. Premiums effectively lower a bond's interest rate. See also *bond, discount, par value*.

# R

**rate of return**  The profit an investment produces, expressed as a percentage of the investment's value. For example, an investment made for $1.00 that produces $.10 of profits has a 10 percent rate of return, because $.10 is 10 percent of $1.00.

# S

**stock**  An ownership share, or "slice," of a corporation. Collectively, the people who hold all of the shares or stock in a corporation own the corporation. They benefit when the corporation earns a profit (typically, they benefit by receiving dividends or by seeing the value of their stock increase), and they suffer when the corporation loses money (typically, they suffer when the value of their stock diminishes).

# Index

**A**ccount balances. *See also* bank statements
  adjusting, 50
  bank downloads vs. account register, 129
  cleared transactions vs. bank statements, 48, 50
Account Balances report, 309, 318–20
Account Details button, 12, 23, 91
accounting, cash vs. accrual basis, 289–95
accounting software, 277, 285–86
Account Manager window, 11–12, 56
Account Register window. *See also* accounts
  for checking accounts, 15–20, 29, 46
  for credit card accounts, 58–60
  displaying, 14–15
  for investment accounts, 192–97
  for mutual funds, 201–9
  printing checks from, 29
  for stocks and bonds, 211–21
accounts. *See also* bank accounts
  for assets, 89–94
  common errors, 49
  creating for online services, 105–8
  for credit cards, 55–60
  deleting, 12, 56
  deleting transactions, 21
  displaying account register, 12, 14–15
  displaying transactions, 12, 14–15
  editing transactions, 20–21

accounts, *continued*
  investment (*see* investment accounts)
  liability, 63, 64, 72–73, 302, 308–9
  naming, 10
  for property, 230–39
  reconciling, 45–52
  removing, 12, 56
  selecting which to summarize, 42
  setting up, 7–11
  storing details, 12, 23, 91
  types of, 9
  what records to keep, 38
accounts receivable
  early payment discounts, 292
  monitoring invoices, 295–97
  recording customer payments, 291–92, 294–95
  recording invoices, 290, 292–93
  setting up accounts, 288–89
  using accrual-basis accounting, 292–95
  using cash-basis accounting, 290–92
  using Money for, 287, 288–89, 298
Account Transactions report, 38, 295–97
accrual-basis accounting
  defined, 289
  recording customer payments, 294–95
  recording invoices, 292–93
accrued interest, 245–46

active real estate investments
  and adjusted cost basis, 233–34
  capital improvements vs. maintenance and repairs, 233
  creating income and expense classifications, 231–33
  defined, 229
  vs. passive real estate investments, 225
  recording depreciation, 234–36
  recording payments for capital improvements, 233–34
  reporting on, 239–40
  setting up property accounts, 230
  starting with home ownership, 223
  tracking capital improvements, 233–34
Add Classification dialog box, 232
Add/Remove Programs Properties dialog box, 4–5
American Online, 262
amortization
  of bond premiums, 247–48
  creating schedule, 80–81
  defined, 64, 321
annual percentage rate (APR), 86
applications
  for accounting, 277, 285–86
  installing, 3–6
  uninstalling, 5
appreciation, defined, 321

asset accounts, 89–94. *See also* accounts receivable; property accounts
assets
    backing up records, 94
    defined, 321
    homes as, 93
    insuring, 94
    noting changes in value, 92
    personal property as, 94
    recording with video camera, 94
    record-keeping tips, 93–94
    separate account for home, 93
    setting up accounts, 7, 89–91
    tracking, 7, 92–94
ATM withdrawals, recording, 17
AutoBudget dialog box, 143–44
AutoComplete, 17, 114
automatic bill payments
    cancelling, 121
    cautionary note, 120
    checking records, 122
    reminder, 121
    setting up, 119–20
automobiles. *See* cars

**B**acking up
    asset list, 94
    financial records, 21
Balance Account dialog box, 75–76
Balance Checking dialog box, 46
balances. *See* account balances; bank statements
balance sheets, 318–20

balancing bank accounts, 45–52
balloon payments, 68, 82, 83, 321
bank accounts. *See also* checking accounts; online banking
    common errors, 49
    reconciling, 45–52
    recording electronic transfers, 19–20
    recording transactions, 14–18
    transferring money online, 131–32
    trouble reconciling, 48–50
    what records to keep, 38
bank balances. *See* account balances; bank statements
banks. *See also* online banking
    identification numbers, 103, 106
    routing numbers, 103, 106
    sending e-mail, 109
bank statements
    downloading from bank, 125–28
    electronic payments on, 112, 117
    reconciling accounts, 45–52
    recording cleared transactions, 48
    recording ending balance, 47
    starting vs. ending balances, 10
    trouble reconciling with accounts, 48–50
bills, paying. *See* checks, printing; online bill payment
boats, record-keeping tips, 94
bond discounts, 248–49, 322
bond premiums, 246–48, 323
bonds. *See also* investment accounts
    accrued interest, 245–46
    allocating discounts, 248–49
    amortizing premiums, 247–48

bonds, *continued*
    defined, 321
    effective interest rate, 247
    par value, 214, 323
    recording interest on, 218–19
    recording transactions in investment accounts, 211–16
    specifying prices in Money, 214
    tax-exempt, 193
    U.S. government, 181
    yield to maturity, 247
    zero-coupon, 218, 250
brokerage fees, 208–9, 219–20
Budget dialog box, 142
budgeting, using Money, 142–44
business. *See* small business
business forms, 278–79
buying on margin, 243

**C**alculators
    Currency Converter, 17
    Loan Calculator, 61–62, 77–81
call options, 243, 244
Call Summary dialog box, 116–17, 128, 256
call waiting, 116
capital gains
    defined, 321
    handling lots, 192
    mutual fund distributions, 205, 206, 207
    passive real estate investment distributions, 227, 228
    and sale of home, 93

capital gains, *continued*
>and tax-deferred investments, 188
>when to track in Money, 189

capital losses, defined, 321

cars
>cost of driving, 139
>insuring, 151
>record-keeping tips, 94

cash accounts, 191, 220–21

cash-basis accounting
>defined, 289
>recording customer payments, 291–92
>recording invoices, 290

cash-flow statements, 316–17

cash machine withdrawals, recording, 17

casualty insurance, 94

categories
>for account balance adjustments, 50
>adding to downloaded bank transactions, 130
>adding to list, 16, 237–38
>for business use, 280–83
>for credit and debit card transactions, 58, 130
>for loans, 70
>new, 16, 237–38
>optimizing for income taxes, 263–66
>for payroll expenses, 303–5
>for real estate investments, 236
>selecting, 16
>splitting transactions among, 18–19

CD-ROM, installing Money from, 5

CDs (certificates of deposit), 250

Chart of the Day, 14

charts. *See also* reports
>printing, 36–37
>storing favorites, 35
>switching to reports, 35
>viewing on-screen, 34–35

checkbook, benefits of computerizing, 13

checking accounts. *See also* online banking
>adjusting check numbers, 15
>adjusting dates, 15
>balancing, 45–52
>common errors, 49
>copying check information, 16–17
>displaying account register, 14–15
>problems reconciling, 48–50
>recording ATM transactions, 17
>recording checks and deposits, 14–18
>recording electronic payments, 112–14
>recording withdrawals, 17
>setting up, 8–10, 11
>starting vs. ending balance, 10
>steps in reconciling, 46–48
>uncleared transactions, 10

check numbers, adjusting in account register, 15

checks. *See also* computer check forms
>for business, 278–79
>categorizing transactions, 16
>copying account register information, 16–17
>handwritten vs. electronic payment, 112
>marking cleared, 48
>payroll, 305–8
>preventing forgery, 51–52
>printing, 25–32

checks, *continued*
>pros and cons of printing, 25–26
>recording in account register, 15–17
>signing, 31
>splitting among categories, 18–19
>voided, recording, 31

children
>custodial accounts for, 179–80, 181
>and income taxes, 179

cigarettes, 139, 143, 165–66

classification feature, 231–33

cleared transaction balance, 48, 50

closing costs, 84–85

collections, 297

college
>calculating how much to save, 173–78
>choices for savings, 180–83
>cost of, 169, 170–71, 178
>custodial funds for, 179–80
>determining need to save, 170–71
>financial aid, 171–73
>financing from income, 183
>investing for, 180–83
>as investment, 169–70
>printing of plan summary, 177
>return on investment, 170
>saving for, 173–83
>using retirement savings for, 180
>ways to reduce cost, 184–86

commodities, 250

comparing loans, 80

comparing mortgages, 82–87

competitors, 316

CompuServe, 262

computer check forms
   choices in, 26–27, 31
   cost of, 25
   describing for printing, 28
   how often to print, 29
   ordering, 28
   printing, 29–31
   pros and cons of using, 25–26
   safeguarding, 32
   signing, 31
   and types of printers, 26–27
   using extras, 31
   voiding, 31
consumer debt, 79–80, 272–73
contractors vs. employees, 300
Control Panel, 4, 99
corporations, 280
correcting mistakes, 20–21
Create New Investment dialog box, 193, 202
credit and collections, 297
credit card accounts, 56–60
credit cards
   accountant's way of tracking use, 55–60
   calculating payment amounts for paying off, 61–62
   categorizing transactions, 54, 58, 130
   getting out of debt, 61–62
   interest on, 79–80
   investing in paying off, 62
   lazy way of tracking use, 54
   overuse of, 141
   printing account reports, 59
   reasons to track in Money, 53

credit cards, *continued*
   reconciling accounts, 59
   recording transactions, 58–60
   setting up accounts, 55–57
   tracking use of, 54–60
Currency Converter calculator, 17
custodial accounts, 179–80, 181
customer invoices
   collection efforts, 297
   discounts for paying early, 292
   printing, 278–79
   producing, 287–88
   recording in Money, 290
   tracking, 295–97
Customize Report dialog box, 41, 42, 43, 296–97, 310–12, 314
cutting expenses, 138–42

**D**ata entry. *See* Transaction Forms
dates
   adjusting in account register, 15
   changing report range, 40–41
debit cards
   categorizing transactions, 130
   when to use, 124
decision making, 137, 166
deductions
   bunching, 270–72
   taking, 269–70
   when to itemize, 270–72

defined benefit retirement plans, 154–56
defined contribution retirement plans, 156
deleting
   accounts, 12, 56
   transactions, 21
Deluxe Business Systems, 28
deposits
   marking cleared, 48
   recording in account register, 17–18
   splitting among categories, 19
depreciation
   defined, 322
   recording in asset account, 233, 234–36
derivatives, 243–44
details, storing, 12, 23, 91
Dialing Properties dialog box, 116, 127, 255
disability insurance, 146, 147
discount points, 83, 84, 322
discounts, bond, 248–49, 322
distributions
   mutual fund, 205, 206, 207
   passive real estate investment, 227–28
dividend reinvestment programs (DRIPs), 215–16
dividends
   mutual fund, 205, 206, 207
   passive real estate investments, 227–28
   as return of capital, 241–42
downloading
   bank statements, 125–28
   stock market prices, 253–56
down payments, 82–83

**E**arnings insurance, 146–51
Edit Scheduled Withdrawal dialog box, 120
effective interest rate, defined, 247
electronic payments. *See* online bill payment
electronic transfers
    recording in account register, 19–20
    between two online bank accounts,
        131–32
e-mail, sending to banks, 109
emergency fund, 146
employees
    vs. independent contractors, 300
    payroll tax and reporting requirements, 300,
        301, 302, 307
    withholding taxes from paychecks, 300, 308
employee stock options, 245
employer pension plans, 154–56
employers
    employee vs. independent contractor issue,
        300
    overview of responsibilities, 299–300
    payroll tax and reporting requirements, 300,
        301, 302, 307
    remitting income taxes for employees, 300,
        308–9
employer tax identification number, 300
ending balance, 10, 47
errors
    in balancing checking accounts, 49
    fictitious transactions, 51
    in loan account balances, 74–76
    unrecorded transactions, 50
estates, 145, 181, 322

even lots, 217
expenses
    business, 279, 284–85
    defined, 322
    tax-deductible, 7
    tips for cutting, 138–42
exporting
    Money data to tax-preparation software,
        268–69
    reports, 39–40
Export Report dialog box, 39
fictitious transactions, 51
File Backup command, 21
File Open command, 21
File Print command, 36
files, passwords for, 102
financial aid, 171–73
financial leverage, defined, 224
financial planning
    long-term goals, 144–45
    safety net, 145–51
    short-term budgeting, 135–44
financial records
    backing up, 21, 94
    how long to keep, 38, 39
    rebuilding after data loss, 38
fixing mistakes, 20–21
forgery, preventing, 51–52
forms. *See* business forms; computer check
    forms
    401(k) plans, 164, 165, 188
    403(b) plans, 164, 165, 188
FSEOG grants, 173

**G**azingus pins, 140
Givens, Charles, 270
Global Network Navigator, 260

**H**ealth, 139, 165–66
home. *See also* real estate
    deducting mortgage interest, 272
    exceptions to capital gains tax, 93
    improvements to, 93
    ownership as investment, 223
    record-keeping tips, 93
    setting up asset account, 93
    tracking market value, 93
home banking. *See* online services
home equity loans, 272–73
homeowner's insurance, 151
household employees, 299, 301

**I**mmigration and Naturalization Service, 301
impact printers, 26–27
importing tab-delimited files, 40
income, defined, 322
income taxes. *See also* Internal Revenue
    Service
    bunching deductions, 270–72
    children's, 179
    and consumer credit, 272–73
    marginal rate, 166, 193
    optimizing categories for, 263–66

income taxes, *continued*
    printing summary report, 267–68
    remitting for employees, 300, 308–9
    reporting real estate profits and losses, 236–37
    and retirement planning, 164–65, 272
    summarizing data for, 266–68
    taking deductions, 269–72
    tips for tax savings, 269–72
    use of tax-preparation software, 268–69
    using Money for record-keeping, 263–69
    using separate Money file for each taxpayer, 265
    what records to keep, 38
Income vs. Spending report, 313–16
independent contractors vs. employees, 300
index funds, 179, 182, 197, 322
Individual Retirement Accounts (IRAs), 164, 165, 188
inflation rate, 148, 149, 150, 159–60, 176, 177, 178, 322
inkjet printers, 27
installing
    modems, 98–99
    Money, 3–6
insurance
    and asset record-keeping, 94
    automobile, 151
    backing up records, 94
    casualty, 94
    disability, 146, 147
    homeowner's, 151
    life, 147–51
    for property, 94, 151

interest
    on bank accounts, 47
    on bonds, 218–19
    on mutual funds, 205, 206, 207
    on passive real estate investments, 227–28
interest rates, 69, 83, 247
Internal Revenue Service. *See also* income taxes
    and bond discounts, 249
    and bond premiums, 247
    federal payroll tax and reporting requirements, 300
    making tax deposits, 308
    Schedule C, 281
    Schedule E, 240
    Small Business Taxpayer Education Programs, 306
Internet. *See also* Outernet
    mailing lists, 259
    newsgroups, 257–58
    overview, 257
    World Wide Web sites, 259–61
investment accounts. *See also* property accounts
    adding stock and bond names to account, 212
    associated cash accounts, 191, 220–21
    calculating return on investment, 215
    describing portfolio, 192–96
    how often to update records, 204
    naming, 190
    recording mutual fund transactions, 201–9
    recording other income and expense, 219–20

investment accounts, *continued*
    recording passive real estate investment transactions, 224–29
    recording stock and bond transactions, 211–16
    recording stock splits, 217–18
    setting up, 189–92
    updating portfolio prices, 196–97
    viewing portfolio, 198–99, 253
    whether to keep in Money, 187–89
Investment Portfolio window, 198, 253
investments. *See also* retirement planning
    for college, 180–83
    defined, 322
    handling lots, 192, 195
    home ownership as, 223
    levels of risk, 181–83
    loans as, 66
    mutual funds, 201–9
    real estate, 223–40
    researching online, 257–62
    setting up accounts, 189–92
    specialized, 241–50
    stocks and bonds, 211–21
    whether to track in Money, 187–89
Investments report category, 36
invoices. *See* customer invoices
IRAs (Individual Retirement Accounts), 164, 165, 188

**J**unk fees, 85

**L**aser printers, 27
liabilities, defined, 322
liability accounts
    defined, 63
    recording loan payments, 72–73
    setting up for loans, 64
    using for payroll, 302, 308–9
life insurance
    calculating how much to buy, 147–50
    re-examining need for, 150–51
    term vs. cash-value, 151
    timing of cancellation, 151
life style, money-saving ideas, 138–42
lightning bolts, 108, 112, 132
liquidating dividends, 241–42
loan accounts
    balancing, 75–76
    defined, 63
    fixing balance errors, 74–76
    recording loan payments, 73–74
    setting up, 65–72
Loan Calculator, 61–62, 77–81
loans. *See also* credit cards; mortgages
    calculating, 77–81
    calculation variables, 68
    categorizing transactions, 70
    comparing, 80
    extra principal payments, 78–79
    interest calculations, 67
    interest vs. principal, 64, 73
    as investments, 66
    other charges, 70, 83, 84
    recording payment, 72–74

loans, *continued*
    shopping for, 76–81
    tracking, 63–76
    using mortgage brokers, 76
loan service fees, 83, 84, 323
long-term goals, 144–45. *See also* college;
    retirement planning
lots
    defined, 323
    how to handle, 192, 195
    odd and even, 217

**M**ailing lists, 259
marginal tax rate, 166, 193
margin interest, 243
memos, 16, 18
Microsoft Excel, using with Money, 39, 40
Microsoft Money. *See* Money
The Microsoft Network, 262
mistakes, correcting, 20–21
modems
    installing, 98–99
    internal vs. external, 98
    overview, 96–97
    speeds available, 97–98
    upgrading, 98
    what to buy, 97
    and Windows 95, 99–100
Money
    backing up files, 21
    exporting reports to Excel, 39, 40

Money, *continued*
    installing, 3–6
    online services, 100–109
    passwords for files, 102
    printing checks, 25–32
    printing reports, 33–43
    setting up accounts, 8–10, 11
    starting, 8
    and tax record-keeping, 263–69
    using for budgeting, 142–44
    using in business, 277–86
    ways to use, 7
money managers, 197
money-market funds, 191, 193
money-saving ideas, 138–42
Monthly Cash Flow report, 43, 316–17
mortgage brokers, 76
Mortgage Planner, 81–88
mortgages
    annual percentage rate (APR), 86
    closing costs, 84–85
    comparing, 82–87
    vs. consumer debt, 79–80
    deducting interest, 272
    discount points, 83, 84
    down payments, 82–83
    interest rates, 83
    for investment property, 230, 236
    junk fees, 85
    loan fees, 83, 84
    loan payments, 85
    making extra principal payments, 78–79
    paying off, 79, 183

mortgages, *continued*
  refinancing, 87–88
  shopping for, 76–81
  using mortgage brokers, 76
MSN, 262
mutual funds. *See also* investment accounts
  account maintenance fees, 208
  defined, 201, 323
  downloading prices, 253–56
  entering market symbols, 252–53
  how to select, 203
  recording other income and expenses, 208–9
  recording transactions in investment accounts, 201–9
  reinvesting distributions, 206–7
  return on, 163, 164, 215

**N**aming accounts, 10
nannies, 299, 301
net worth, 189, 318–20. *See also* asset accounts
New Account Wizard, 6, 8–10, 11, 12
New Category or Subcategory dialog box, 237–38, 282
New Mutual Fund dialog box, 194
New Properties or Sub-Properties dialog box, 232–33
newsgroups, 257–58

**O**dd lots, 217
one-person businesses, 278

online banking
  adding downloaded transactions to account register, 128–31
  creating Money account for, 105–8
  defined, 101
  downloading account records, 125–28
  how it works, 123–24
  keeping manual backup, 124–25
  list of participating banks, 123, 124
  overview, 123
  safety of use, 101–2
  signing up for, 102–8
  switching banks for, 132
  transferring money between accounts, 131–32
online bill payment
  automatic payments, 119–22
  canceling payments, 117–18
  checking status, 122
  creating Money account for, 105–8
  defined, 101
  entering payments, 112–14
  fee for using, 111
  how it works, 111–12
  payee information, 113–14
  sending payments, 115–18
  signing up for, 102–8
  timing of, 112, 113, 115
  tracking unreceived payments, 118
online quotes
  defined, 101
  entering market symbols, 252–53
  fee for, 251
  how it works, 251

online quotes, *continued*
  setting up, 252
  signing up for, 102–8
online services. *See also* Outernet
  creating Money accounts for, 105–8
  equipment needed, 96–100
  learning about, 101
  making changes to, 109
  overview, 95–96
  passwords for files, 102
  phone number for accessing, 104–5
  PIN numbers, 101
  safety of use, 101–2
  setting up, 102–8
  signing up for, 102–8
Online Services dialog box, 254
Online Services Setup Wizard, 103–8
on-screen reports, 33–35
opening files, 21
options, stock, 243–44, 245
Outernet, 262
owners equity, 280

**P**artnerships, 280
par value, 214, 323
passive real estate investments
  vs. active real estate investments, 225
  creating reports, 229
  defined, 223
  recording distributions, 227–28
  recording purchases, 224–25
  recording sales, 226–27

passive real estate investments, *continued*
  return of capital, 228–29
  setting up in Money, 226
passwords, 102
Payees and Categories window, 231–33, 265, 282, 304
payment, discount for early, 292
Payment Calendar, 71, 119, 121
payment status, checking, 122
payroll
  paying federal taxes, 300, 308–9
  preparing checks, 305–8
  printing transaction report, 310–12
  setting up liability accounts, 302
  splitting check information among categories, 306
  state and local taxes, 301, 302, 307
  tax and reporting requirements, 300, 301, 302, 307, 308–9
  using Money for, 299–312
  withholding taxes, 300, 308
Peachtree Accounting, 285–86
Pell grants, 172
pension plans, 154–56
Performance by Investment Account report, 215
Performance by Investment Type report, 215
Perkins loans, 173
personal archives
  creating, 37–38
  how long to keep records, 38, 39
  what to keep, 38
personal liability insurance, 151
personal property, record-keeping tips, 94

phone numbers
  for accessing online services, 105
  setting up to dial, 116
PIN numbers, 101, 255
Planning Wizards
  Loan Calculator, 61–62, 77–81
  Mortgage Planner, 81–88
  Retirement Planner, 147–50, 158–62, 173–78
plug and play, 99
PLUS loans, 172
portfolio, defined, 323. *See also* investments
Portfolio window. *See* Investment Portfolio window
post-retirement return, 162–63, 164
precious metals, 250
premiums, bond, 246–48, 323
pre-retirement return, 162–63, 164
principal, loan, 64, 73, 78–79
Print Checks dialog box, 29–31
printers
  setup, 33
  types of, 26–27
printing
  balance sheets, 320
  business forms, 278–79
  cash-flow statements, 317
  charts, 36–37
  checks, 29–31
  college savings plan summary, 177
  multiple copies of reports, 37
  profit and loss statements, 316
  reports, 36–37

printing, *continued*
  retirement planning summary, 162
  selected pages of reports, 37
Print Report dialog box, 36–37
Prodigy, 262
professional money managers, 197
profit and loss statements, 313–16, 317
programs
  for accounting, 277, 285–86
  installing in Windows 95, 3–6
  uninstalling in Windows 95, 5
Programs menu, 3, 8
property accounts
  and adjusted cost basis, 233–34
  categories for real estate investment transactions, 236–38
  creating income and expense classifications, 231–33
  recording depreciation, 233, 234–36
  recording investment property income and expenses, 238–39
  setting up, 230
  tracking capital improvements, 233–34
  tracking investment property mortgages, 236
property classifications, 231–33
property insurance, 94
put options, 243, 244

QuickBooks, 285–86
quotes, stock. *See* online quotes

**R**ainy-day funds, 146
rates of return, 159, 162–63, 164, 215, 323
real estate. *See also* home
  active investments, 229–40
  active vs. passive investments, 225
  passive investments, 223–29
  why to invest in, 224
real estate investment trusts (REITs). *See* passive real estate investments
receivables. *See* accounts receivable
reconciling
  defined, 48
  how to balance bank accounts, 45–48
  postponing, 49
  problems with, 48–50
record-keeping
  backing up, 21, 94
  for homeowners, 93
  how long to keep records, 38, 39
  for personal assets, 93–94
recycling, 140
refinancing mortgages, 87–88
register. *See* Account Register window
reinvesting
  mutual fund distributions, 206–7
  stock dividends, 215–16
reminders. *See* Payment Calendar
removing accounts, 12
renaming asset accounts, 91
replacement income, 147–50
Report And Chart Gallery window, 33–34

reports
  Account Balances, 309, 318–20
  for accounts receivable, 295–97
  Account Transactions, 38, 295–97
  for active real estate investments, 239–40
  calculating return on investment, 215
  categories of, 35–36
  changing appearance, 40–43
  changing column widths, 43
  changing date range, 40–41
  changing fonts, 43
  for credit card accounts, 59
  customizing, 40–43, 296–97
  defined, 33
  exporting, 39–40
  Income vs. Spending, 313–16
  list of types, 35–36
  Monthly Cash Flow, 43, 316–17
  for passive real estate investments, 229
  for payroll transactions, 310–12
  Performance by Investment Account, 215
  Performance by Investment Type, 215
  printer setup, 33
  printing, 36–37
  retitling, 311, 314, 319
  selecting accounts to summarize, 42
  storing favorites, 35
  switching to charts, 35
  Tax-Related Transactions, 38, 43, 264, 266–68
  undoing customization, 43
  viewing on-screen, 33–35
  What I Have, 36

Retirement Planner
  calculating savings needed, 157–62
  using to calculate college savings, 173–78
  using to calculate replacement income, 147–50
retirement planning
  calculating savings needed, 157–62
  exploiting tax savings, 272
  funding early, 183
  and pension plans, 154–56
  printing summary, 162
  and rates of return, 159, 162–63, 164
  setting income goal, 156–57
  and social security, 153–54, 157, 158
  using savings for college, 180
return. *See* rates of return
return of capital
  passive real estate investments, 228–29
  stocks and bonds, 241–42

**S**aving money
  for college, 173–83
  how it adds up, 158, 161
  ideas for, 138–42, 164–66
  for rainy day, 146
  for retirement, 157–62
savings accounts, 8–10, 11
savings bonds, 181
security, online banking, 101–2
Select Accounts dialog box, 42
Select Checks dialog box, 30

Select Transactions dialog box, 297, 314–15
Set Up Automatic Payment dialog box, 120
short sales, 242–43
signing checks, 31
sign-up forms, for online services, 104–5, 107
small business. *See also* payroll
    accounting software for, 277, 285–86
    creating categories for transactions, 280–83
    keeping books using Money, 280–85
    measuring profits, 313–16
    Money vs. accounting systems, 278–79
    owners equity, 280
    preparing payroll using Money, 299–312
    printing checks, 278–79
    profit and loss statements, 313–16
    recording expenses, 279, 284–85
    recording income, 283–84
    tracking assets and liabilities, 279
    using Money in, 277
Small Business Taxpayer Education Programs, 306
small capitalization stocks, 216
SmartFill, 114
smoking, 139, 143, 165–66
social security
    paying payroll tax, 308–9
    and retirement planning, 153–54, 157, 158
software
    for small-business accounting, 277, 285–86
    for tax preparation, 268–69
Spending Habits report category, 36
Split Shares dialog box, 217–18

splitting. *See also* stock splits
    bank deposits among categories, 19
    checks among categories, 18–19
    credit card payments among categories, 54
    loan interest and principal, 73
    payroll check information among categories, 306
Split Transaction dialog box, 18–19, 54, 306
Stafford loans, 172
Standard & Poor's 500, 316, 322
Start button, 3, 4, 8
starting
    Money, 8
    New Account Wizard, 11, 12
starting balance, 10
state and local taxes, 301, 302, 307
stock index funds, 179, 182, 197
stock market, alternatives to, 183
stock options, 243–44, 245
stock quotes. *See* online quotes
stocks. *See also* investment accounts
    buying on margin, 243
    for college savings, 182
    defined, 323
    downloading prices, 253–56
    entering market symbols, 252–53
    investing in directly, 211
    liquidating dividends, 241–42
    minimizing risk, 183
    puts and calls, 243, 244
    recording splits, 217–18
    recording transactions in investment accounts, 211–16

stocks, *continued*
    reinvesting dividends, 215–16
    return on, 160, 162–63, 215
    short sales, 242–43
    small capitalization, 216
stock splits, 217–18
Stop Payment orders, 118
subcategories, defined, 16. *See also* categories

**T**ab-delimited text files, 39
Tab key, 15
TaxCut, 268
tax deductions, 269–72
tax-deferred accounts, 164–65, 188, 190, 205
taxes. *See* income taxes; Internal Revenue Service; payroll
Taxes report category, 36, 38
tax-exempt bonds, 193
tax-preparation software, 268–69
Tax-Related Transactions report, 38, 43, 264, 266–68
thankfulness, 136–37
Transaction Forms, 22
transactions
    in date order, 22
    deleting, 21
    editing, 20–21
    entering, 14–18
    fictitious, 51
    forgotten, 50
    viewing information about, 22–23
    viewing list, 22

transfers. *See* electronic transfers
TurboTax, 268

**U**ncleared transactions, 10, 50
unemployment taxes, 309
uninstalling programs, 5
universal life insurance, 151
Update Price dialog box, 197
U.S. government bonds, 181

**V**erify Modem dialog box, 100
video cameras, using for record-keeping, 94
View triangle menu, 12, 22
voided checks, recording, 31

**W**-2 forms, 309–12
W-3 forms, 309–12
W-4 forms, 305
*Wall Street Journal* Web site, 260
weighted average return, 163, 164
What I Have report category, 36, 318–20
What I Owe report category, 36
Who Is Getting My Money report, 310–12
whole life insurance, 151
wills, 145

Windows 95
　installing modem, 99–100
　installing programs, 3–6
　Programs menu, 3, 8
　Start button, 3, 4, 8
withdrawals, recording, 17
withholding taxes, 300, 308
wizards
　defined, 6
　Loan Calculator, 61–62, 77–81
　Mortgage Planner, 81–88
　New Account Wizard, 6, 8–10, 11, 12
　Online Services Setup Wizard, 103–8
　Retirement Planner, 147–50, 158–62,
　　173–78
work-study programs, 173
World Wide Web, 259–61

**X**fer. *See* electronic transfers

**Y**ahoo Web site, 260–61
yield to maturity, defined, 247

**Z**ero-coupon bonds, 218, 250

# Stephen L. Nelson

**Stephen L. Nelson** writes and consults about using computers for personal and business financial management. The author of over 50 books and more than a 100 magazine articles, Nelson is the best-selling author on using computers for personal financial management. Nelson's books have sold more than 1,500,000 copies in English and have been translated into eleven different languages.

Nelson, a certified public accountant, holds a bachelor of science degree in accounting from Central Washington University and a masters of business administration degree in finance from the University of Washington.

Nelson lives in the foothills east of Seattle, Washington with his wife, Susan, and the kissing bandits, Beth and Britt Marie.

**T**he manuscript for this book was prepared and submitted to Microsoft Press in electronic form. Text files were prepared using Microsoft Word for Windows 95, version 7.0.

**Cover Designer**   Greg Erickson

**Interior Graphic Designers**   Kim Eggleston, Amy Peppler Adams (designlab)

**Page Layout and Typography**   Stefan Knorr

**Copy Editor**   Paula Thurman

**Technical Editor**   Beth Shannon and Kaarin Dolliver

**Indexer**   Julie Kawabata

**Photography**   Nancy Medwell

**Cover Color Separator**   Color Control

Pages were composed by Stephen L. Nelson, Inc., using PageMaker 6.0 for Windows, with text in Garamond and display type in Formata. Composed pages were delivered to the printer as electronic prepress files.